Educators Review The Full Value School

After some 40 years as an educator the foundational needs of students willing and able to learn have never changed. What has changed is the need for us to create a more safe, and introspective environment in order for our students to cope with the myriad of inputs we call the 21st century. Which is why we embraced the Full Value program. Working with Dr. Maizell we have followed a path that placed our students and staff on a continuum of self-awareness and mindfulness that has benefited all involved and contributed to our mission of supporting student success and creating lifelong learners. This book serves as an essential guidepost for implementation.

- *James J. Opiekun, Superintendent of Schools, Kinnelon Borough Public Schools*

At first glance, Full Value may seem to be a separate entity from the academic classroom; but with a little creativity, teachers can use Full Value/Project Adventure activities to simultaneously cover content and character building. I've been able to examine conflict in Romeo and Juliet using the "Helium Hoop" and highlight learning from success and failure in Homer's epic the Odyssey using the "Pathway" activity. However, the moment that validated the inclusion of this program into my High School ELA classroom was witnessing a disengaged, emotionally traumatized student willingly participate in the Pitfall (Minefield) activity and smile for the first time. Not only did Full Value improve the dynamic of my classroom, truly making it a safe and engaging learning environment for all, but it also improved my effectiveness as an educator. This book is essential to creating an emotionally safe learning environment for your students.

- *Kelly DeAraujo, High School Teacher, Vernon Township Public Schools*

Cultivating an educational environment that incorporates social emotional learning starts with building trust between students and teachers. As the faculty applied Full Value training to establish behavioral awareness and accountability during classroom interactions, the opportunity for integration within lesson delivery proved to be a logical and powerful extension. Overall, the depth of student growth was quite impressive. Richard Maizell, Jim Schoel, John Grund have provided the blueprint for Full Value implementation that can enrich academic integrity, while emphasizing important life skills.

- *John P. Hynes, Superintendent of Schools*

Full Value empowers students to create a classroom environment where they can learn, thrive, and gain skills to become a valuable community member inside and outside of the classroom.

- *Terry Lummer, 5th Grade Teacher, Kinnelon Borough Public Schools*

I have found Full Value to be essential in establishing a sense of community in our school. The Full Value behaviors are concise and easy to understand, while at the same time having a scope wide enough to have a positive impact on all of our daily interactions.

This is supported by a common language that enables all of us to communicate about what really matters as we collaborate, problem solve, or resolve conflicts. Full Value is integral to the character of our school.
- *Mark Mongon, Principal, Pearl R. Miller School*

When Dr. Maizell first shared the Full Value norms with me, it became crystal clear that our planet would be a better place if we could all live by these simple, yet so powerful tenets. I am proud to have been part of the initial "Full Value Cadre" in my school district. Dr. Maizell provided mentoring and support that empowered teachers and students to engage in social-emotional learning that led to student empowerment and greater self-regulation. Leading a school community dedicated to developing kind, empathetic, caring humans will remain a career highlight.
- *Jodi Mulholland, Principal, Stonybrook Elementary School*

One of my favorite things about being part of a full value community is that as I worked alongside the students and my colleagues there was always this common understanding and shared value system that never failed. Even in the most tense or difficult situations, it is what invariably brought us together. It is and was a great feeling!
- *Lisa Nafash, High School Counselor, Kinnelon Borough Public Schools*

I knew that I had already formed some strong bonds in just one day with some teachers from other buildings I didn't even know. I knew that whatever I was involved in was going to change my life.
- *Sarah Tinney, Full Value Schools training participant, Primary School Counselor, Kinnelon Borough Public Schools*

As each new school year approaches, educators bring bright hopes of creating a classroom climate & culture that offer an engaging & emotionally safe environment for learning. Teachers & administrators seek meaningful connections between the integration of curriculum & character education. They are keenly aware of the need to find a balance between the two. Our district's solution was Full Value. Beginning with one school, some curious teachers attended a training & discovered how enthusiastic students became when taught content-based lessons using Full Value activities. The message traveled, K-12, to all eight schools. The momentum grew, creating Full Value classrooms in every school & finding the balance that educators sought. With Full Value, the balance you seek is well within your grasp. This book will serve as an invaluable resource for character education & academic integration.
- *Iris Wechling, Director of Education, West Milford Township School*

The Full Value School

A Social Emotional Learning Community

By Richard Maizell & Jim Schoel, with John Grund

Cover Art and Illustrations by Anna Rampelt

Full Value Communities
Calais, VT

Fair Use: Books and articles quoted or cited in the text under fair use allowances are acknowledged in the notes and references.

ISBN-13: 978-0-578-48079-4

Library of Congress Control Number: 2019908698 Full Value Communities, Calais, VT

THE FULL VALUE SCHOOL: A SOCIAL EMOTIONAL LEARNING COMMUNITY by Richard Maizell, Psy.D. & Jim Schoel, with John Grund

Copyright © 2019 Full Value Communities, LLC. All rights reserved. No part of this publication may be reproduced, stored in a retrieval system, or transmitted, in any form or by any means, electronic, mechanical, photocopying, recording, or otherwise, without the written permission of the copyright owners.

Come visit us at: www.fullvaluecommunities.org

TABLE OF CONTENTS

DEDICATION x

Some Thoughts From Mr. Fred Rogers xi

INTRODUCTION – THE FULL VALUE SCHOOL

Our Purpose xii
Who is the Book For? xiii
SEL - A Different Way of Being Smart xiii
Living a Full Value Life xv
Full Value & CASEL Core Competencies xv
How is this Activity Book Different from Other Activity Books? xvii
What's Inside the Cover? xvii
Cross Categories xviii
Activity Difficulty Level & Materials xviii
How and Why do I Find Time for This? xix
Some Notes About Co-Authorship xxi

CHAPTER 1 FULL VALUE

Origins of Full Value 1
No Discount Contract 1
From No Discount to Full Value 2
Full Value Commitment Replaces Full Value Contract 2
The Balance of Full Value 3
Full Value Today 3
Full Value Outcomes 3
An Overview of Each Full Value Behavioral Norm and Their Outcomes 4
Be Here 4
Be Safe 5
Be Honest 6
Set Goals 7
Let Go & Move On 11
Care For Self & Others 12
Full Values Working Together 14
Control to Empowerment & Full Value 14
Some Thoughts About Educator Participation 15
Full Value Behavioral Norms & Trauma Work 15
Summing Up 17

CHAPTER 2 THE IMPACT OF FULL VALUE ON AFFECT & ABSTRACT REASONING

A Brain That Can't Feel Can't Make Up Its Mind 18

We Feel – Therefore We Learn 19
ABC Triangle 21
Full Value & Metaphorical Abstract Reasoning 23
Metaphorical Activity Structures 24

CHAPTER 3 CO-CREATING FULL VALUE COMMITMENTS & CHALLENGE OF CHOICE

About Co-Creation 28
Co-Creation & Trauma Work 28
Global Full Value Activities 29
Full Value Commitment 36
    The Being 36
    The Village 37
Full Value Commitments Across Age Groups 37
Primary/Elementary & Special Needs Students 37
Middle & High School 41
Full Value Commitment & Curriculum 42
Whole School Full Value Commitment 43
Whole School Integration Projects 43
Challenge by Choice to Challenge of Choice 44
Challenge of Choice & Trauma Work 46

CHAPTER 4 ASSESSMENT & REFLECTION STRATEGIES

GRABBSS Assessment for Full Value Communities 47
What is GRABBSS? 47
The Life Cycle of Groups 47
Using GRABBSS with Students 48
Using GRABBSS for Program Design and Implementation 54
Some Thoughts on High School Programs 57
Summing Up 59
Reflection Practices 60
What, So What, Now What? & The Adventure Wave 62

CHAPTER 5 CALLING GROUP

The Why of Calling Group 67
Types of Groups 68
How Calling Group Aligns with Full Value 69
Control to Empowerment in Calling Group 69
The How of Calling Group 70
Calling Group Techniques 71
The When of Calling Group 71
Sequencing the Calling Group Process 71
Calling Group & Trauma Work 73

CHAPTER 6 BE HERE

Outcomes of Be Here 74
Activities 74

CHAPTER 7 BE SAFE

Outcomes of Be Safe 102
Activities 103
The Trust Sequence 114

CHAPTER 8 BE HONEST

Outcomes of Be Honest 122
Activities 123

CHAPTER 9 SET GOALS

Set Goals 134
Set Goals & Full Value Commitment 135
Activity Example 135
The Focus of Goal Setting 136
Directed or Self-Directed Goal Setting 136
Goal Setting & Distractors 137
Goal Setting with Primary School Students 137
Goal Setting with Elementary School Students 138
Goal Setting with Middle and High School Students 139
The Ideal Self 139
SMART Goals 140
4 Square Goal Setting Worksheet 141
Set Goals & Trauma Work 142
Outcomes of Set Goals 142
Activities 142

CHAPTER 10 LET GO & MOVE ON

Outcomes of Let Go & Move On 168
Activities 168

CHAPTER 11 CARE FOR SELF & OTHERS

Outcomes of Care for Self & Others 192
Activities 193

CHAPTER 12 FULL VALUE & ACADEMIC CONTENT AREAS

Integration into Content 213
Tools for Lesson Planning..221
Content Areas & Full Value Activity Connections 222
Project Adventure Physical Education Cycles & Full Value..224
Summing Up 225

CHAPTER 13 MINDFULNESS & FULL VALUE

Overview 226
Be Here: In the Present Moment...228
Be Safe: Non-judgmentally 230
Be Honest: Awareness that Emerges 230
Set Goals: Attention on Purpose 232
Let Go & Move On: Unfolding of Experience 233
Care of Self & Others: As if Your Life Depended on It..234
Full Value & Mindfulness in Action 235
Bringing Mindfulness to Schools...236
3 New R's of Education 237
Activities That Support Teaching Mindfulness 237
Brain Basics...237
Mindfulness Activities 239

CHAPTER 14 MODEL PROGRAMS & SUSTAINABILITY

Under the Big Tent of Full Value 248
    How Full Value Supports the Responsive Classroom 249
    How Full Value Supports the Resolving Conflict Creatively Program 251
    How Full Value Supports Restorative Practice 254
Primary Prevention 254
Best Practices in Schools 255
Kinnelon Borough Public Schools...255
Peer Leadership – Bernards High School...260
Sustainability...265
Summing Up...265

CHAPTER 15 ODDS & ENDS

Creating Small Groups 267
Activity Resources..268
Mindfulness Resources...269
Full Value Communities 272
    What We Do 272
    Who We Are 272

CHAPTER 16 PRINTABLE MATERIALS

Lesson Planning Template.. 274
Behavioral Norms & Desired Outcomes Table 275
SMART Goals... 276
4 Square Goal Setting Worksheet... 278
Bridge-It Group Language 279
Bridge-It Sample Timeframes.. 280
Alligator River Rankings 281
Accepting Yourself... 282

REFERENCES 283

INDEX 291

ACKNOWLEDGEMENTS... 296

DEDICATION

This book is dedicated to Karl Rohnke, an international leader in experiential education. In 1971, Karl co-founded Project Adventure, adapting the principles of Outward Bound to the public schools. Karl's skills to invite engagement, play, and commitment have shaped the world of experiential learning. He remains the touch point for many of us who continue to do this transformational work. The field of experiential learning owes him a lasting debt of gratitude, as do we. "Life is serious. But not that serious."

What do you do with the mad that you feel? When you feel so mad you could bite. When the whole wide world seems oh so wrong, and nothing you do seems very right. What do you do? Do you punch a bag? Do you pound some clay or some dough? Do you round up friends for a game of tag or see how fast you go? It's great to be able to stop when you've planned the thing that's wrong. And be able to do something else instead—and think this song—

I can stop when I want to. Can stop when I wish. Can stop, stop, stop anytime... And what a good feeling to feel like this! And know that the feeling is really mine. Know that there's something deep inside that helps us become what we can. For a girl can be someday a woman, and a boy can be someday a man.

- Fred Rogers in Testimony Before the US Senate Commerce Committee, May 1, 1969 (Used with permission from Fred Rogers Productions)

INTRODUCTION

THE FULL VALUE SCHOOL

Our Purpose

The purpose of this book is to teach and demonstrate how Full Value norms (Be Here, Be Safe, Be Honest, Set Goals, Let Go & Move On, Care for Self & Others) can create an effective social emotional learning (SEL) primary prevention program in K-12 public and private schools.

School districts recognize that social emotional learning is at the core of their work.

> It is our mission to prepare each student to be a contributing member of society and to participate successfully in the global community. We guide students to achieve academic skills and facilitate their social and emotional development so they can become lifelong learners and reach their fullest potential.
> -Kinnelon Borough Public Schools, NJ

The Kinnelon Mission Statement, prominently featured on the district's home page, represents what can be found on websites of every school across the United States, from urban to rural. Our larger society craves more civility, empathy, and compassion but struggles to find solutions. So, it makes sense that the process of fostering emotional intelligence is supported within the schools, and as early as possible. Yet only recently has the response to this need begun to accelerate beyond mission statements to mission action.

In many instances, the response has been haphazard and fragmented. Districts often rely on outside providers who offer lesson plans, workbooks, and videos. We call this "doing" social emotional learning. A lesson is taught, perhaps weekly, in isolation from the rest of the curriculum, with few opportunities to practice skills across school settings. SEL becomes just another deliverable, taught at students but not with students. It is not often that students are invited to co-create classroom behavioral norms or given tools to facilitate their use.

SEL programs are often specific to a limited grade span. It becomes confusing to students who learn the terminology for a program introduced in the primary grades, only to start all over again when they enter elementary, middle, or high school. In this book, we provide a very different model that establishes common SEL language across all grade levels, fully engages students in creating behavioral norms, and connects SEL to all elements of the instructional and social school experience. Full Value Schools is not a standalone program. It is an integral part of students' K-12 school life. In a Full Value community, students and teachers experientially co-create and practice behavioral norms together. Along with the empowerment to define these norms (under the teacher's guidance) comes the responsibility to model them during every interaction between students and with adults. Full Value is a partnership between students and educators, not a prescribed top down didactic process or a program that dictates rules and shapes behavior. We have also learned that if practiced with fidelity, Full Value can be transformative for students and educators.

Some readers may choose not to delve more deeply into this book as they are already invested in an existing SEL program that helps their students. However, we would gently invite you to keep reading. Many elements and tools of The Full Value Schools model can be utilized to broaden, deepen, and sustain the impact of existing programs. After understanding the unique characteristics of Full Value, a discussion of sustainability in Chapter 14 defines how our model provides meaningful enhancements to many existing SEL programs.

Who Is This Book For?

Our intended audience includes teachers, administrators, board members, school counselors, child study team members, paraprofessional educators, parents, and any other adults who interact with students, including cafeteria and playground aides, school bus drivers, and maintenance and custodial staff. In addition, in the larger community, this text will be helpful to any agency working with young people.

SEL – A Different Way of Being Smart (Elias et al., 1997)[1]

The term social emotional learning emerged in the mid 1990s to describe many disparate programs supporting character education. A prime mover in this effort was and is the Collaborative for Academic, Social, and Emotional Learning (CASEL). The organization has identified five core competencies: Self Awareness, Self-Management, Social Awareness, Responsible Decision-Making, and Relationship Skills (Core SEL Competencies, 2007).[2] CASEL has also created the acronym SAFE to describe their philosophy:

> Sequenced: Connected and coordinated activities to foster skill development.
> Active: Active forms of learning to help students master new skills and attitudes.
> Focused: A component that emphasizes developing personal and social skills.
> Explicit: Targeting specific social and emotional skills. (CASEL guide, 2015)[3]

Foundational to this philosophy is the importance of integrating SEL into all aspects of student life, from the classroom to the playground. Continual and systemic exposure to concepts as well as opportunities to practice them through participation, is essential. This integration should also extend into the larger community and, where possible, into the home. Primary prevention work is hard, requiring sufficient training and ongoing support. The work must happen every day and permeate every interaction.

- Social Emotional Learning (SEL) is not a luxury; it is essential to becoming a fully actualized member of society.

- True leaders display social emotional maturity, including empathy, compassion, listening, affirmation, critical self-reflection, and wisdom.

- SEL can and must be efficiently and effectively woven into the fabric of our children's daily lives.

- Success is assured if educators integrate SEL into their own lives. Therefore, Full Value must be more than prescriptive; it must be participatory.

- Only by thoroughly blending SEL into all aspects of the curriculum will it be accepted and integrated by students.

- SEL strengthens abstract reasoning and enhances cognitive functioning and associated behaviors.

The idea of systemic infusion has found its way into federal law. The Obama administration initiated this under the Every Student Succeeds Act (ESSA). The law requires that interventions must be "sustained (not stand-alone, one-day, and short-term workshops), intensive, collaborative, job-embedded, data-driven, and classroom focused" (pg. 401).[4]

Under this legislation, Title 1 funding will be set aside for implementation at the state level. In many states, including Massachusetts, Connecticut, and New Jersey, legislation already exists that requires adopting and implementing primary prevention SEL programs to address harassment, intimidation, and bullying.

It is often an assumption that a clear definition exists for what social emotional learning is. However, the first question educators often ask when participating in one of our trainings and workshops is, "What is SEL?" We focus on two essentials: the ability to self-regulate and the wherewithal to have a voice that can positively influence the world around you. These essentials are described in detail in the outcomes associated with each Full Value (Chapter 1) and reflect what CASEL defines as:

> ...the process through which children and adults understand and manage emotions, set and achieve positive goals, feel and show empathy for others, establish and maintain positive relationships, and make responsible decisions.[5]

Drilling down into this process, we look at the skills and competencies of well designed, systemic SEL programs. These include:

1. Cognitive skills, including executive functions such as working memory, attention control, flexibility, inhibition, and planning, as well as beliefs and attitudes that guide one's sense of self and approaches to learning and growth.

2. Emotional competencies that enable one to cope with frustration, recognize and manage emotions, and understand others' feelings and perspectives.

3. Social and interpersonal skills that enable one to read social cues, navigate social situations, resolve interpersonal conflicts, cooperate with others, and work effectively in a team, and demonstrate compassion and empathy toward others (pg. 15).[6]

Living a Full Value Life

- In our work with children and adults in schools, business groups, and in the community, we find a deep yearning for defining and living a Full Value life with norms that are developed together rather than imposed. These norms must be universal, teachable, comprehensive, easy to understand, and sustainable and inspirational. In the Full Value and associated outcomes, we find these qualities. However, we have learned that while the desire is there, often the process to get there is missing.

- We want to be present with each other, but do not know how to bring our focus to bear. Many internal and external distractions and preoccupations can get in the way.

- We feel a deep need to feel physically and emotionally safe. Unfortunately, this can often take the form of defensiveness and aggression rather than support and trust.

- We crave affiliation but often suffer from loneliness and isolation.

- We want to be honest with each other but shy away from the potential for conflict, hurt, and alienation associated with honesty.

- We are continually involved in goal setting, but lack the skills to define what is important to us, the help we will require, the internal resources we will need to commit, and how we know we've succeeded. These skills are rarely taught.

- We want to resolve conflicts and continue to have relationships, but often don't know how. As a result, we experience confrontation as being a bad thing rather than growth enabling. Fixable situations become irresolvable, compromising relationships that did not have to end.

- And finally, we need to become better at tending to our own needs as a prerequisite to becoming good at nurturing those around us.

In the following chapters, we will offer insights into how to teach Full Value and why it is of critical value from a pragmatic perspective.

Full Value & CASEL Core Competencies

We have highlighted the evolving work of CASEL to frame how the Full Value Schools model aligns with what is defined as critical needs and effective interventions. The bedrock behavioral norms of Full Value dovetail with CASEL's five core competencies.

We believe that these competencies are directly supported by the Full Value Behavioral Norms with significant crossover, as indicated in the following table:

FULL VALUE	CASEL CORE COMPETENCIES
Be Here	Self-Management, Social Awareness
Be Safe	Social Awareness, Self-Awareness
Be Honest	Relationship Skills
Set Goals	Responsible Decision Making
Let Go & Move On	Self-Awareness, Self-Management
Care for Self & Others	Self-Management, Relationship Skills, Social Awareness

While these norms will be reviewed in detail in our book, their primary intent can be easily derived. Beyond the CASEL competencies, the six Full Values embrace the critical SEL components of trust, presence, commitment, mindfulness, physical and emotional safety, giving and receiving feedback, defining and achieving measurable goals, relinquishing anger and hurt to maintain meaningful relationships, and generativity.

The CASEL model of best practices is embedded in the DNA of Full Value work.

- The teaching and implementation of Full Value are activity-based. For example, students and teachers may engage in games and initiatives that model and practice the behavioral norms and/or use the learning process in the classroom.

- Full Value activities can be connected to curriculum content areas such as language arts/literacy, reading, science, mathematics, physical education, and the performing and visual arts. They become part of the natural tapestry of the classroom experience.

- Students are active participants in co-creating how Full Value norms are used in their classrooms and school.

- Public acceptance of mindfulness is an essential aspect of Full Value.

- Students learn and are empowered to identify and discuss their differences and to resolve them in a way that avoids shaming, guilt, and blame.

- The focus is squarely on developing specific social-emotional skills.

- Full Value provides a common language and process that can be used at all developmental levels and across grade levels. As a result, there is no need for students to start over in new grades, classrooms, and schools as they move through their K-12 educational experience.

- In order to maintain simplicity, the three vital components of (1) co-creating behavioral norms, (2) goal setting, and (3) student led group discussions can be conveyed to staff via a short intensive training session.

- Sustainability training has been developed to ensure that internal experts can support school staff.

Finally, ongoing outcome evaluations would indicate a direct correlation between the systematic implementation of Full Value and a concurrent reduction in harassment, intimidation, and bullying incidents, as well as a reduction in disciplinary referral rates. Also noted are improvements in grade point average and attendance. This parallels the results of the CASEL meta-analysis (Durlak, 2011).[7]

How is This Activity Book Different from Other Activity Books?

A casual online search for experiential activity books yields hundreds of titles. They are usually focused on promoting team building, self-efficacy, self-esteem, goal setting, and problem solving with populations ranging from corporate groups to students. In this text, we apply activities specific to the creation of a Full Value Commitment. This purposeful application is unique, structured to offer an experiential approach to Full Value and social emotional learning. We also make direct connections to academic content areas, which further promotes the integration of SEL into all aspects of student learning.

For a detailed review of the background of this work, please read our earlier text, *Exploring Islands of Healing* (Schoel & Maizell, 2002).[8]

It has long been accepted that peer-to-peer learning and cross-age interactions between students are hugely beneficial. We will whet your appetite concerning the integration of peer leadership training with Full Value.

We hope that our efforts will provide a clear roadmap and a broad array of resources to support training and implementation in your school as we strive to develop a more empathetic, compassionate, and emotionally sophisticated community of learners.

What's Inside the Cover?

The book begins with a history of Full Value and an overview of each behavioral norm. Following this is a chapter discussing the impact of Full Value on fostering abstract reasoning skills and the associated effect on the mastery of complex academic material. This chapter also includes research on how the teaching of affective regulation positively impacts behavior and cognition, from the classroom to the workplace to the community. While it is crucial for us to convey that the Full Value model comes with clear theoretical underpinnings, we will then leave theory behind and focus primarily on providing the necessary tools for implementation.

Chapters include:

- Co-creating a Full Value Commitment with students

- An activity-based goal-setting process

- Full Value specific concepts, including Calling Group (the way students problem solve and celebrate their successes)

- Challenge of Choice

- The Control to Empowerment continuum, which allows students the freedom to take ownership of the Full Value process with adult guidance

- GRABBSS, an assessment tool used for activity selection and for examining the necessary elements of successful program implementation and sustainability

Following this is a chapter on connecting Full Value to academic content areas. There will be examples of lesson plans and a tool for developing content-based lessons. A chapter will explore mindfulness and Full Value (with activities). Also provided will be information on the application of Full Value to train peer leaders and to use students as program ambassadors with their peers.

While this seems like more than enough for one text, the preponderance of the book provides several hundred activities to use in teaching Full Value to students, organized under each behavioral norm. Activity write ups include necessary materials, the level of presentation difficulty, how the activity is done, suggestions for reflection, and other Full Value cross categories where the same activity can be used for different purposes.

Cross Categories

Once you become more familiar with the activities it will become apparent that they can be used to teach many areas of Full Value. Activities can be used again and again, depending on how they are introduced by you or co-created with students.

We think that defining cross categories for activities will free you to tap into your personal creativity in using them for more than one purpose and for more than one age group. For example, a tag game can help students learn to be present and engaged with each other, but can also be applied to issues of physical and emotional safety, honesty, and Let Go & Move On. The purposes and difficulty level of activities can be adjusted for different developmental stages and varying cognitive and physical capacities. Activities can also be used to teach multiple Full Values at the same time. We encourage and applaud creativity when engaging in activity selection and design with students.

Activity Difficulty Level & Materials

Activities are rated for ease of preparation, presentation, and facilitation based upon reviews by outside readers unfamiliar with them. An activity receives a rating of 1 for easy to 4 for the most complex. The complexity of an activity should not discourage its use, but we thought that a rating system would be helpful for teachers experiencing some entry anxiety into this process.

Understanding that most schools have limited resources, we have chosen activities that require minimal use of materials and supplies. Most of what you will need can be found in your kitchen, basement, attic, or garage (e.g., tarps, Beanie Babies, Popsicle sticks, eggs, balls for juggling, carpet squares, rope, buckets, etc.). Some suggestions for purchasing items are listed within the activity chapters and in the appendix.

While it would be impossible to categorize the thousands of activities that have been invented over the years by experiential practitioners, our many examples will hopefully lead to look at what exists in many books through the lens of teaching Full Value.

How and Why Do I Find Time for This?

In the past you may have chosen to post a set of rules on the classroom bulletin board, explain them, reinforce them, and then enforce them (often again and again with the same students). Or perhaps you tried another more inclusive method for establishing your classroom climate and culture. In either instance, it all takes time. Creating and sustaining a Full Value Commitment is no different. However, once established, with students taking responsibility for their own behavior and feeling more empowered, increased instructional time becomes available with associated improvement in academic performance while also teaching students the essential skills of self-regulation and having a voice when their peers violate established classroom norms (Zins, Bloodworth, Weissberg & Walberg, 2007; Payton, Weissberg, Durlak, Dymnicki, Taylor, et al., 2008; McCormick, Cappella, O'Connor, McClowry, 2015; Schonfeld, Adams, Fredstrom, Weissberg, Gilman, et al, 2015; Corcoran, Cheung, Kim, Xie, 2018).[9]

Teaching Full Value can be frontloaded into the beginning of the school year using the activities we provide to familiarize students with the program, leading to the creation of a classroom Full Value Commitment. This might involve using the initial period each morning during the first week or two of school at the primary and elementary levels. Once the Commitment is developed, it is adjusted over time depending on the needs of the class. The practice of the behaviors connected to each Full Value occurs naturalistically during individual, small group, and class interactions. Further on in the book, you will see how Full Value can be wholly integrated into academic content areas (Chapter 12).

Another implementation option is to use daily classroom activities and interactions to teach Full Value, which can be more effective with middle and high school students. This involves developing an understanding of how behaviors elicited by daily interactions in the classroom are connected to each Full Value Behavioral Norm. For example, if a class has difficulty settling down and paying attention during the framing of a lesson, this can be used as a Be Here issue. The lesson stops, and group is called. Students are prompted to co-create a list of behaviors (predicated on what just happened) that will support being here when they begin the lesson. This conversation will also include distractors that need to be avoided. The co-creation of the classroom Full Value Commitment flows out of this conversation without the need for a specific activity other than what is happening during the lesson.

Often the most effective path is a combination of the two: using activities designed to elicit behavior that focuses on one Full Value in combination with integration into the day-to-day interactions in the classroom. The activities are particularly effective as they are targeted, experiential, novel, and fun. Aside from focusing on a particular Full Value, they build students' capacity to work together on a goal as a group and all of the various skills that entail.

Finally, and most importantly, we continue to grapple with repeated episodes of self-injurious behavior and unspeakable, aggressive violence in our schools and communities. At the root of this are children who feel marginalized at an early age and are never given the tools to self-regulate or have a voice when feeling overwhelmed or threatened. We have seen these children as early as preschool. They are very easy to identify. They are either too quiet or too agitated. They are not provided with a safe and affirming environment to communicate their needs, fears, hopes, and aspirations. They feel alone and isolated. These are the students whose pain becomes transmuted into anger or self-harm and who, as they become older, have increasing access to resources to do harm to themselves or others.

Feelings of marginalization, depression, and hopelessness are not limited to a small group of students. The California Adverse Childhood Experiences (ACE) Study (1998)[10] surveyed 17,000 adult Californians and reported that two-thirds of the adult respondents experienced at least one ACE, and 12.5% experiencing four or more ACEs during their public school experience. ACEs are shown to have a causative link with nearly every major public health problem in America, including depression, suicide, substance abuse, and decreased life expectancy.

At the core of many children's mental health issues is the experiencing of trauma. In a study conducted by the Data Resource Center for Child & Adolescent Health (2013), it was estimated that nearly thirty-five million children between the ages of 0-17 had experienced one or more episodes of severe trauma in their families. This is close to half of our nation's children. According to Dr. Christina Bethell, Professor, Bloomberg School of Public Health, Johns Hopkins University:

> If more prevention, trauma-healing and resiliency training programs aren't provided for children who have experienced trauma, and if our educational, juvenile justice, mental health and medical systems are not changed to stop traumatizing already traumatized children, many of the nation's children are likely to suffer chronic disease and mental illness.[11]

As noted, the study indicates that building resilience serves to inoculate students against many of these catastrophic outcomes. The Full Value School provides a systemic culture and climate to support resiliency. This includes the development of behavioral norms (co-creation), providing opportunities for students to make choices about how they participate in the program (Challenge of Choice), control and empowerment through goal setting, and a forum for discussing issues and celebrating successes within a nurturing and supportive group process (Calling Group). Full Value components, and their positive impact on mitigating trauma will be discussed within this book.

No matter how we choose to do it, primary prevention SEL work is essential to maintain safe schools and a safe and healthy society. We have wasted far too much time debating its importance.

> We must educate our children for civic participation at every level, so that they and we come to see more committed, generous, and heroic actions as part of everyday life, not just a reaction to crisis. We must prepare our children for the tests of life, not a life of tests (2001).[12]
>
> - Maurice Elias, Professor of Psychology at Rutgers University and creator of the NJ Safe and Civil Schools initiative

* * * * * *

Some Thoughts About Co-Authorship

This text involved the work of Richard Maizell, Jim Schoel, and John Grund with a total of over 135 years of experience in the field of education, social work, psychology, counseling, teaching, administration, and experiential learning. The blending of their skills and expertise has resulted in a product that imparts essential theoretical knowledge and implementation strategies to support your efforts to integrate social-emotional learning into your particular setting. Every effort has been made to have the authors speak with one voice. Where our individual experiences are essential to enrich your understanding of the material, breakout boxes will contain this information. We hope you enjoy the fruits of this collaboration as much as we have.

CHAPTER 1

FULL VALUE

Full Value is a growth enabling process with the capacity to respond to the social-emotional needs of individuals and groups. The six guiding principles explained below rely on student contributions to develop what Full Value means to *them* in their unique setting. In order to encourage participation and to model shared responsibility, students must invest in the norms that are developed. Student buy-in most likely occurs when they have a direct say in the process.

For any group to function, it needs to establish a set of agreed-upon guiding norms. For our country, it is the Constitution. In business, this often takes the form of bylaws, charters, and contracts. In schools, this may be a set of rules posted by the classroom teacher at the beginning of the year. In society, we adhere to basic social contracts like stopping for red lights, not yelling fire in a movie theatre, standing in line when waiting for a bus, etc. Societal acceptance of behavioral norms provides a foundation for safe and cooperative living.

Origins of Full Value

Full Value traces its history back to the Outward Bound movement (Miner, 2002).[13] A group of Outward Bound instructors working in conjunction with educators was instrumental in bringing the Outward Bound experiential and expeditionary learning process to American public schools. Supported by a US Department of Education Grant, Project Adventure was founded in 1971 and housed at Hamilton-Wenham Regional High School in Massachusetts. Its mission was to adapt wilderness-oriented Outward Bound cooperative and challenge activities to public and private schools. It became evident early in its implementation that a process-oriented tool was needed to support group development and functioning, leading to adoption of the No Discount Contract (Medrick, 1977).[14]

No Discount Contract

As Project Adventure (PA) applied it, No Discount sought to ensure that participants devalued neither themselves nor others during their experience together. PA groups used three constructs from the No Discount Contract: Safety, Goal-Setting, and Feedback. Because of the risk factors inherent in the physical activities, a primary purpose for establishing the contract was to ensure the physical safety of group members when participating in activities that could result in injury if people were not looking out for each other. Devaluing behavior that could compromise physical safety included losing focus, fooling around, and taking unnecessary risks. Aside from affecting physical safety, these types of behavior impacted on the emotional safety of group members.

Project Adventure activities were, and are still, goal focused. No Discount (and its successors) had an individual and a group layer tied to goal setting. The individual layer asks for a commitment on the part of the person to set personal goals that would support the larger group goals, and further:

> Each person agrees to be confronted when his behavior does not match the behavior he identified as a goal. Similarly, he agrees to confront others when their behavior does not match what they identified as goals (Medrick, p. 197).

An individual goal in service of the group goal might be, "I will speak up when I have an idea about how to solve a problem."

The group layer supports grappling with a problem and finding ways to solve it. However, in order to be effective, each group member must have a voice in the process, honestly assess their strengths and areas of need, ask for help, offer encouragement, and contribute ideas and actions leading to a solution. Thus, a group goal connected to the No Discount Contract might be, "Let's agree to support each other."

Within a transactional framework (Berne, 2011)[15], decision-making around personal and group goals is practiced. Feedback is a way for the group to participate in the growth of its individual members. The practice of feedback laid the groundwork for what has become *Be Honest*. The safety, goal setting, and feedback commitments were spiraled out beyond the group's operation into family, community, work, and school-related interactions.

From No Discount to Full Value

The No Discount contract formed the basis for all that the group aspired to become. Naming a representation of group aspirations with a double negative, "No Discount" worked against its purposes. The introduction of the term "Full Value" provided a positive reframe that groups responded to favorably. In addition to eliminating negative terminology, the scope of Full Value was expanded to include *Let Go & Move On*, and *Care For Self & Others* (Schoel & Maizell, 2002).[16] These additional elements dramatically broadened the range of behavioral norms contained within Full Value Contracts and provided access to a wide-ranging set of learning outcomes.

Full Value Commitment Replaces Full Value Contract

Although Full Value is a social contract, it can be confused with a signed legal document. Contracts are a way of quantifying behavior based on common and case law. When contracts are broken, lawsuits often result. Once signed, participants in contracts are forced to comply with its rules. The glue that holds a contract together is based on the threat of punishment resulting from the violation of its stipulations. Contracts are not considered to be dynamic (i.e., easily changed when their focus shifts). If the intention is to create an asset-based community, framing it with an agreement rooted in negative consequences is counterintuitive.

A commitment differs from a contract as it is based in affect. It is a social-emotional bond. People commit to rather than contract with each other in relationships. We speak of being committed to an idea or a cause. While we sign an employment contract, our level of commitment drives the amount of time, energy, and devotion we bring to the work.

When Full Value Behavioral Norms are broken, it is an affective experience for students. They may feel hurt, angry, sad, or betrayed. Awareness, learning, and a reformulation of commitments result from this breach of trust. Contrary to a contract, it is assumed that violations will occur, providing crucial information for the group to process. Violations become learning opportunities. In fact, groups creating Full Value Commitments are asked to define these violations as *distractors*. It is built into the structure of the document. A Full Value bond between people within a group resides in their affective experience and expectations.

Full Value encourages groups to alter their commitments as they learn and grow from experience, renegotiating their operating norms, goals, and expectations. While contracts can be renegotiated, this typically occurs due to a violation or misunderstanding. Therefore, altering a contract is not considered to be positive. Our understanding of the ordinary meaning of *contract* and how it markedly differs from the intention of the group process led us to change the terminology from Full Value Contract to Full Value Commitment.

The Balance of Full Value

Considering each value and its outcomes led to the discovery of the *balance* of Full Value. For example, trust forms the basis for all relationships, yet maintaining a healthy mistrust can keep us out of trouble in making ill-advised commitments. Goal setting can lead to success. However, it also holds the potential for failure. Failure can be a great teacher. Grappling with failure as a learning experience reframes it as an opportunity for growth.

Full Value Today

The six Full Value Behavioral Norms are:

- Be Here
- Be Safe
- Be Honest
- Set Goals
- Let Go & Move On
- Care for Self & Others

Full Value Outcomes

We have identified specific social/emotional outcomes that result from implementing of a classroom Full Value Commitment. They are important to keep in mind and may be used as a template for backward design when planning academic lessons or specific activities to teach the Full Value Behavioral Norms. For example, outcomes associated with Be Here include:

- Active listening
- Becoming comfortable in one's own skin (aloneness)
- Building relationships
- Reflecting on information

These outcomes specifically relate to mindfulness practice and are reviewed in Chapter 13, Mindfulness & Full Value:

- Attunement
- Awareness of slipping into the past and future
- Emotional self-awareness
- Integration
- Optimism
- Organizational awareness

An Overview of Each Full Value Behavioral Norm and Their Outcomes

Be Here:

Attention in a classroom is an increasingly elusive commodity. Committing to Be Here asks that we focus on participating despite all distractions that impact us. A preschooler being present in class is very different than the presence reflected in the behavior of a high school student. Yet at any level, working on being here, wherever you are, is where education begins. Being present fosters engagement with others and leads to active listening, contributions, and learning. As evidenced by the number of times Be Here is listed as a cross-category within the activities chapters, it is clear that much of what we communicate requires developing skills in this area. Being present in the experience requires understanding the task, asking clarifying questions, having the necessary materials, and keeping track of time.

Be Here Outcomes

Active Listening: Listening is an essential skill to develop with students, as it is the basis for effective communication. It requires becoming skillful at parsing out external and internal distractions.

Becoming Comfortable in One's Own Skin: In our culture, being unplugged from our social lives has become increasingly difficult. We are not comfortable with silence. We are often afraid to be alone with our thoughts and feelings. Our feelings of isolation are reflected in the obsession with social media. It is essential to embrace our thoughts and feelings and to cherish time alone. Being OK with being alone promotes the ability to operate as an individual who develops personal opinions and unique perspectives.

Building Relationships: Once communication is established by practicing active listening, the potential for establishing and deepening relationships exists. Part of being here is learning something more about how people live their lives, what is important to them, and what causes happiness or hurt. It is the beginning of vulnerability, which is also at the root of building relationships. It allows for authentic and meaningful communication and supports the ability to work together more effectively. Connecting with others within any activity involves shared ownership and responsibility, leading to the pride of accomplishment and feelings of increased self-efficacy and self-esteem.

Self-Reflection: As part of the Be Here process, students are offered options for self-reflection. These include journaling, creating a physical representation such as a collage, drawing, or sculpture, and group and paired sharing of experience. Self-reflection contributes to affective growth and abstract reasoning.

Be Safe:

The violation of the physical and emotional safety of students in schools is commonplace. This may take the form of bullying, humiliation, intimidation, harassment, rejection, cliques, and gangs. Learning about who and what to trust provides strategies for surviving these violations. There are degrees of trust, of course. Trust is relational, building connections with other people. In teaching about trust, an understanding of mistrust is essential. Mistrust provides us with wisdom in decision-making. It teaches us to ask questions and to develop a critical eye. When we teach the differences between trust and mistrust, we aim to give students wisdom that will last a lifetime. Trusting self is also an aspect of Be Safe.

<u>Be Safe Outcomes</u>

- Trust
- Mistrust
- Responding Rather Than Reacting
- Self-Regulation
- Feeling Secure
- Welcoming Authentic Interaction

Trust: When we have come to believe that those around us have a genuine and demonstrable concern for our well-being, we feel emotionally safe. This trust is gained via repetitive experiences where this concern is demonstrated consistently over time.

Mistrust: Given that not every interaction will be emotionally safe, it is vital for students to have a clear sense of when this is happening and how to respond without self-blame and doubt. They must not be victimized.

Responding Rather Than Reacting: This involves practicing self-regulation, pausing, taking a breath, and not going with your first instinct to lash out when feeling emotionally compromised. It also recognizes the psychological feedback from one's body (e.g., clenching fists, tightness in the chest, etc.) and understanding what this might mean in terms of the potential for overreaction.

Self-Regulation: The ability to self-regulate is essential to maintaining a school environment free of harassment, intimidation, and bullying. When confronted with an interaction that holds the potential for wielding hurtful power and control over another student, this skill initiates a process where the students know to stop, walk away, and, if need be, ask for help. Self-regulation also works to prevent piling on, when a crowd of students forms around two antagonists to derive some vicarious pleasure. If there is no one to pile on, when one of the two antagonists refuses to be victimized, the bully is left powerless.

Feeling Secure: Forming secure attachments with those around us begins very early in life. Caregivers who provide unconditional positive regard and who resonate with the feelings of their children build and maintain emotional safety. Their responsiveness legitimizes feelings that children have while providing a safe space for talking about how the thoughts and behaviors connected to those feelings can affect others. Beyond showing empathy for the experience of another, a secure attachment offers opportunities for emotional healing and the repair of compromised relationships.

Welcoming Authentic Interaction: The willingness to listen. The desire to take risks in self-disclosure.

Be Honest:

Striving for compassionate honesty in the communication of thoughts and feelings is the focus of this behavioral norm. For communication to be effective, honesty must permeate all aspects of individual and group communication. However, there is a caveat to this. Honesty can be used for less than honest intentions. There may be an agenda to humiliate the recipient with negative feedback to gain power and influence. Brutal honesty may be an act of revenge for perceived slights or humiliation. When offered in a caring way, honest feedback provides an invaluable perspective to the recipient who can then better hear it without becoming defensive. Honest feedback must always be offered with the intention of encouraging growth, or it becomes a violation of the receiver's emotional safety. The essential question is, "Will my feedback help my classmate to grow?" Courage is a crucial component because honesty can mean you are not sure you are right and are willing to say, "I think this, but I could be wrong." This connects to self-assessment as well as assessing the intentions that drive feedback received from others. We should always strive to be compassionately honest.

<u>Be Honest Outcomes</u>

- Practicing an Ethical Code of Behavior
- Exploring the Truth
- Integrating Feedback
- Values

Practicing an Ethical Code of Behavior: While the Full Value Behavioral Norms fit nicely into a code of ethics or conduct, honesty would seem to be at the core of ethical behavior. It is being true to your beliefs even when no one is watching you. Connected to reflective practice is self-honesty projected outward in all communications with others.

Exploring the Truth: True explorers investigate what is unknown and try to make sense of it. Honesty is an essential tool of the student explorer, particularly when considering the thoughts and feelings of classmates. If I am the recipient of feedback, am I pushing past my initial perception of events and through my defensiveness? Am I really hearing what is being said? Am I asking questions that are focused purely on developing an understanding of what happened? Am I opening up my belief system to change? If a student can ask themselves these questions, they are exploring the truth during and after the activity.

Integrating Feedback: Integrating feedback is a courageous and stressful process. It may mean altering preconceived notions and experiencing the disruption of what might be many years of thinking about things in a certain way. Conversely, it can also involve careful consideration of feedback, associated self-reflection, and concluding that the offered feedback is not on target. Not owning the feedback around a situation can be a reasonable outcome. People can agree to disagree.

Values: This means holding true to one's values and not compromising them when in a situation where that could occur. For example, in an activity, there may be the potential for compromising one's value system in perceived service to the group. The successful completion of an activity could require disclosing if he or she, or another student, loses contact with an object to avoid a pyrrhic victory. Self-reporting this infraction or reporting what is observed will cause the entire group to have to start over. The choice for the student built into the activity is to either hold true to the value of honesty or diminish the success of the group by compromising successful completion of the task. There are, of course, social risks associated with being faithful to one's values. Reflection after the activity provides opportunities for this to be processed, and students who support cheating as a strategy to be confronted by their peers.

Set Goals:

The ability to set clearly stated personal and professional goals is the basis for a fulfilled life. Unfortunately, all too often, students find themselves exiting their senior year with either an ill-defined set of goals or on a trajectory to fulfill someone else's plan for their future.

According to the National Center for Educational Statistics:

> The 6-year graduation rate in 2014 was 60 percent for first-time, full-time undergraduate students who began their pursuit of a bachelor's degree at a 4-year degree granting institution in fall 2008. The 6-year graduation rate was highest for Asian students (71 percent) and lowest for Black and American Indian/Alaska Native students (41 percent each).[17]

The commitment of time and money associated with this life choice is enormous, yet these dismal statistics reveal that the goal-setting process that led to attending college for many students was ineffective.

Goal setting includes brainstorming, planning, and learning to make informed choices. Setting and achieving goals is a primary life experience. Persistence is also a

> At a recent presentation on Full Value I asked a group of 180 educators how many had been taught a formal goal setting process prior to entering college. Only a handful of people raised their hands. This is a serious content omission in post-secondary teacher training -Richard

significant, learned attribute. Sumner Redstone said, "Success is not built on success. It's built on failure. It's built on frustration. Sometimes it's built on catastrophe."[18] While experiencing success is essential to maintaining motivation, experiencing failure and learning from it is also necessary. The balance between success and failure provides students with necessary learning experiences.

Goal setting should result in an honest assessment of what the student wants to achieve, how to get there, know when you've been successful, and what internal and external supports will be necessary. This last point holds excellent growth potential, for it empowers the student to ask for help from others as an essential step in goal achievement. The honing of goal-setting skills has ramifications for working collaboratively in all future endeavors with family, friends, and in the employment setting. Specific to the work setting, engaging in the cooperative development of a shared mission is at the forefront of employer desired twenty-first century workplace readiness skills.

Goal setting provides opportunities for cooperation rather than competition. For if an agreed upon goal is achieved, our propensity for fairness is rewarded. Practicing fairness spills into all areas of social emotional learning, promoting sharing, generosity, and self-sacrifice.

Set Goals Outcomes

- Growth Oriented
- Cooperation Versus Competition
- Intention into Action
- Brainstorm and Plan
- Achievement
- Failure
- Accepting Help
- Defining Clear Objectives
- Empowerment
- Independence
- Intelligent Risk Taking

Growth Oriented: Central to goal setting is that growth occurs from choosing an objective and fulfilling it. A goal that does not involve growth and change is not worthy of consideration.

Cooperation Versus Competition: The goal-setting process we describe in Chapter 9 asks students to set personal and school related goals that are theirs alone, with support asked for and provided by classmates. As each plan is individually based, the competitive process is eliminated. Non-competitiveness is also the structure of all activities that are described in the book. It is always the group working collaboratively together, rather than competing against each other to reach a goal.

Intention into Action: Having the intention to change is an essential place to begin, but it must be followed by action. Engaging in a deliberate goal-setting plan and the work of achieving the goal demonstrates a willingness to define and commit to change.

Brainstorm and Plan: Brainstorming feeds the creative process. It liberates the student from having to determine a goal without true exploration. Planning tools in this text focus on content and process.

Achievement: The outcome of this process is to achieve a desired goal. When a student does the hard work of defining a goal and working diligently to achieve it, there is a tremendous feeling of satisfaction and accomplishment.

Failure: The expression "failing forward" describes the upside of a student's struggle with goal setting. If failure is reframed for students as an opportunity to learn rather than as a shameful experience, then failure just becomes part of the process. It may be that a student selected an unrealistic goal. A goal may seem desirable, but then lose its luster over time. The goal might be too vast and require smaller, achievable subgoals in order to get there. Words and phrases like change, rethinking, reconsideration, smaller steps, other resources, and a different goal are all asset based and optimistic. This is how the experience of failure can be viewed as a growth-oriented tool. Finally, we all sometimes fail, and rallying from that experience and moving forward is crucial to building resiliency. This is the ability to not internalize the failure to the point where it causes paralysis and self-doubt. If we did not experience failure, we would not know how achievement feels. This is the balance of Full Value.

Accepting Help: We exist in a society that rewards independence, self-reliance, and autonomy. If pulling yourself up by your bootstraps was a successful approach, we would not have the National Alliance on Mental Health reporting that 20 percent of students ages 13-18 live with a mental health condition. This number represents approximately 10 million students enrolled in public and private schools, grades 9-12.[19] The deliberate inclusion of asking for outside support to reach a goal begins to break down this maladaptive process for students. Practicing supportive collaboration is essential.

Defining Clear Objectives: Defining relevant and measurable objectives can be difficult. With the tools provided for students in this text, it becomes easier. Teachers working with students and students working with each other are essential to generating clear objectives. The defining of measurable objectives is built into all provided activities.

Empowerment: The successful completion of an individual or group goal is an empowering experience. Measurable success brings pride of accomplishment, increasing self-confidence, and an understanding that it is possible to negotiate difficult terrain with sufficient planning.

Independence: Mastering the ability to set goals and achievements, even when asking for help during activities in the classroom, builds a sense of independence. It offers students a window into the possibility of setting and achieving goals throughout their personal and professional lives.

Intelligent Risk Taking: Students, particularly adolescents, tend to become involved in risk taking behaviors. Taking risks can be growth enabling or can be stupid, resulting in self-harm. Implicit in goal setting is that a chance must be taken. For without risk, change is limited. The following reading from The Essene Book of Days illustrates this and is a powerful metaphor for introducing goal setting to middle and high school students. It is called The Parable of the Trapeze: Turning the Fear of Transformation into the Transformation of Fear.[20]

> Sometimes I feel that my life is a series of trapeze swings. I'm either hanging on to a trapeze bar swinging along or, for a few moments in my life, I'm hurtling across space in between trapeze bars.
>
> Most of the time, I spend my life hanging on for dear life to my trapeze-bar-of-the-moment. It carries me along at a certain steady rate of swing and I have the feeling that I'm in control of my life. I know most of the right questions and even some of the right answers. But once in a while, as I'm merrily (or not so merrily) swinging along, I look ahead of me into the distance, and what do I see? I see another trapeze bar swinging toward me. It's empty, and I know, in that place that knows, that this new trapeze bar has my name on it. It is my next step, my growth, my aliveness coming to get me. In my heart-of-hearts I know that for me to grow, I must release my grip on the present, well known bar to move to the new one.
>
> Each time it happens to me, I hope (no, I pray) that I won't have to grab the new one. But in my knowing place, I know that I must totally release my grasp on my old bar, and for some moment in time hurtle across space before I can grab onto the new bar. Each time I am filled with terror. It doesn't matter that in all my previous hurtles across the void of unknowing, I have always made it. Each time I am afraid I will miss, that I will be crushed on the unseen rocks in the bottomless chasm between the bars. But I do it anyway. Perhaps this is the essence of what the mystics call the faith experience. No guarantees, no net, no insurance policy, but you do it anyway because somehow, to keep hanging onto that old bar is no longer on the list of alternatives. And so for an eternity that can last a microsecond or a thousand lifetimes, I soar across the dark void of, "the past is gone, the future is not yet here." It's called transition. I have come to believe that it is the only place that real change occurs. I

mean real change, not the pseudo-change that only lasts until the next time my old buttons get punched.

I have noticed that, in our culture, this transition zone is looked upon as a "no-thing," a no-place between places. Sure the old trapeze-bar was real, and that new one coming towards me, I hope that's real too. But the void in between? That's just a scary, confusing, disorienting "nowhere" that must be gotten through as fast and as unconsciously as possible. What a waste! I have a sneaking suspicion that the transition zone is the only real thing, and the bars are illusions we dream up to avoid the void, where the real change, the real growth occurs for us. Whether or not my hunch is true, it remains that the transition zones in our lives are incredibly rich places. They should be honored, even savored. Yes, with all the pain and fear and feelings of being out-of-control that can (but not necessarily) accompany transitions, they are still the most alive, most growth-filled, passionate, expansive moments in our lives.

And so, transformation of fear may have nothing to do with making fear go away, but rather with giving ourselves permission to "hang-out" in the transition between trapeze bars. Transforming our need to grab that new bar, any bar, is allowing ourselves to dwell in the only place where change really happens. It can be terrifying. It can also be enlightening, in the true sense of the word. Hurtling through the void, we just may learn how to fly.

Let Go & Move On:

Let Go & Move On provides opportunities to practice the skill of working with others when there is anger, misunderstanding, and hurt feelings. It means to co-exist even when one disagrees, which facilitates working toward a common goal. In some instances, this provides an opportunity to practice forgiveness. But in situations where one can't or won't forgive, there is often still the need to get along, work together, and share responsibilities. This is true in schools, in the community, and for families. It also means accepting that change is inevitable and often beyond our control. Family dynamics are altered by something as joyous as the coming of a new baby, to the loss of a parent. In the work setting, the retirement of a beloved leader can breed resentment and destructive behavior toward a successor. The shifting sands of popularity in the classroom can cause a student to feel newly accepted or rejected. Acceptance of change requires letting go of what was or will be, and making healthy choices around how to work effectively within changed circumstances.

<u>Let Go & Move On Outcomes</u>

- Revenge Versus Reconciliation
- Resiliency
- Accepting Unenforceable Rules

- Accepting Difference
- Accepting Complexity

Revenge Versus Reconciliation: When we are hurt somehow by a perceived negative interaction, there is a tendency to lash out. This can escalate rather than move past a conflict. Practicing the skill of finding common ground and compromising on some of the strong beliefs that feed hurt and anger involves reconciliation. Conflict breaks down connections. Reconciliation requires a commitment to finding a win-win solution to disputes.

Resiliency: This is learning the skills to keep moving forward in relationships, going past some of the more painful interactions to continue to work toward the group's goals. It is learning to become more comfortable with being uncomfortable. This connects to failing forward in relationships, and that connections between students can become stronger through the successful resolution of conflict.

Accepting Unenforceable Rules: An example of an unenforceable rule is, "My teacher had my sister, who was an outstanding student, so I will be favored by the teacher, as well." Learning to let go of preconceived beliefs that are not rooted in the actual experience is an important element of this commitment.

Accepting Difference: Our personalities and associated behaviors are part nature, part nurture. We each come from a unique place. When students develop this understanding, it changes the nature of experience from objective to subjective. It makes it easier not to personalize disagreements as students work to understand the concept that we all come from a different place.

Accepting Complexity: If life were simple, if there were no gray areas, then there would be no need for the 1.3 million lawyers[21] (as of 2018) practicing in the United States. Therefore, it is vital for students to be exposed to activities where ambiguity is modeled and can be discussed. Recognizing these gray areas builds tolerance, acceptance, and mature social judgment.

Care for Self & Others:

Caring for others involves compassion and empathy. Caring is reflected in listening and responding, following through to completion (it is one thing to want to do something, quite another to get involved enough to do it), compassionate reaching out to a group member who feels out of place, coping with excluding and judgmental language, honoring the commitments and insights of others, and understanding and responding with feeling.

Caring for self (i.e., being attentive and responsive to self needs, as distinguished from vanity) is also a reflection of empathy. It is challenging to teach self-care if the teacher is not practicing it.

Educators and other service providers are notorious for ignoring their own needs, impacting their physical and emotional health, and compromising their ability to work effectively with students. Empathic self-care encompasses the whole definition of the word. Unfortunately, the time and emotional pressure of doing a job that seemingly has no end, with demands to serve on every level, can cause educators to make poor choices in this regard. Maintaining a daily ritual of self-care that allows for no distractions is a solution. A strategy to maintain the ritual is to have at least one fellow professional commit to being a care buddy, a person to check in with, if only as a reminder that one isn't alone.

Care for Self & Others Outcomes

- Recognizing Self-Worth
- Recognizing Personal Needs
- Self-sacrifice
- Personal and Social Responsibility
- Interdependence
- Self-Empathy/Empathy
- Self-Compassion/Compassion

Recognizing Self-Worth: An activity presented in Chapter 11, Care for Self & Others, is called Accepting Yourself. Students develop a list of their strengths as members of the class. After reading from the list, the rest of the class is invited to add to it. Students often find the acceptance and disclosure of positive attributes as being quite challenging. They have been told that this is bragging, egocentric behavior. In fact, we are often our own harshest critics, and the self-recognition of strengths with further affirmation from a group of peers is the essence of caring for oneself. It is the recognition of the unique qualities we bring to our interactions with others and a public affirmation of these strengths.

Recognizing Personal Needs: Through practicing caring for oneself, students understand the importance of nurturing one's own needs as a foundation for being an effective caregiver. Doing for others without this recognition ultimately leads to resentment and a deep sense of loss. Students learn that to care for self is not selfish but rather essential to leading a balanced emotional life. This also means teaching students the value of taking time for personal growth and renewal.

Self-sacrifice: Another word for this is altruism, which is selfless attention to the needs of others. This behavior is most often demonstrated by students who understand the importance of self-care, providing them with the emotional strength to extend themselves to others without expecting emotional reciprocity. This is the stuff of heroic deeds! Activities associated with this Full Value Behavioral Norm provide opportunities for demonstrating self-sacrifice at many levels.

Personal and Social Responsibility: In working within a social group, using agreed upon norms/values, students learn that they are part of a larger system where the individual moving parts affect the whole. Care for Self & Others can be connected to our democratic structures at the middle and high school levels. Programs such as Social Security, Medicare, and Medicaid, as well as the requirement to pay taxes to fund schools and social services, all represent the personal and social responsibility reflected in this Full Value Behavioral

Norm. Developing this social/emotional outcome contributes to a citizenry that more fully participates in society because they understand the need for shared responsibility.

Interdependence: This is the realization that taking care of oneself supports taking care of others. Unresolved anger, harboring hurt feelings from an interaction, or not taking care of one's physical self can all impact the ability to care for others.

Empathy: Teaching the skill of resonating with the emotional life of another is critical to building and maintaining intimate relationships. Many of the activities used to teach Full Value in this book allow students to practice this social/emotional outcome.

Self-Compassion/Compassion: The way we treat a very good friend is how we should be treating ourselves. We would never speak to a good friend with the words we use in our heads to evaluate our own behaviors. Being incessantly self-critical does not help us grow. Compassion is empathy put into practice. When a student witnesses a peer struggling with their ability to succeed and lends a helping hand, empathy and compassion are both at work.

Full Values Working Together

One might be tempted to see Full Value as a hierarchy. It isn't. We do not first teach students to Be Here before we move on to Be Safe. In reality, no one Full Value holds sway over another. When students truly live their Full Value Commitment, they can apply all of the Full Values simultaneously. For example, one can Be Honest, but if honesty is not offered with the recipient's emotional safety kept in mind, the honesty can be destructive. When participating in a meaningful exchange with significant emotional content, students need to be in the moment, tuned in, and present with each other.

Control to Empowerment & Full Value

Full Value invests significant decision-making authority with students to craft the behavioral norms they agree to live by. This democratic experience can be messy. As teachers, we may be tempted to jump in and overly guide the process, becoming directive. Wait time is an essential tool to get participation from a student who may need a more extended period to formulate a contribution. Rather than being directive, more open-ended prompts can help move the process along. Conflict, while sometimes painful to experience, can be productive and growth enabling. Students need to practice constructing an artful argument, expressing their beliefs passionately, brainstorming, compromising, and coming to a resolution. They also need to learn that with empowerment comes responsibility.

Power sharing with students does not mean the surrendering of authority. Whether it is guiding the creation of a Full Value Commitment, facilitating an activity or lesson, or Calling Group (Chapter 5), the readiness of students to act responsibly and not abuse the power they have been granted is continuously being assessed. At the end of the day, the teacher is responsible for his or her students' emotional and physical safety.

The Control to Empowerment Scale (Simpson & Gillis, 1998)[22] provides a graphic representation of this process as discussed in Exploring Islands of Healing (Schoel & Maizell, pg. 97).

Control										**Empowerment**
	1	2	3	4	5	6	7	8	9	10

As teachers, we understand the importance of being firm at the beginning of the school year (Control) and lightening our touch as student behavioral patterns become more familiar (Empowerment), and relationships build. This is true when developing a Full Value Commitment and Calling Group. The teacher must bring students back to the process if things get out of hand. The teacher must initially ensure that groups are called for good reason. However, as long as civility is maintained and ideas, not personalities, are the focus of attention, students must be invested with the power to propose and come to a consensus around the norms that they will be asked to live by. We know that without this power, classroom rules become imposed and, therefore, usually ineffective.

Some Thoughts About Educator Participation

For Full Value to be embraced by students as a way of life, all educators in the school really need to embrace it, as well. It can't be do as I say, not as I do. As noted above, Control to Empowerment is the safety valve to maintain supervision where necessary. And there should be no hesitation about intervening when the physical safety of students is at risk. However, the primary thrust of Full Value is responsible empowerment. We want to teach students how to fish! Your participation in activities and contribution to Full Value Commitments is also essential. It is a modeling process that students need and will appreciate. They need to know that you are in this with them, not as a dispassionate observer. You will note that some activities require participation to guide their content and outcomes. Your participation facilitates building stronger relationships with students. Your presence becomes more real as they learn about you. This does not necessarily mean significant personal disclosure, but participation in and of itself helps to engender closeness.

Full Value Behavioral Norms & Trauma Work

"Being able to feel safe with other people is probably the single most important aspect of mental health; safe connections are fundamental to meaningful and satisfying lives" (Van der Kolk, 2014, pg. 352).[23]

Anyone working in education should become aware of the profound impact trauma may have on themselves, our colleagues, and especially our students. The educator's primary role regarding trauma is to develop awareness and to do no harm. Traumatic experiences scar students with an extreme sense of losing control and an inability to respond to the world in a competent manner. These experiences can be one-time events or ongoing exposure to an environment that induces fear and an overall feeling of being unsafe. Trauma doesn't just impact our thoughts and feelings but also our bodies. People suffering from PTSD develop nervous systems that remain on high alert that can be triggered at any moment and by seemingly innocent stimuli. Being on guard impacts how we process information, learn, and relate to others, and leaves many hyper-vigilant and drained. One of the most crucial understandings to develop is that we have no idea what other people have experienced and how these traumatic experiences affect them.

Trauma comes in many sizes. A traumatic event can be an accidental or violent act, either personally experienced or witnessed. It could be a dangerous inner-city neighborhood or a highly competitive suburban high school. The reasons may be very different in nature, but both environments leave many students stressed and unable to function optimally. Unresolved trauma lingers under the surface of many people's psyches and can surface without warning.

A common reaction to trauma is through disassociation, which is an attempt to cope by distancing oneself from emotions, thoughts, feelings, or even one's own body. Educators need to be informed of all of this, but are not responsible for healing it. Well-trained support teams of mental health professionals need to work closely with educational staff members to identify and provide interventions and referral services to anyone impacted by trauma.

Full Value offers the following container for trauma:

Impact of Trauma	Full Value Offering
Disassociation	Be Here: Offers the experience of being in the present moment with sensations, emotions and thoughts. Mindfulness is the opposite of dissociation.
Loss of Safety	Be Safe: Offers the experience of physical and emotional safety. The student is empowered to co-create their environment.
Loss of Trust	Be Honest: Offers the opportunity to develop authentic relationships by speaking their truth and having the permission to have their needs met.
Loss of Control	Set Goals: Offers the opportunity to gain a sense of control through intention and purpose. The goal setting process offers the student the chance to ask for support from others.
Shame	Let Go & Move On: Offers the permission and practice to move on from the things we cannot change or that just don't work.
Loss of Self-Worth	Care for Self & Others: Offers the student the opportunity and permission to practice self-care. This agreement also

	offers the opportunity to practice and receive empathy and compassion.

Summing Up

In reading through this material, you may conclude that primary prevention is hard work. There is no way around it, it is! But the rewards are manifest and life changing. Socially appropriate behaviors need to be practiced repetitively and linked to authentic experience with carryover into the home whenever possible. Students need to be active participants in defining what pro-social behaviors look and feel like, or the result will be reduced to another set of externally imposed rules. The commitment students make to social emotional learning must become integrated into all interactions throughout the school, inseparable from any academic content area.

Of equal importance is the extent to which school staff agree to embrace and live the commitments they have co-created with their students. While it is recognized that authority remains invested with the adults, teachers must strive to empower students to self-regulate and have a voice whenever possible. When a Full Value School is implemented with fidelity, teachers find that they have much more time to do what they love to do: teach. This happens by creating a truly collaborative effort with students and the concomitant release from the stressful, repetitive, and ineffective disciplinary hamster wheel.

CHAPTER 2

THE IMPACT OF FULL VALUE ON AFFECT & ABSTRACT REASONING

Educators are overwhelmed, as are public schools in general. Schools are increasingly asked to serve in the role of in loco parentis. The list grows longer every year, from monitoring inoculations to pre and post-school care, nutrition, sex education, cyberbullying, and homelessness. Content area requirements, testing, and evaluation continue to become more complex and demanding. It is no wonder teachers are hesitant when asked to "teach" social emotional learning.

But what if teaching personal responsibility, empathy, and compassion for others added demonstrable value to academic achievement? What if equipping students to take responsibility for self-regulation and for each other reduced distracting and off task behavior? What if students were better equipped to set academic goals and define a path to genuine achievement? What if the data demonstrated that teaching students to understand and regulate their affective lives and give voice to their concerns accelerated progress in content areas? What if this were also true for the development of more effective abstract reasoning skills?

The short answer is that social emotional learning and Full Value supports all of these areas when implemented systemically and with fidelity. Contrary to the stereotypical belief that social emotional learning is just another time waster in an already oversubscribed day, it is foundational to increasing the capacity to learn more effectively. Let's look at why.

A Brain that Can't Feel Can't Make Up Its Mind

In an article entitled *Feeling our Way to Decision* (Lehrer, 2009)[24] we learn about Elliot. Elliot was a high functioning man with a complicated job and a family. He was successful by every measure until surgery in the prefrontal area of the brain compromised his ability to experience affect. His lack of emotional responsiveness was confirmed by exposing Elliot to stimulating images that should have produced sweat from the glands in the palms. No response was noted. Elliot's IQ remained in the top 3 percent, but now he was unable to use it. As an outcome of this disconnection, Elliot lost his job, got divorced, and moved in with his parents. As Lehrer notes:

> This was a completely unexpected discovery. At the time, neuroscience assumed that human emotions were irrational. A person without emotions - in other words, someone like Elliot - should therefore make better decisions. His cognition should be uncorrupted. The charioteer should have complete control.

> What, then, had happened to Elliot? To Damasio, Elliot's pathology suggested emotions are a crucial part of the decision-making process. When we are cut off from our feelings, the most banal decisions become impossible. A brain that can't feel can't make up its mind (pg.15).

The seat of this emotional control appears to reside in the orbital-frontal cortex. Damage to this area prevents emotions from filtering a flood of excessive cognitions that would otherwise paralyze decision-making. Lehrer indicates:

> The crucial importance of our emotions - the fact that we can't make decisions without them - contradicts the conventional view of human nature, with its ancient philosophical roots. For most of the twentieth century, the ideal of rationality was supported by scientific descriptions of human anatomy (pg. 17).

We Feel – Therefore We Learn

A paper titled *We Feel, Therefore We Learn: The Relevance of Affective and Social Neuroscience to Education* (Immordino-Yang & Damasio, 2007)[25] posits, "Emotion-related processes are required for skills and knowledge to be transferred from the structured school environment to real-world decision making because they provide an emotional rudder to guide judgment and action" (pg. 3).

The authors nest their hypotheses in brain-based research by examining the responses of brain-injured subjects in the pre-frontal area and how that causes a disconnect between what is learned and how the learning is used. Damage to the pre-frontal area, while not compromising hard skills (such as the ability to calculate, reason, and read), causes people to begin to make decisions antithetical to the purposes of their work.

> These patients' ability to make advantageous decisions became compromised in ways that it had not been before. In fact, there was a complete separation between the period that anteceded the onset of the lesion, when these patients had been upstanding, reliable, and foresightful citizens, and the period thereafter, when they would make decisions that were often disadvantageous to themselves and their families. They would not perform adequately in their jobs, in spite of having the required skills; they would make poor business deals in spite of knowing the risks involved; they would lose their savings and choose the wrong partners in all sorts of relationships (pg. 4).

A more traditional explanation would be that those affected have lost the capacity for logical-rational thought. However, assessment indicated that the patients had no loss of IQ and could convey the appropriate rules of behavior associated with their work, but were incapable of behaving appropriately or responding to or learning from the emotional feedback in their environment. As noted, their *emotional rudder* was compromised.

These findings have significant implications for the critical nature of social emotional learning that extends well beyond the importance of creating and maintaining a safe and civil society. The essential point is that with the absence of affect, cognitive functioning becomes compromised. That affect is fundamental to the decision-making and problem-solving process in the cognitive domain. The authors provide a striking visual image when describing the importance of emotions in managing cognition:

> Emotions are not just messy toddlers in a China shop, running around breaking and obscuring delicate cognitive glassware. Instead, they are more like the shelves underlying the glassware; without them cognition has less support (pg. 5).

However, we know that unregulated affect can be destructive. The fight/freeze/faint/flight response is an example of the primitive displays of affect that, in times past, may have protected us from saber-toothed tigers but now serve to compromise relationships between people. Un-modulated affect works at cross-purposes for the implementation of ideas, which requires compromise, openness, and empathy. Primitive affect manifests in behaviors that can be emotionally and physically dangerous.

It has long been accepted that different components of intelligence transcend the traditionally measured areas of the Intelligence Quotient (IQ). These assessments focus on subscales that assess verbal comprehension and working memory, and performance scales that assess perceptual organization and processing speed. Nevertheless, IQ is typically used as a predictor of academic success.

Interestingly, while not outlined in the Wechsler Individual Achievement Test (WIAT III, 2009)[26] manual, a body of work has focused on using these same IQ scales as a projective tool in order to assess for the emotions that are embedded in responses. There can be clear pathological responses that questions can elicit. For example, when asked what to do with a stamped and addressed letter found on the street, a normal response would be to mail it. A more anti-social reply would be to open the letter, read it, then throw it in the trash. When asked what to do when smelling smoke or seeing fire in a movie theatre, an affectively healthy response would be to quietly tell the manager. More pathological would be to stand up and yell "fire," then run for the exit.

> A more personal observation of the essential interplay between cognitive capacity and emotional intelligence is instructive. During a clinical internship at Greystone State Psychiatric Hospital in Morris Plains, New Jersey I had occasion to conduct IQ assessments on the involuntarily committed clients. While their Full-Scale IQ scores often totaled in the Very Superior Range of Intelligence, they were completely unable to function. Most were on the locked ward for the criminally insane. This was a striking example of high cognitive capacity absent the necessary self-regulation that a healthy affective life or emotional intelligence provides. - Richard

Daniel Goleman's (1995)[27] contribution of emotional intelligence (EQ) have broadened the view of intelligence as it applies to human capacities, conceptualizing five areas encompassing EQ. These include self-awareness of your emotions, managing your own emotions, self-motivation, awareness and understanding of the emotions of people around you, and managing relationships.

He points to an emerging body of rigorous evidence that supports the strong connection between embedding social emotional learning programs in schools and the associated rise in academic performance. Goleman debunks the antiquated notion that academic learning has nothing to do with students' social and emotional environment. He cites current research in the neurosciences.

> The emotional centers of the brain are intricately interwoven with the neuro cortical areas involved in cognitive learning. When a child trying to learn is caught up in a distressing emotion, the centers for learning are temporarily hampered. The child's attention becomes preoccupied with whatever may be the source of the trouble. Because attention is itself a limited capacity, the child has that much less ability to hear, understand, or remember what a teacher or a book is saying. In short, there is a direct link between emotions and learning (Para. 5).

He also points to the crucial importance of weaving social emotional learning into the fabric of school culture and climate.

> As a William T. Grant Foundation study has revealed, the active ingredients in the programs that worked were largely the same, no matter their ostensible target problem. The best SEL programs were implemented throughout each year of schooling. They shaped the entire school climate, and they used developmentally appropriate lessons. They also taught children specific social-emotional skills like self-awareness, self-management, empathy, perspective taking, and cooperation. In short, they were lessons in emotional intelligence (Para. 2).

The two summative points to be made are that (1) affective regulation can and must be taught in order to be used effectively in the service of cognition and behavior, and that (2) without access to modulated affective functioning, thinking and acting can become significantly compromised.

ABC Triangle

The Affect-Behavior-Cognition (ABC) Triangle (Maizell, pg. 24)[28] captures the essence of this conclusion. In the experiential learning process is the affect that undergirds and integrates the outcomes of thought and behavior.

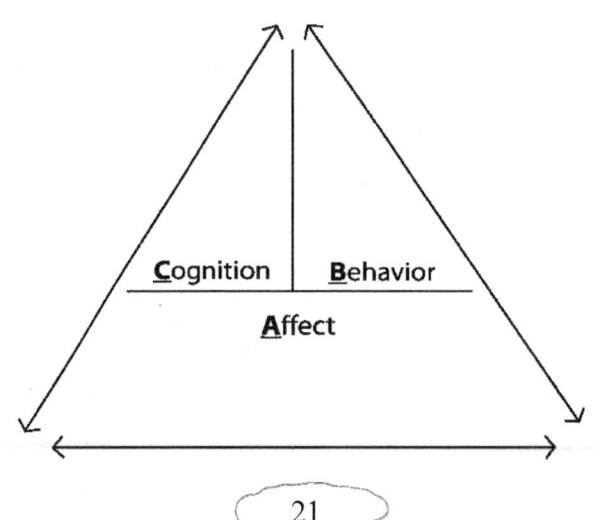

Full Value work is experiential. Students do things together to build affective connections and associated thoughts and behavior. This sets it apart from other social-emotional learning programs, which reside almost solely in the cognitive or behavioral domains. Doing things together might be the day-to-day work of learning in the classroom. Depending on their developmental age, students work in groups, take turns, present information either individually or as teams, have snack time, line up and go to recess, eat lunch together, ride the bus, etc. These events can all be viewed through the lens of activities that have emotions and associated cognitions and behaviors affiliated with them. Full Value uses these activities as naturalistic opportunities for social emotional learning. Doing things together can involve prescribed activities that teach elements of Full Value. It can also mean participating in an activity-based lesson focused on a particular academic content area.

In cognitive programs, students may watch videos with interactional scenarios, asked to describe what is happening (e.g., bullying, put downs, marginalization), then to provide alternate behavioral solutions for the video's actors. Other programmatic strategies promote student engagement in guided discussions, attendance at inspirational assemblies, or utilizing a more didactic instructional approach. Unfortunately, these types of methods keep students at an emotional arm's length from the actual experience of interacting with peers. Further, in responding to scenarios or guided discussions, students may expose their vulnerabilities absent a group process that maintains an emotionally safe and caring environment within which to self-disclose.

There may also be a goal-setting process to reduce incidents of put-downs or other anti-social behaviors. Progress may be charted and discussed. While the goals are worthy, how is the goal-setting operationalized for success? Where is the connection to the emotions that drive the behavior? What tools are students provided to replace anti-social with pro-social behaviors? How are students taught to not only self-regulate, but also to hold others accountable for their behavior?

While many of these programs evidence measurable change in how students treat each other, we believe that the Full Value experiential model provides a much more authentic and sustainable integration of the core social-emotional competencies common to many character education programs.

The intention of Full Value, as illustrated in the ABC Triangle, is to connect affective experience to cognitions and to discuss associated behaviors. Thus, there is always a circling back to the feelings evoked by the experience. Via this process, new learning becomes more thoroughly integrated as the line drawn from affect to behavior and cognition solidifies connections.

Living within the guidelines of behavioral norms means dealing with the complex areas of relationships and feelings. It is a highly conceptual process. A question then arises: aside from the benefits of teaching, modeling, and living a process that engages students in learning about self-regulation, empathy, compassion, and kindness, are there other benefits? An answer lies in the emerging body of literature suggesting that emotional awareness and intelligence are intrinsically linked to enhanced mastery of academic content areas, and more effective functioning in family, work, and community settings.

The more we can create and sustain a culture encouraging the development of affective sophistication, the more likely there will be an effective transference to how we think and behave, and, further, to how we apply this understanding to all content areas, from social science to literature to the applied sciences and to the living of our lives.

Full Value & Metaphorical Abstract Reasoning

We have provided an overview of the essential role that affect serves in energizing the cognitive process. Revisiting Bloom's Taxonomy of Educational Objectives (Anderson & Krathwohl, 2001)[29] we know that the cognitive process is scaffolded, ranging from simple recall of facts to analyzing and synthesizing complex ideas. The activity-based methodology at the core of teaching, practicing, and implementing Full Value draws upon a number of techniques that have students engage in highly conceptual tasks to grow, maintain, and strengthen their Full Value School.

For example, the co-creation of behavioral norms in a Full Value Commitment requires significant conceptual reasoning. As their developmental level allows, students must first understand the six core behavioral norms and how they can be set into motion. A kindergarten student might identify sitting quietly while a peer speaks, or listening to directions in the lunchroom, as Be Here behaviors. A high school student might list such Be Here behaviors as coming to class prepared, participating in discussions, taking notes during a lecture, or being attentive to a friend who is in crisis. The process of understanding the core norms and associated behaviors is rooted in adaptive emotional functioning and not relegated to the recall of facts.

A second-grade class in the Kinnelon Borough Public Schools agreed upon the following behavioral norms to aspire to for their Full Value Commitment in the Be Here area: listen, try hard, share supplies, keep friends company, and learn. Beyond determining what each Full Value Behavioral Norm looked like when practiced, students also agreed on what distractors were present in their lives that might compromise their effectiveness. The class developed the following distractors: being negative, shouting out, name calling, lying, talking over the speaker, bragging, running, pushing, stealing, and making annoying noises.

It is critical to stress that these were not teacher-imposed behavioral characteristics. They came from students, and, further, the students negotiated the behavioral norms and distractors included in the classroom Full Value Commitment. Some items were close to being duplicates, and others were not deemed necessary via a consensus-building process facilitated by the teacher as part of creating the Full Value Commitment.

In co-creating this commitment, students needed first to identify a representation of their work that would reflect the goals of the classroom. In this instance, students decided upon a road symbolizing a forward-moving journey. Distractors were described as litter along the side of the road that needed to be picked up and attended to. Twenty-two classmates negotiated the norms that would be included on their road. This winnowing process was complex. All of this falls under the category of abstract reasoning.

Metaphorical Activity Structures

We believe that many significant experiences are metaphorical, represented in our lives through natural inferences that students discover for themselves through just living, and/or through deliberate connections that a teacher makes in framing an experience. We have found that there are metaphorical activity structures unique to experiential learning. For example, Calling Group always takes place in a circle. Circles put everyone on an equal footing. There is no place to hide, eye contact can be made with everyone, and there is the potential for all to be heard. The circle naturally eliminates the hierarchy found in rows of students facing the whiteboard with the teacher at the helm.

Individualizing is another important metaphorical activity structure. Individuals are both parts of a group and also singular contributors. In the classroom, they set goals for themselves and participate in the larger landscape of group goals. The group is also an experiential archetype. The group may be representative of family, community, or team.

The second graders' choice of a highway with Full Value cars on a journey passing by detritus on the side of the road is rich in abstract metaphorical thinking. The students' agreement helps them to make linguistic, visual, and experiential connections. As noted, there is a journeying element to their representation that supports the idea that the class will be moving forward together, carrying their aspirations and distractors along for the ride. The association of trash along the side of the road (which we have all experienced) offers a powerful reminder of the behaviors needing to be attended to, examined, processed, and cleaned up.

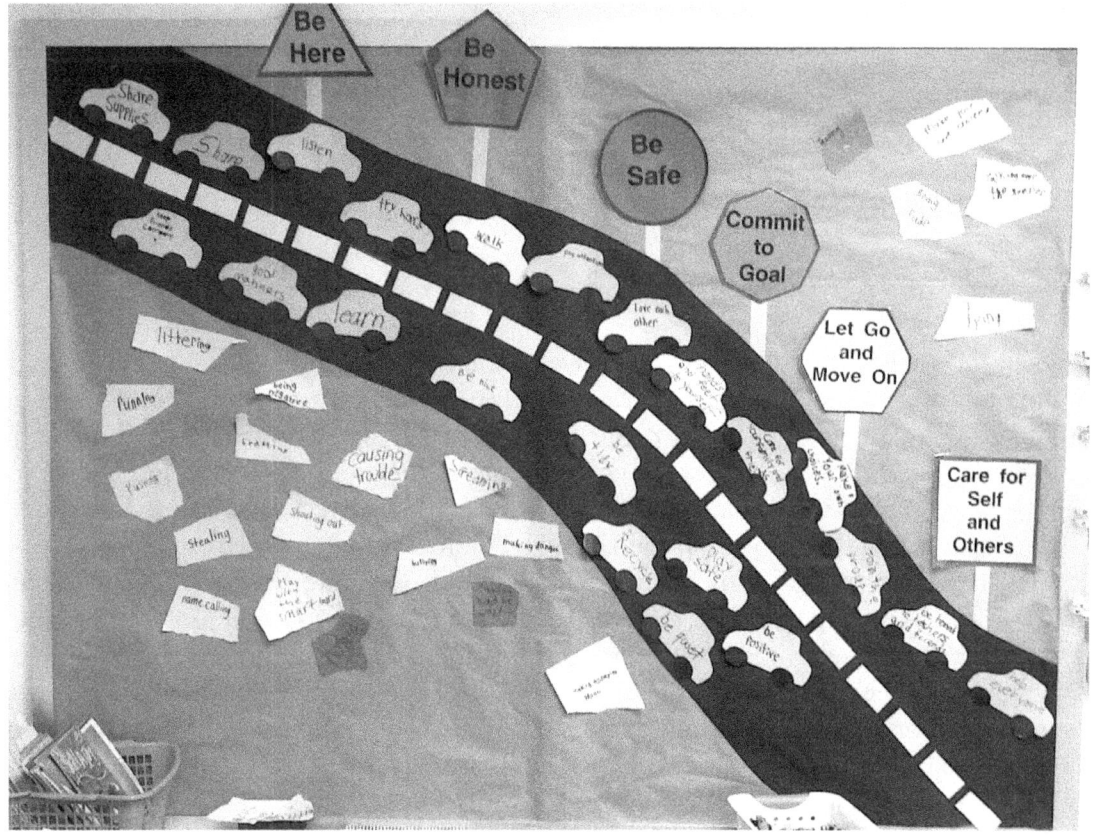

For further examples of the co-creation of Full Value Commitments across grade levels and types of classrooms, the reader is referred to Chapter 3.

Metaphorical abstract reasoning has been identified to support knowledge acquisition in a number of academic content areas, including mathematics, reading, science, and social studies (Kincade, 1991).[30] The value of metaphors is that they help students to link their life experience with exposure to novel concepts. For example, in understanding the impact of the size of roads and traffic flow, a civil engineer offers an explanation using the metaphor of pipe diameters. As pipes are connected from larger to smaller diameters, the flow of cars becomes more constricted.

As noted, Calling Group is also fertile ground for abstract reasoning. It is the circling of students to address issues, share information, and celebrate successes. Calling Group will be discussed in some detail in Chapter 5. For example, if a group is called to address the violation of behavioral norms, the following must occur:

- A consensus is reached on what actually happened. Who did what to whom?

- The *What* of the experience is connected to agreed upon Full Value Behavioral Norms.

- The group's Commitment is revisited.

- Behaviors are connected to feelings.

- Students take responsibility for their behavior.

- Appropriate consequences are negotiated between group members.

- Key learning from the experience is identified.

- Agreements are reached as to how to move forward.

On their morning ride to school, a group of elementary school students was behaving badly on their bus. One student, in particular, was the target of nasty comments. The process has a number of the above-listed components. Using a fleece ball to award *Speaker Power* (Elias & Arnold, eds., 2006)[31] to whichever student possessed the ball, an Information Group was called to help students reach a consensus on what had occurred on the bus. The injured party told his side of the story, supported by many of his bus mates. Next, the process moved to a Feelings Group. Again, the student expressed his feeling of being embarrassed and afraid of using I statements. The main provocateurs began to cry and took responsibility for their behavior. Each student in the group of fifty had an opportunity to voice an opinion, concerns, and feelings. This moved to an Outcome Group where students took responsibility for their behavior and apologized. The closing discussion focused on how to prevent similar incidents from occurring again. This was a group of second graders.

In a study entitled *What Effective Schools Do* (West et al., 2014)[32] thirteen hundred eighth grade public school students were assessed to determine the effect of crystalized or fluid intelligence methodology (Cattell, 1963)[33] on improved academic performance, as reflected in standardized test scores. Fluid intelligence, which we believe to be most affected by the Full Value experiential learning model, "are the abstract reasoning capabilities needed to solve novel problems (such as the ability to identify patterns and make extrapolations) independent of how much factual knowledge has been acquired" (West, pg. 74). The essential questions the researchers asked were, "Do Schools that succeed in raising test scores do so by improving their student's underlying cognitive capacities? Or do effective schools help their students achieve at higher levels than would be predicated on measures of cognitive ability alone?" (West, pgs. 73-74).

Cognitive psychologists have identified three elements of fluid intelligence: processing speed, working memory, and the ability to engage in novel problem solving. The authors of this article note, "Schools that are particularly effective in improving standardized test scores may do so by improving fluid cognition along one or more of these dimensions" (West, pg. 73). In this study, comparisons were made between standardized achievement testing and, among other data, assessment of fluid reasoning skills. Significant correlations were obtained between fluid reasoning and scores on mathematics and reading assessments, accounting for over thirty percent and sixteen percent, respectively. Thus, the impact of fluid reasoning on academic achievement was significant.

The Full Value model dovetails completely with engaging in novel problem solving, whether it be via the creation of Full Value Commitments, activities that teach Full Value Behavioral Norms, or sorting out differences via Calling Group.

In summarizing their findings, the authors write:

> Indeed, perhaps the most important implication that we draw is that educators seeking to innovate should get about the business of developing and rigorously testing the effects of interventions to raise these fluid cognitive skills. Improved abstract-reasoning capacity likely has important benefits in its own right and is highly related to important skills such as reading comprehension. Deficits in students' fluid cognitive skills may also prevent even the most effective schools from raising all of their students' academic performance to the desired level (Para. 31).

The immersion in the abstract reasoning process to form and maintain a positive school climate and culture is directly connected to academic mastery, creative problem-solving, fostering and maintaining relationships, working as a high functioning team, and exercising leadership skills. These are all skills that are essential to employers in the 21st century.

The rapid evolution of business practices, the impact of technology, and the almost desperate search for new ideas and related products require employees who can be fully present in the workplace. This means developing skills to respect and appreciate differences of personality and ideas, and give and receive honest feedback that does not shut down openness to change. It involves setting goals predicated on honest self-assessment. The ability to function autonomously while knowing when to seek guidance is essential. Engaging in creative and aspirational thinking and problem-solving without fear of crossing boundaries provides the fuel for development. Using failure (distractors) as a growth opportunity and experiencing confrontation as healthy and necessary for change are essential ingredients. And finally, the ability to extend compassion to colleagues experiencing difficult times serves to maintain an affirming work environment. Living in a Full Value community at school provides students with systemic practice of a process that continually models all of these aspirational traits.

Social-emotional learning programs have, in many instances, limped along in educational settings. Their continued existence is often due in considerable measure to a champion within a school who understands the critical importance of educating the whole child, and the intuitive perspective that nurturing affect has a lasting impact on learning. There are some encouraging signs that this is changing. For example, the Boston public schools have recently hired an assistant superintendent for social-emotional learning. This indicates recognition in a major urban district with over 54,000 students that this work is essential, not an add-on to be discarded due to cyclical budget concerns. Schools that wish to be truly high performing must also equip their students to be affectively connected to themselves and to their peers. Even if a school's focus is entirely on achievement, the argument can no longer be made that social emotional learning distracts from academics. In fact, the reverse would appear to be true. Students connected to their affective experience and who are afforded the opportunity to develop and practice their abstract reasoning abilities are more effective learners and better able to apply these skills as collaborators and leaders with family, community, and the workplace.

CHAPTER 3

CO-CREATING FULL VALUE COMMITMENTS & CHALLENGE OF CHOICE

Full Value Commitments are the keystone of a wondrous arch that supports all of the social interactions that transpire in a classroom. An architectural term, the keystone is "The wedge-shaped piece at the summit of an arch, regarded as holding the other pieces in place" (Random House Dictionary of the English Language, 1967).[34] An arch is one of the most robust load bearing structures in building design. When viewed metaphorically, the arch is the classroom structure that cannot stand without individual commitment but is immensely strong when properly supported by positive values and behaviors. The students and teacher each become a keystone for the other.

About Co-Creation

Co-creation is at the heart of our Full Value work. Students must have a legitimate say in developing structures that will influence their lives in school. Co-creation should be utilized when introducing an activity and in the development of the classroom Full Value Commitment. Student participation in frontloading the purpose of an activity will depend on their developmental capacities. The ability to think symbolically must be present to make conceptual connections between the activity and whatever issue is being worked on. For example, suppose a student is given a balloon with a behavior on it (Be kind to others) and asked to protect it (not break the balloon). In that case, they must be able to make the metaphorical connection (balloon is kindness) and understand the symbolism associated with not breaking it (keeping kindness safe).

Some would argue that the ability to think abstractly does not begin until age eleven (6th grade). However, we have routinely witnessed much younger students making metaphorical and symbolic connections, and ascribe this in large part to the engaging nature of the activities. The experiential process promotes multi-sensory integration of concepts. Specific examples of students in primary and elementary school successfully utilizing metaphorical abstract reasoning and making symbolic connections can be found in this chapter.

If co-creation is not possible, teacher framing of an activity helps ensure that student outcomes are more than just having fun (which is always part of the goal). For example, younger students may not independently come to the conclusion that keeping a balloon unbroken with "Be kind to others" written on it correlates with actually honoring those feelings, but when explained to them in simple language, students do understand and integrate the message.

Co-Creation & Trauma Work

Trauma is synonymous with powerlessness and victimization. Co-creation empowers the student to reassert control over their environment. Instead of an outside authority (as benevolent as that person might be) imposing the purposes of an activity, the student has an authentic voice. What they contribute matters. The course of events can be changed. Control is reasserted.

Co-creation may provide a profound antidote to the outright lack of control that trauma inflicts on many students, especially if a student's source of trauma is through an adult's inappropriate or violent behaviors, which is not an unusual circumstance. If a student has had limited positive experiences with adults, re-patterning through co-creating with empathetic and stable adults offers a corrective experience of connection and relationship. This experience is built on trust and value rather than arbitrary and irrational behavior. We should appreciate the potential of seemingly minor events that may trigger trauma in others. We should also be aware of the opportunities within Full Value that may serve to offer a path to begin resolving this trauma.

This chapter will drill down into the various options for co-creating a Full Value Commitment with students. The visual form they take is only limited by your class's imagination. The content will be individualized to your students' age, cognitive capacities, and stage of development. The activities below offer experiential methods to help students understand the structure and use of Full Value Behavioral Norms and their representations, supporting the creation of the classroom Commitment. In some instances, students can choose a Full Value to work on in small groups or in pairs, brainstorming behaviors and distractors. This can happen in a large group discussion as well. Behaviors and distractors can then be applied to activities or the day-to-day happenings in the classroom. Or, the norms can evolve via the activity itself. This is particularly effective as the behaviors displayed during the activities can be used to create a Full Value Commitment. In addition, they are less abstract as they can be immediately connected to student experience.

All Full Value Commitments should contain positive behaviors described either by a word, a phrase, or with drawings or pictures. These should be placed on the inside of whatever physical representation you and your students choose to create. On the outside of the representation, distractors should be placed that are likely to get in the way of living the behaviors you and your students feel are necessary for building and maintaining a Full Value classroom and school community.

Global Full Value Activities

These activities are designed to introduce the Full Value Behavioral Norms and how they can be defined and modeled.

Activity Difficulty Scale

1 (Easy) ------- 2 (A bit harder) -------- 3 (Pretty complicated) --------- 4 (Difficult)

The Activity: Full Value Boop   Time: 60+ minutes

Materials: 9-inch to 12-inch diameter balloons,   Difficulty: 1

Beanie Babies, rubber critters, mouse traps, etc.

How you do it:

Decide on a method that best suits the age of your students to develop a list of Full Value behaviors and distractors. This might be via pairs, small groups, large groups, using pictures, etc. Or, the activity can be used without behaviors and distractors, which can then be added during subsequent rounds.

Option 1: Depending on class size, blow up enough balloons to make it a challenge to keep all of them up in the air at once. Make sure you have adequate space for moving and a high ceiling. The objective is to keep all the balloons aloft without hitting the ground. Students may not double tap balloons. They can use any part of their bodies to tap with. Ask the class to think about what it takes to keep all the balloons going at once without touching the ground. Also, ask them to think about how certain behaviors might get in the way of their success. Spread the various objects (Beanie Babies, rubber critters, etc.) around the floor. Explain that they represent the behaviors they want to avoid while keeping the balloons aloft. The more capable the group, the more objects (distractors) you want to spread around. Either determine with students or decide on a reasonable number of balloon drops and distractor contact (with the objects on the floor) that would result in starting over. Or you may collectively decide to time a round and count the drops and touches. Encourage students to self-report drops and touches. This may not happen as the action tends to get somewhat frantic, so you might want to keep track of them, as well.

Option 2: Work with students to determine, before beginning the activity, what Full Value behaviors they want to protect and what distractors they want to be aware of and avoid. The behaviors are written on the balloons, and specific distractors, represented by your collection of objects, are labeled. The rest of the activity proceeds as above.

Reflection:

Option 1: The behavioral outcomes of Boop become the focus for developing positive behaviors and distractors. Some questions for students might include:

- If there was a time for planning, were your ideas considered?

- Did you listen to and consider the ideas of your classmates?

- What are your thoughts about the need for planning?

- What were some of the strategies you used to keep the balloons aloft?

- How did you work with others?

- Did your attention wander, and did it affect how well things went for you?

- Were you able to bring your attention back, and if so, how?

- How did having lots of people around you trying to keep balloons up affect you?

- Did you bump into people, or were you bumped into? How did you feel about that, and why?

- Were you honest about balloon touches and stepping on the objects on the floor?

- What positive behaviors can we take from this activity to include in our Full Value Commitment?

- What distractors do we want to work on and include in our Commitment?

Option 2: Since the behaviors and distractors have already been identified, the reflection would focus on how the positive behaviors were honored and how the labeled distractors impacted the group's success.

After a round or two, ask students to do some thinking around how to most effectively protect their positive behaviors. This equates to how best to keep all of the balloons up for the longest period of time. If they don't come up with any ideas of their own, suggest that perhaps the balloons could be tied together. This becomes a metaphor for teaching how all of the behaviors work with each other to maintain a Full Value classroom and school.

Cross Categories: Be Here, Be Safe, Set Goals, Care For Self & Others, Let Go & Move On

---

The Activity: Full Value Speed Rabbit   Time: 60+ minutes

Difficulty: 2-3

How you do it:

Looking for ways to motorically, spatially, and thematically integrate the conceptual dimensions of Full Value? To avoid the embarrassment of appearing not to understand the previous incomprehensible sentence, just nod your head, "yes," and read on. Let's lay out the generic version first.

The forming of three animal shapes is taught to the group:

Elephant: A student stands between two peers and holds out a left or right arm as a waving trunk. The students on either side form large ears with their arms connected in a circular shape to the trunk (the student standing between them).

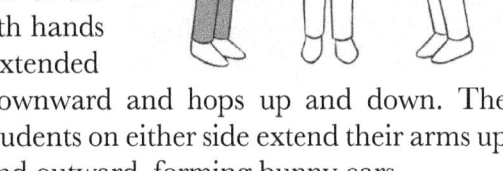

Rabbit: The student in the center of the trio puts hands in, elbows out, with hands extended downward and hops up and down. The students on either side extend their arms up and outward, forming bunny ears.

Gorilla: The student in the center makes gorilla noises while scratching under an armpit. The students on either side pretend to groom the student in the center as gorillas and monkeys are wont to do.

Have the group divide itself into groups of three, with you or a volunteer standing in the middle of a large circle. Each threesome must know how to form all of the animal representations. The volunteer has a simple yet crucial job: to point at a trio and yell either "elephant," "rabbit," or "gorilla." Rather than thinking the yeller quite mad, the trio who have been pointed to must form the critter they have been assigned. If the group gets their animal together within five to ten seconds (depending on age and capabilities), the person in the middle points to another trio, and so on until one group can't get it done in time. The center positioned member of that trio becomes an expatriate, leaving their group of three and moving into the center, while the person in the center becomes a part of that trio.

The next step is to have students co-create representations of Full Value behaviors rather than animals or other objects. For example, ask the group how they might represent *trust*, *compassion*, *strength*, or *honesty*. The game is played in the same manner, but the trio formations now take on a different meaning.

Cross Categories: Be Here, Let Go & Move On

The Activity: Full Value Call Time: 40 minutes

Difficulty: 2

How you do it:

> Here is a way for groups to decide on positive behaviors for their Commitment and say it like they mean it. Form pairs and ask them to spend just a minute or two deciding on two behaviors they feel would be important to have as basic ground rules for effective group functioning. For example, a pair might choose *faith* and *listening*. Split the pairs to the far corners of a gym or an open field. Hand them blindfolds or have them close their eyes. At your command, and with their bumpers up (arms extended with hands flat and up) to avoid unfortunate collisions, have them yell their behavior as loudly as possible, while listening for their partner's behavior at the same time. While yelling, they must find their partner in the cascading (but nurturing) mayhem of screams from other pairs who are searching for each other. Once all pairs are reunited, a conversation can occur around the behaviors each pair selected for inclusion in the group's Full Value Commitment and what it felt like to be seeking each other out. Before the Full Value Call begins, make sure you have enough spotters on hand to avoid collisions with bleachers, chuckholes, or goal posts.

Cross Categories: Be Here, Be Honest, Let Go & Move On

The Activity: Full Value Human Sculpture Time: 45 minutes

Difficulty: 2

How you do it:

> Six to eight students work together to form a human sculpture primarily using their bodies. Props are allowed to enhance the representation. The sculptures can depict everything from single to multiple Full Value Behavioral Norms. For example, during a Full Value training, a group of teachers formed a sculpture of the soldiers planting an American Flag on Iwo Jima to represent Set Goals. Have each group share with classmates the thinking that went into their creation.

Cross Categories: Set Goals, Care for Self & Others

The Activity: Mind Mapping Time: 60 minutes +

Materials: Poster paper, markers Difficulty: 2-4

How you do it:

First popularized by Tony Buzan (2015)[35] mind maps provide a visual brainstorming tool for students across age groups to organize their Full Value Commitment. Divide students into small groups (six is an ideal number) and distribute six sheets of paper, each labeled with one Full Value Behavioral Norm surrounded by a brain shape. Around the brain, students use colored markers to list words and phrases representing what each Full Value means to them. These words and phrases should be written at the end of lines coming from the central brain. As each behavior is written at the end of the primary curved lines, additional line extensions are added to refine and expand on primary words or phrases. For students with limited written expression, provide an array of magazines, newspapers, etc. They can use pictures from these sources to represent behaviors on the mind map.

Have students flip the paper over and list or represent, via drawings or pictures, distractors that can get in the way of using identified positive behaviors. Provide sufficient time for students to brainstorm. Gather the small groups in a larger circle. Ask each group to describe their maps. Spend some time helping the whole group come to a consensus on the behaviors and distractors for each Full Value Behavioral Norm. Scribe the finished product for transfer to the classroom Full Value Commitment.

The Activity: Toxic Waste (Protect those values!)   Time: 1 hour

Materials: See list below   Difficulty: 3+

How you do it:

A terrific way to get students thinking about their chosen behaviors to reside within their Commitment is to have them cared for by the group. Your Toxic Waste kit should include all the following items (and can be purchased commercially – See Chapter 15):

- A bicycle inner tube, cut
- Large rope, enough for a thirty-foot diameter
- Smaller rope, enough for a five-foot diameter
- When tied together, a bunch of ropes will allow for lengths to reach ¾ of the way across the circle's thirty-foot diameter. Use yellow polypropylene, some retired nine mm rope, harness webbing, and a few lengths of bungee cord

- Miscellaneous toys to add distractors
- Two #10 tin cans (the kind baked beans and sauce come in for institutional kitchens)
- Two gym spot markers or plastic plates
- Permanent markers and masking tape
- Six to ten small diameter plastic or rubber balls, like Pensie-Pinkies, hollow and light. (For those of you who have never had the transcendent experience of whacking a Pensie-Pinkie with a stickball bat, they are now manufactured again. It is the highest and smoothest bouncing pink ball on the planet)

Lay out two circles of rope, a large outer ring with a diameter of approximately thirty feet, and a smaller rope circle centered in the larger one, about five feet across. Call an Information Group (Chapter 5) and ask students to talk about the positive behaviors they have been carrying with them throughout their group experience. Write each behavior they recall on masking tape, and then attach each to a ball. The balls should then be carefully deposited in one of the cans. Now, place the empty #10 tin can on a spot marker inside the smaller circle. Next, place the can containing the group values (labeled balls) on the second spot marker just outside the smaller circle.

Position the group around the outside of the larger circle. Hand them the bag filled with ropes, an inner tube, and other assorted retrieval items. Using these resources, the group must transfer their positive values from the can bobbing in the sea of toxic waste to the blissfully serene can in the inner circle. It is imperative that no behaviors are desecrated by tumbling into the toxic waste during the transfer process from one can to another. The group may not cross into the outer circle without risking their corporeal lives.

There are many solutions to this most challenging of initiatives. The inner tube figures prominently in the most common solution paths. If you are feeling particularly strict, blindfold any participant whose hand breaks the plane of the outer circle when holding onto a rope. They may continue to hold the rope, but a sighted helper must now direct movements. This strategy maintains the integrity of the challenge and will ensure that members of the group unanimously dislike you, at least for the duration of this activity.

Cross Categories: Be Here

Full Value Commitment

<u>The Being</u>

One of the earliest and most successful representations of a Full Value Commitment was The Being, which is still widely used. Created by a youth worker at The Harbor for Boys and Girls in East Harlem, New York, it became a game-changer for the teaching of Full Value. Its success revolved around the symbolism of embodiment, where young people participate in creating a physical and personal representation of the positive behaviors they can express and wish to practice in their lives. The Being is created by tracing the outline of a student volunteer with a magic marker who lies face up on a large piece of butcher

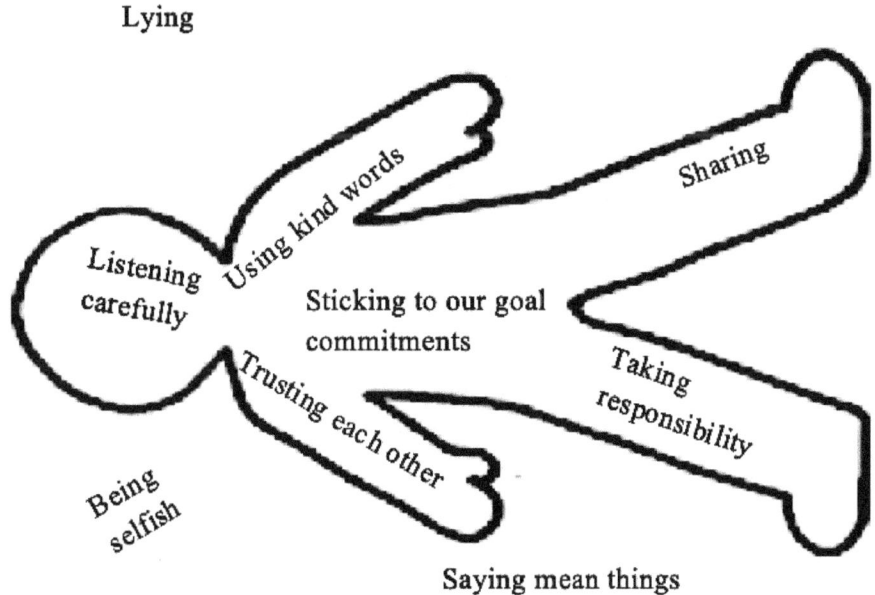

paper. The next step is for the group to brainstorm those positive behaviors, then reduce them to eight to ten essentials. These essentials are written *inside* the body. Students then agree upon distractors that might get in the way of living their positive behaviors. These are placed *outside* of the body.

The beauty of The Being is that it can work well with both younger and older students. Young children connect best to either physical or pictorial representations. Instead of writing on The Being, students can draw pictures or cut out photographs (making a large commitment collage) that represent their behaviors and distractors.

<u>The Village</u>

The creation of a classroom village also works well for younger and older students. The added benefit of this for the Full Value Commitment is the opportunity to add student goals. The creation of positive behaviors and distractors is the same. Students then draw their own small hut inside the village. Within their hut is placed a personal and school related goal that they have developed for the year. With younger students, a drawing or pictorial representation of their goal(s) can be used. Older students can simply write them inside the hut.

Full Value Commitments Across Age Groups

For students to understand Full Value and define what each outcome means for them individually and as a group, the language must suit their level of development. As a matter of practicality and experience, Full Value language has been refined to meet these different needs. Here is an overview of developmentally appropriate language to build Full Value Commitments by grade level:

<u>Primary (Grades PreK-1)</u>

Be Kind
Be Gentle
Be Safe

<u>Grades 3-5 through High School</u>

Be Here
Be Safe
Set Goals
Be Honest
Let Go & Move On
Caring for Self and Others

Depending on the comfort level of the teacher and the capacities of their students, a more sophisticated version can be used for primary students.

<u>Primary/Elementary & Special Needs Students</u>

Younger students (pre-k, 1) and students with significant language deficits (e.g., students with Autism and multiple disabilities) often benefit from physical representations of the Full Value Commitment.

Here is an example of how a classroom teacher utilized Beanie Babies to communicate elements of Full Value to her students. She added Challenge of Choice to the mix (pg. 44):

Material Needed: Four Beanie Babies: lion, lamb, zebra, and a skunk (or whichever ones you and your students decide will represent classroom behavioral norms).

Each animal represents the following Full Value concepts: Play Safe, Be Gentle, Play Fair, and Challenge of Choice.

LION: As the representative of the king of the jungle, the lion tells us to play safe.

LAMB: The lamb tells us to be as gentle as a lamb.

ZEBRA: The zebra represents a referee (hopefully the stripes make this one obvious). The zebra tells us to play fair and follow the rules.

SKUNK: The skunk tells us not to be a stinker. Meaning… participate as fully as you can by finding a way to become involved.

Other Beanie Babies can be used to represent different behavioral norms.

- OWL: Think, study, or be wise
- BEAVER: Work hard
- RABBIT: Be quick
- TURTLE: Be tough. Get into your shell when you need to.

In providing this example, the point is that the classroom teacher (and students) can be creative and imaginative in implementing Full Value. There is no one right way to do this. Once one understands the norms and their associated outcomes and students' capacities for grasping the information, what the agreement looks like becomes a co-creation between the teacher and students.

As noted above, there is really no limit to the creativity that can be brought to bear. For example, as described in Chapter 2, there is a Full Value Commitment created by Ms. Sarah Tinney and her second-grade class. Their Commitments took the shape of a road with cars representing positive behaviors and litter along the side of the road as distractors. But Ms. Tinney and her class went a lot further. They developed a Driver's Manual, which included all of the behaviors that the class had agreed to practice. Below is a table listing their Set Goals behaviors.

> **Commit to Goals**
> **What does it look like?**
> Students doing what they are asked to do
> Try hard when a goal is set even if it's hard
> Never give up
> Learning new things
> Students listening
> Students doing their work
> Sitting or standing and listening
> Standing up for someone who is being bullied
> because our goal is to be nice
>
> **What does it sound like?**
> Whispering
> People encouraging others to do their goal
> Saying to someone off our road, "Can you
> please start?" (Say the goal)
> Telling someone, "Hey you're doing great!"
> Saying, "Keep up the good work!"
> Saying, "Don't let the hard stuff get in the way."
> Telling friends to, "Get on the road!"
>
> **What does it feel like?**
> You're encouraged and cheered
> Excited
> A "sweet" feeling
> Like you're at an extravaganza or a fiesta!
> You're having a good time

Ms. Tinney and her class chose to approach each Full Value by defining what they look like, sound like, and feel like. This helped students to make connections with this conceptual reasoning process more easily. Students then signed the manual to formalize their commitments. As a way of evidencing pride of membership in the classroom, Ms. Tinney and her class also developed Full Value Driver's Licenses, which each student displayed on their desks.

Below are some additional Full Value Commitments from Kiel (Pre-K, K-2) and Stonybrook (3-5) Schools in Kinnelon, NJ.

The island on the previous page was created by second grade students (with the artistic help of the teacher and classroom Paraprofessionals). Students connected with the idea of either being on the island or off the island as representing their commitment to Full Value. Palm trees contain agreed upon positive behaviors. The floating bottles hold distractors.

Some of the student created behaviors include, "Keep hands away from other kids' food, help kids do math, walk in the halls quietly, share snack if a friend needs it, stop doing annoying things when people ask you."

Kindergarten and First Graders created this Pop-Up Full Value Commitment with the help of their school librarian:

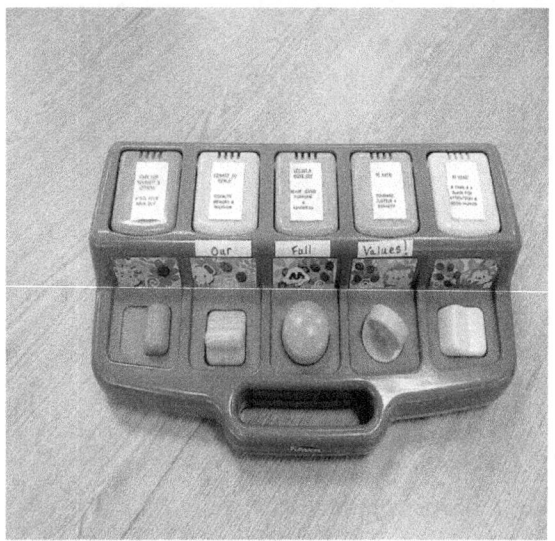
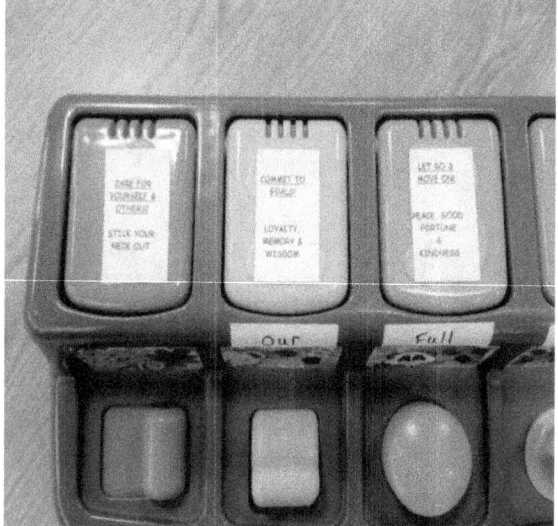

Middle School & High School

Just as the complexity of the language varies, the implementation of these values does, as well. Older students will be more able to use language to articulate behavioral norms when co-creating commitments with their classmates, and when processing the use of their agreed upon norms as problems arise.

Here are examples of a Full Value Commitment from Kinnelon High School, NJ (9-12). The language is clearly more sophisticated, and the design business-like. It is also interesting to note that the behaviors are more academically focused (increasing group and individual performance) rather than a primary focus on maintaining positive relationships.

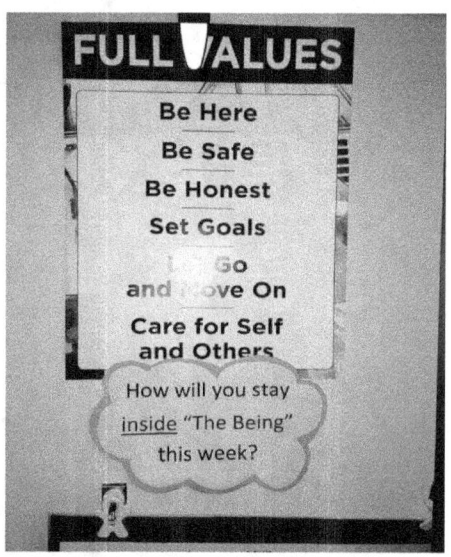

This is similar to the Full Value Commitment developed by students at Pearl R. Miller Middle School in Kinnelon, NJ. Again, the language is more sophisticated with a minimum of graphic embellishments. Teachers have reported that students in upper grades find that pictorial contracts are too childish for them. As students progress through the grades and become more capable of abstract reasoning, it is predictable and appropriate that contracts will become more language based. Interestingly, at the middle school level, which is more transitional in terms of the shifting focus from the importance of relationships to academics, the positive behaviors are a mix of both. For example, under Let Go & Move On are listed, "Accept a decision, Forgive and forget, Give people a chance, Acknowledge your feelings and then start over."

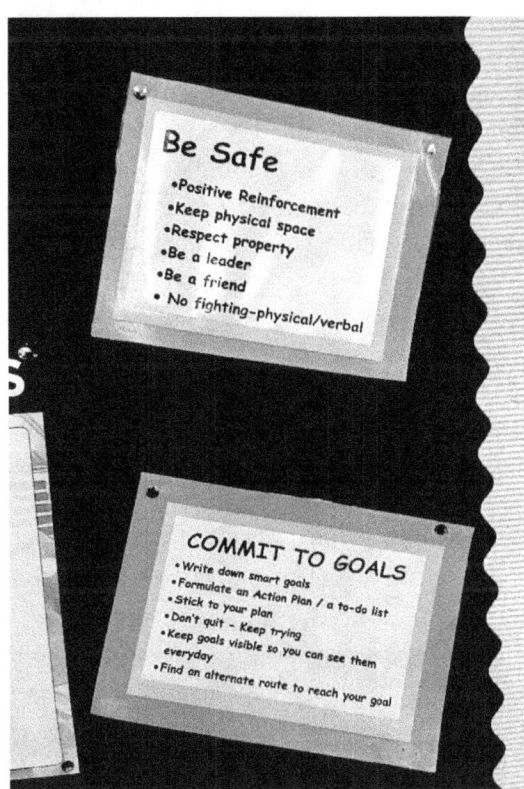
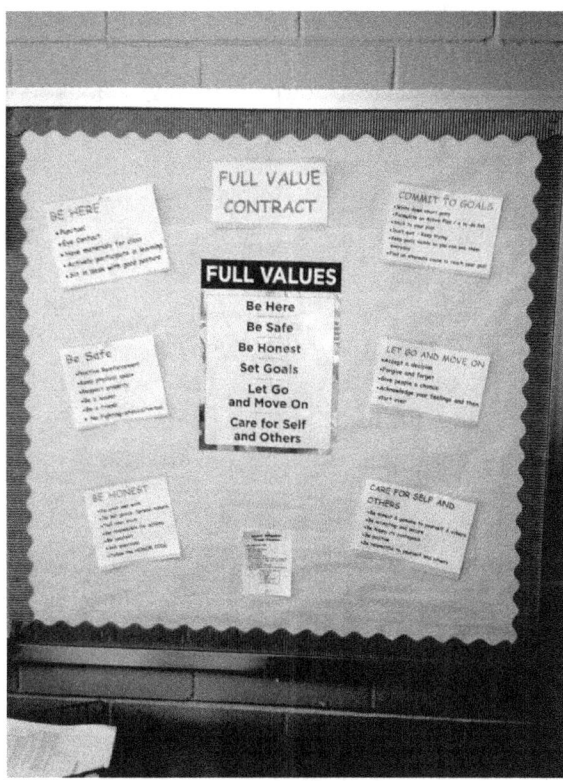

Full Value Commitment & Curriculum

A middle school science teacher combined the study of plant biology with creating and caring for the class's Full Value Commitment. Each area of Full Value was described and discussed with students. They were then asked to investigate plants in small groups and link regionally grown plant characteristics to each Full Value Behavioral Norm. Small groups presented information on their selected plant to the large group, emphasizing the Full Value metaphor associated with their plant. The plants were then purchased and brought into the classroom. Students went through the process of determining behaviors for each Full Value plant. These were written on Popsicle sticks and pushed into the soil around them. Distractors were written on the outside of the plant pots. Caring for their values was represented by the class commitment to keep the Full Value plants healthy. This provided a direct experiential connection for students.

Whole School Full Value Commitment

Because of the departmentalized structure in most middle and high school programs, developing a Full Value Commitment for each classroom can become unwieldy and confusing. The option exists to establish a commitment for either each grade level or the entire school. This process can be linked to our representative democracy, providing opportunities for integration into the history and social studies curricula. After presenting an overview of each Full Value Behavioral Norm and engaging students in activities to teach them, students develop a list of behaviors that reflect each commitment, along with associated distractors. Next, two representatives are chosen to attend a meeting with students from other classes. At this student congress, behavior and distractor lists are presented. Often, there will be significant commonalities. A draft list of agreed upon behaviors and distractors is brought back to each classroom for further discussion. During this second round, students discuss how the behaviors might be depicted. This information is brought back to the student Congress to further discuss behaviors and their representation within the Commitment(s). The final product is reviewed and presented in each classroom for a majority vote. This could be integrated into an existing student government model.

Whole School Integration Projects

With the administration's support, creative thinking is unleashed for students and teachers in representing Full Value for an entire school or district. For example, at the Kiel School, the art teacher, Sona Santigato, collaborated with a general education teacher to create a Full Value playground area outside the school. This space is used for activities that teach Full Value and is the location for Calling Group. The painting was completed with students and teachers working together (see below).

In the Stonybrook School, a public way has been found to honor students who exemplify the practice of Full Value with their peers and teachers. Each month, a particular Full Value Behavioral Norm is recognized. The bulletin board, located adjacent to the school's main entrance, recognizes students for successfully demonstrating Be Here behaviors. It is one of many examples of building administration and staff taking ownership of the program and exercising their creativity to put it into practice.

Challenge by Choice to Challenge of Choice

Challenge by Choice as a guideline for participation in experiential learning first emerged from Project Adventure (PA), an organization that promotes activity-based learning. Its CEO and a founder, Karl Rohnke, has been attributed with the primary development of the initial concept (Chase, 2009)[36]. Challenge by Choice was applied to encourage participation on Ropes or Challenge Courses, a series of activities on the ground and at height that offered perceived, growth-oriented risks for participants. In his dissertation, Exploring Challenge by Choice in an Adventure Setting, Daniel Chase lists the following elements:

- The chance to try a potentially difficult and potentially frightening challenge in an atmosphere of support and caring.

- The opportunity to back off when performance pressures or self-doubt become too strong, knowing that a chance for a future attempt will always be available.

- The chance to try difficult tasks, recognizing that the attempt is more significant than performance results.

- Respect for individual ideas and choices (p. 2).

One of the more glaring frustrations of this approach, particularly with more oppositional populations, was their choice to do nothing. Unfortunately, this was also the option for participants who were intimidated by the nature of some activities, where completion rather than going for the perfect try was the only measure of success. Rohnke's desired outcome was to encourage student engagement in experiential learning, not give them an out to sit on the bleachers.

In Exploring Islands of Healing (Schoel & Maizell, 2002)[37] the first hint of a shift in thinking around Challenge by Choice was revealed:

> Since the advent of Challenge by Choice, we have noticed leaders complaining that their participants use it to get out of engaging in activities. This was not our intention. To counter the problem, there are two suggestions. First, Challenge by Choice means that participants choose their level of challenge. It does not mean to opt out of the challenge. Secondly, for some groups, Project Adventure has introduced the phrase Challenge of Choice. The slight change in language is meant to express that participants choose their level of challenge but stay within the challenge (pg. 14).

In this book we fully endorse the small but significant change in language. The "of" communicates that choosing means finding a way to participate meaningfully. In an academic setting, the choice to do nothing isn't acceptable. Furthermore, there are often times when the options offered around assignments are limited. While the instructional process may be differentiated, as is the depth of content, what is taught is defined by state standards. However, within these constraints, giving students a voice in how they learn is essential.

When engaged in an activity to teach or practice Full Value, Challenge of Choice means "Go For The Perfect Try." An array of options can be offered, from providing encouragement, observing and taking notes, spotting, and full participation. The nature of the activity must be completely explained, allowing for an intelligent choice to be made as to the degree of participation. Also, of importance is to stress that trying an activity is as meaningful as finishing one. So, for example, during The Gauntlet activity (Chapter 7), a fearful student just slightly leaning from side to side while walking through the line could be a major accomplishment that must be recognized. An all or nothing (outcome-product approach) can dissuade a student from trying at all. Conversely, a gradual process will often encourage the student to go further than they had initially committed to.

Challenge of Choice can also be applied to the academic setting. For example, in project-based learning, Challenge of Choice can be helpful for students to define their roles. One student may be more comfortable taking notes while another enjoys doing research. Challenge of Choice will set the stage for participation in some way and at some level.

Understanding *challenge* and what that means to a student is also important. An appropriately selected challenge will be growth enabling, whereas a mismatched challenge will result in stagnation or failure. Whether confronting fears and anxieties around a group activity or an academic demand, challenge can provoke a wide array of feelings. For example, the challenge of an assignment can lead to confidence or despair. Understanding this helps the teacher guide the choice as to how the student can participate in a meaningful way without becoming paralyzed by feelings of inadequacy or self-doubt. Conversely, if a student engages in a challenge that does not in any way stretch their limits, little growth will occur.

As a bedrock concept of Full Value, it is crucial that students at all grade levels understand what Challenge of Choice means and how they may use it when engaging in any classroom activity.

To Go For The Perfect Try[38]
-Sarah Smeltzer & Joe Petriccione in Gold Nuggets

Growth is a never-ending process
that can be accomplished
under the most adverse circumstances.
Growth can be achieved
from one's attempt to …
"Go for the perfect try."

Challenge of Choice & Trauma Work

Trauma is antithetical to choice. A child who experiences trauma may not have any ability to make autonomous decisions. Depending on the nature of the trauma, this may extend to the compromising of physical and emotional boundaries.

Challenge of Choice is foundational to empowering students. For example, in an activity that involves holding hands, a student can choose a buddy rope (a short strand of rope that connects people without holding hands). This helps students approximate the experience of physical contact, does not isolate the student from participating, and recognizes that trauma can be pervasive. It may be that the thought of any physical contact is too painful for a student. Challenge of Choice provides opportunities for students to offer suggestions, serve as process recorders, provide encouragement, and problem-solve.

Students may have experienced years of emotionally devaluing behaviors, being told they will never amount to anything, are ugly, or stupid. Challenge of Choice provides the opportunity for engaging in levels of leadership, or staying in the background if that is in the student's current comfort zone.

As the core element of Full Value is the inclusive group experience, students who have experienced the trauma of isolation are no longer ignored or isolated. Instead, they are part of an affirming community of peers and adults. Challenge of Choice is one of the components that act as a bulwark against continued victimization and can extend beyond the classroom to the family and the community.

CHAPTER 4

ASSESSMENT & REFLECTION STRATEGIES

GRABBSS Assessment for Full Value Communities

What is GRABBSS?

GRABBSS is an assessment tool for the Full Value classroom and school. Its purpose is to provide a framework to view student thinking, behavior, and affect, and how they connect to Full Value Commitments and associated activities. Each letter of the acronym is packed with the potential for finding answers to important questions regarding how students relate to each other and to you in the classroom. It can be used effectively for in the moment decision-making as well as long range planning. There are seven elements to the tool: Goals, Readiness, Affect, Behavior, Body, Setting, and Stage of Development. Components will be described below as they relate to life in your classroom and school. Familiar scenarios will be provided, followed by a discussion of how a specific assessment element can be helpful to sort out what is going on, which then leads to activity selection, direct teaching, and group reflection. The scenarios and suggested questions will serve as a jumping off point for applying GRABBSS to a wide range of school situations you will encounter with students.

The Life Cycle of Groups

When using GRABBSS, it is vital to understand the context of your assessment. Groups are not static. They evolve over time. The Readiness of a class in September to form relationships and work together will be different from November. When using GRABBSS, the stage of development of a group should be taken into account, or your assessment may miss the target. For example, the Readiness focus during the first week of school may involve showing students where things are in the classroom, how to get to the playground, learning the morning routine and daily schedule, or finding their bus. As these skills are acquired, the focus will begin to shift more toward group work and individual preparedness.

There is a pattern to group development clearly explained by Bruce Tuckman (1965 & with Jensen, 1977)[39]. Five stages have been identified and described:

- Forming: Think about when your class arrives on the first day. Most everyone is on their best behavior. Students are checking each other out, looking for commonalities and acceptance. Most students try to come prepared and concentrate. It is the honeymoon period.

- Storming: During this stage leaders and followers emerge. Habitual behaviors may also start to surface. For example, if seats are not assigned in a secondary school class, those who participate will be up front, and those who don't will try to hide in the back of the room. Some social niceties will begin to fall away as students become more familiar with each other. This knowledge allows for some 'button pushing' to occur.

- Norming: Toward the end of the first two or three weeks, more group cohesiveness begins to emerge. By this time students have been engaged with each other in some sort of group work. There is more communication, interdependence, and a sense of community. Friendships have formed, which allow for a sense of safety that comes from deeper affiliation.

- Transforming: In this stage students are fully engaged in the demands of the classroom. There will still be outliers, but generally students have developed a working relationship with preferred partners, receive the support they need to master the curriculum, and are experiencing enough success and non-judgmental learning from failure to feel effective.

- Adjourning (1977): This process occurs at the end of the year when students experience a sense of loss and sadness. There is the hiatus of summer and the possibility that the group will not be reunited in the fall.

It is important that your use of **GRABBSS** connects to Tuckman or some other group process model. It may be perfectly normal that a small group struggles to succeed in the early weeks of school as they are in the Storming phase of development. The reason why an ordinarily placid student suddenly becomes sullen or withdrawn at the end of the year may very well be related to the anticipated loss of friends. Tuckman informs GRABBSS.

Using GRABBSS with Students

Goals:

To set and achieve goals is foundational to all learning. As we will extensively review in Chapter 9, this involves a set of skills that are not often taught but are always in play in our lives, whether in school, at home, in the community, or at work. It is, therefore, essential to know how effectively students can use a goal-setting process when working individually and in groups. Any assignment is a springboard for teaching the process of how to set and achieve goals.

Scenario: A group of eighth-grade students has been assigned a long-term project to research, write, and produce a short film documentary on recycling. You have outlined some preliminary resources and also defined roles that each member of the group can assume. They include Director, Writer, Cinematographer, and Editor. As you circulate among groups in the classroom, a GRABBSS G assessment for goal setting may raise the following questions:

- Have I clearly communicated what I want the group to accomplish?

- Do students understand the topic focus?

- Can they identify steps to complete the assignment?

- Have students been able to articulate what they are willing to do and what help they might need from their peers?

- Have they established a fair and equal workload?

- Have students established criteria for when they can all agree that the project has been completed and is ready for presentation to the class?

Your **GRABBSS** Goals assessment of the group will determine what additional resources and interventions may be needed to equip students to successfully complete the project. As you circulate the room, you may find that a number of groups are similarly struggling with initiating their project goals. You may decide to directly teach them goal-setting skills using the materials outlined in Chapter 9 (SMART Goals or the 4 Square approach). Direct connections can be made between the activity experience and the projects that are being worked on. The activity and associated behaviors, thoughts, feelings, and learning can also be looped back into the classroom Full Value Commitment. One can ask the following questions:

- Are we using the behaviors we have agreed upon under Set Goals effectively?

- Do we need to revisit them?

- Are there distractors that we need to review?

- Are there new distractors that we have experienced as part of our activity work together that we need to add?

Readiness:

Students come to your classroom with varying levels of readiness across physical, cognitive, and emotional domains. The recognition of this variety leads to differentiated instruction in the area of content and process. Educators have come to recognize that a one-size-fits-all approach in terms of methodology is not adequate. Students do not all learn the same way or at the same rate. Some have strengths as visual learners; some rely more on auditory or tactile processing. Students also often evidence differing levels in their fine and gross motor skills. Teachers in primary grades have long understood this when it comes to reading instruction. Students are typically broken into small groups depending on their reading fluency and comprehension. Social-emotional readiness can also be quite variable. Some students are willing to share; others are not. Some exhibit patience and thoughtfulness; others are more spontaneous and reactive. Social-emotional readiness affects all aspects of academic and social learning. The R of **GRABBSS** helps to focus us on student readiness in the classroom.

Scenario: A third-grade class will be attending an hour-long assembly on recycling. There will be a lecture, a short movie, and opportunities for some interactive student participation. Four classes will be attending, which means there will be eighty students in the room. All students are required to attend. Here are some readiness questions to consider:

- When observing your class, what is the best time of day for this type of event to occur? For example, is their readiness level more present in the morning or the afternoon? (This can become a discussion with the building administrator.

- Are there students who should or should not be sitting together?

- Will some students require an intermission due to the length of the assembly? How will that be organized?

- Are there students who can serve as peer mentors, helping to settle classmates more easily distracted or fidgety?

- What information do students need to understand content better and, therefore, be more engaged?

Your observations can lead directly to the Full Value Commitment. The upcoming assembly can be described, and students engaged to reflect on what positive behaviors and information would be helpful for them to have an exciting experience. Potential distractors can also be identified. Potential distractors can also be identified. Post assembly, the experience can be viewed as an activity to draw learning from related to developing new behaviors and distractors or refining existing ones.

Affect:

As discussed in Chapter 2, the control of affect is at the core of self-regulation, guiding how students think and behave. When students are in touch with and have tools to manage their various emotional states, they can effectively interact with their environment. Regulated affect contributes to resilience. A student who learns not to personalize the devaluing behavior of peers will not be bullied. A student who is in touch with their emotional needs and states will be more able to focus and also be able to develop strategies for self-care. Assessing for individual and group affect in your classroom is perhaps the most important element of GRABBSS. Working with a class of students, each with their individual affective states and needs, is a complicated business. As students relate informally and in groups, understanding their interactions around feelings can be daunting. The A of GRABBSS will help sort all of this out and contribute to social emotional learning and academic planning.

Scenario: (Two or More Students) During recess, a group of students is arguing about the rules of a game. The students can't seem to find any compromise or develop a shared understanding of the rules. The anger has escalated to the point where pushing and shoving have started, and students are taking sides.

Some GRABBSS A questions to consider:

- Are there specific students in this scenario who tend to react with anger when they don't get their way?

- Are any of the involved students behaving in a way different from what you would ordinarily expect of them?

- Do you know a school, family, or community issue that could be contributing to an unusual level of anger and sensitivity?

- Is one particular student a target of the larger group's anger or acting to deliberately provoke a dispute?

While a student's affective state can be related to school interactions and academic demands, your assessment should extend to the student's life at home and in the community. Students do not check their home lives at the door. To assume this is naïve. Knowing essential details of a student's history does not prejudge them. Instead, it informs your interactions with empathy and compassion. Illness, divorce, recent relocation, siblings, or family financial concerns all contribute to stress loads on students. Ignoring the potential impact of these and other stressors will contribute to a dysfunctional classroom climate and affect all students.

Scenario: (Individual Student) An eleventh-grade student comes to class without his textbook or notebook. He does not take his usual seat, slumping in a chair in the back. Instead, he seems fatigued, listless, and disinterested. While he is often quiet and needs to be pushed a bit to participate, his affect today is different.

GRABBSS A assessment helps explain and accept, with patience, what may seem exaggerated responses to interactions with you and his peers, fatigue, fluctuating mood, etc. There are several things you can do to temporarily reduce the stress load. Giving the student some space, avoiding confrontation, and letting go of minor oppositional behaviors all communicate to them that you recognize and understand the discomfort. These choices are the result of an accurate GRABBSS assessment. Even without disclosure from the student, which is ultimately their choice, you have encircled the student with compassionate, unconditional positive regard. This will pay long-term dividends as you form an emotional alliance.

Behavior:

As described in Chapter 2, we know that behavior arises from an emotional place. Behavior without affect does not exist. This is also true of our thinking. Our thoughts come from our feelings. Looking at behavior through the lens of GRABBSS provides the opportunity to work backward to the thoughts and feelings associated with how students are acting or acting out.

Scenario: (Two or More Students) A group of students is lined up at the door waiting to depart for lunch. There is some pushing and shoving going on as students jockey for the position of first in line. Some GRABBSS B questions to consider:

- How do the students who are involved usually get along?

- Are their interactions out of character?

- What are their verbalizations telling you?

- Is there a gathering crowd mentality? (Other students circling around to goad the antagonists?)

- Are students willing to help each other?

- Is there bullying going on?

- Do other students from the class take on a leadership role to intervene?

Body:

This element of GRABBSS is used to evaluate how a student's physical state, including health and special education issues, impacts their ability to learn and relate to each other. A student who comes to school with a cold, fever, or is recovering from an injury will typically behave differently than what you have come to expect. A student struggling with reading, organization, or focus due to a learning disability may demonstrate emotional, behavioral, or cognitive concerns. Body issues affect the ability to learn and should guide your instructional strategies. For example, if a student's strength as a learner is auditory processing, then lesson material should support that preferred learning style. Generally, it is helpful for all students to have material presented using multi-sensory instruction. The GRABBSS B assessment helps to be deliberate in designing lessons to reflect this approach. GRABBSS B can impact where students are seated in the classroom during certain lessons, the amount of movement allowed for a particular student, the noise level, or how students are grouped.

Body also extends to self-perception related to body image. A compromised body image alters a student's willingness to present confidently (or at all) in front of classmates, and impact on becoming involved in activities requiring physical participation.

Whenever a student does not respond as expected, it is important to check for GRABBSS B concerns. It is also important to build the capacity for all students to show empathy, compassion, and patience for classmates who are affected by Body concerns. Teaching and modeling these traits are part of building and maintaining a Full Value School and will provide important information and updates to the class's Full Value Commitment. Often, resonating with a student's Body challenges results in the reduction of resistance to learning and more rapid recovery, if illness or accidents are the concern. Given our demonstrable mind-body connection, if a student feels that their uniqueness is valued and supported, positive learning outcomes are more likely to result.

Interestingly, there can be whole class Body issues. There are days when all students are suffering from malaise or are overly restless. This could be a function of the weather, time of the year, or something going on in the school or community affecting everyone. It is important to consider these factors and adjust your instruction accordingly.

Setting:

Students are affected by their setting. A child who comes from a supportive, loving, and stable home, no matter what the parental configuration, will be more able to learn and demonstrate resilience when stressed. A well-nourished child who has access to quality medical care, walks to or from school in a safe neighborhood, and lives in a family with sufficient financial resources is more likely to thrive in the classroom. One of the most significant impacts of Full Value is to create a safe, predictable, and supportive culture and climate for students who, due to personal circumstances, may not experience it anywhere else in their lives. As noted, it is an unfortunate reality that schools are increasingly called upon to fill societal voids for students. Building and maintaining Full Value represents how we foster the capacity for resilience, self-esteem, and self-efficacy to be as important as supporting nutritional needs.

Setting concerns are considered hidden distractors within the Full Value Commitments; in many instances, giving voice to them may cause shame and doubt for students. However, for the teacher they are urgent considerations that will impact learning readiness, interactions between students, level of energy, distractibility, etc. Conversely this area is rich in developing behavioral norms under such areas as Be Safe, Care For Self & Others, and Let Go & Move On.

Setting is also a consideration when planning for individuals and groups of students. The capacity to handle different settings can be variable. Some kids can tolerate the chaos of the lunchroom while others may withdraw or become overly stimulated. A field trip may cause some students to wander off while others follow the rules. A game or initiative may cause students to focus or become overly aggressive or demanding. During a bus ride to school some students will calmly talk to friends or look out the window, while others throw food and harass other students. Interventions to anticipate and adjust the nature of the setting are informed by using this element of GRABBSS.

Stages of Group Development:

This element is most directly connected to our discussion of Tuckman's Stages of Group Development. We focus here on students' stages of development as reflected in the creation and implementation of their Full Value Commitment and their ability to use the Calling Group process. Some questions to ask:

- Are students able to explain each of the Full Value Behavioral Norms and what they mean to them? Can they offer examples of their use?

- Are students able to explain what distractors are and how they can interfere with meeting their Full Value Commitment?

- Do they use Full Value language with each other when sorting out disputes?

- What is their understanding of Calling Group?

- Are groups called and regulated by teachers, or have students been able to do so with varying degrees of supervision?

Determining students' stages of Full Value development will assist in guiding activity choices and infusing Full Value into the content area of the curriculum.

Using GRABBSS for Program Design and Implementation

Just as we have described GRABBSS for activity selection, so too can we look through its lens to plan and begin your school district's program.

Goals:

There are several aspects to goal setting in program design, including the mission of the school district, the mission of a funding organization (if different than the school district), the goals of the staff who will be supervising and facilitating the program, and the expectations and level of engagement with parents and community. Determining district or school goals is critical, as there is a direct connection between this and the level of financial and administrative support the program will receive.

New school initiatives may come from many directions. The staff, school board/administration, or parents may identify a need. Ultimately, no matter what the source, without an active commitment from central office and building-based administrators, SEL programs tend to founder. Goals need to be unambiguously stated and resources, commitments, and outcomes clearly defined.

School-based programs may be recipients of dollars from outside sources, such as state funding for primary prevention programs or private foundations. The goals of external revenue providers must be carefully considered as a component of program design. For example, is there a need for drug and alcohol or trauma components? Are only certain grade levels or buildings funded? Is the attempt to involve parents mandated? Is there a data collection requirement? These considerations can impact the nature of the program and, therefore, may factor into whether to accept certain types of funding, given the strings that may be attached.

Readiness:

The level of organizational readiness is essential to determine before making any commitments to running a social emotional learning program. Poor organizational readiness should not dissuade you from taking the plunge. However, at least you will be diving in with a watertight mask on! Assuring that a school is ready has much to do with the education you provide to significant gatekeepers before formalizing and presenting a proposal. Key staff that has gained an explicit working knowledge of the program's unique qualities are much more likely to line up behind you when your proposal goes to the Board of Education for approval. This process takes time but is well worth the investment.

Establishing organizational readiness can include providing literature, asking administration from schools that have adopted the program to contact your leadership staff, finding an operating program nearby, and arranging a site visit. We have found that the most effective way to establish administrative support is to provide a one-day overview experiential workshop. Even this short immersion is enough for school leaders to understand the power of the approach on a very personal level. But in the end, this program (or any program for that matter) cannot be sustained without administrative support.

An important consideration is to avoid the all or nothing approach. It may be that your school or district is not ready for a full-blown program. An option might be to start a pilot in one building or one grade level, especially if there is a keen interest on the part of a building principal to be the host. This strategy reduces the complexity of implementation dramatically. Teaching staff can visit the pilot program from other district schools. Participating teachers become collegial advocates. This is often much more effective than an outside provider attempting to sell a program, as a level of trust has already been established between colleagues.

A final essential component of readiness has to do with financial and resource commitments to your program. Ascertaining the level of ongoing dollars available and from what sources will significantly impact program design. When will training occur (summer, after school, during professional development days)? Will teachers be compensated either directly or through the use of compensatory days? Is there enough funding for training, textbooks, and equipment? If this is a public school setting, do you have to be accountable for contractual issues related to training and after school activities? Who will prepare the financial reports for outside funding agencies, if any are involved? What is the plan for sustainability? This is not an exhaustive list of questions, but offered to highlight the kinds of concerns you should consider as a function of carefully thinking through a program.

Affect:

The feeling tone of a school can greatly impact how much you will struggle to initiate a successful program. If a school district's focus is primarily on academic achievement, work will need to be done to help the board and administrative team understand the intrinsic connections between social-emotional wellness and academic progress. They are not mutually exclusive and, as we have discussed in this book, serve each other. The bifurcation of academic and social-emotional wellbeing seems most present in high schools. Building administration can experience social emotional learning as an unwanted intrusion, taking up time that would otherwise be devoted to the push for academic excellence. However, research (as discussed in Chapter 2) indicates that social emotional learning increases academic performance by enhancing abstract reasoning, affective maturation, and reducing disciplinary referral rates and absenteeism. Pragmatically, departmentalized programs fragment the day, whereas teaching multiple content areas in one classroom allows for more flexibility in the lower grades. However, via thoughtful program design, Full Value can be seamlessly integrated into a departmentalized setting.

Generally, you will find increased receptivity to a social-emotional learning program in the primary, elementary, and, to some degree, middle school levels. If you find this positive affect is present in your primary and elementary programs, this would be the place to begin. As students progress through the grades, we have found that they bring an expectation into their high school classes that Full Value should exist. It is a tail wagging the dog approach, which we have found to be effective.

Behavior:

The affect of the school toward your program will often be reflected in the level of cooperation from staff, facilities and funding provided, and the level of concern and enthusiasm generated by key players, such as teachers, principals, superintendents, and members of the Board of Education. As a program planner, you must be cognizant of those who walk the talk, as opposed to those who don't follow through on their commitments or who actively construct roadblocks at every turn.

Body:

At first blush this particular **GRABBSS** modality might seem to have little relevance to organizational assessment. However, we see connections in terms of the physical plant of the building and its ability to accommodate activities that may need to occur outside of the classroom. Are there fields or a playground with open areas close to the school? Proximity becomes a factor when thinking about an activity that could take forty-five minutes to complete. If transit time between the classroom and play space is extensive, this may determine activity selection and what should be purchased to support the program. Is there easy access to an all-purpose room or gymnasium should there be inclement weather? These rooms are often intensely utilized and may be difficult to schedule for experiential classroom activities. Working closely with the physical education department and co-planning activities for your class that can take place within the physical education program can be a win-win for all concerned.

Setting:

The setting of the school will have a significant impact on your program structure. In particular, it is essential to understand the mores of the school and the larger community it serves. It is a truism that the climate within a school often mirrors the desires and aspirations of the outside community. For example, a vocational school setting where learning a trade and entering the workforce is the primary agenda will differ significantly from a school district that prides itself on sending 95 percent of its graduates to college. Likewise, the climate of a private day placement for children struggling with emotional concerns will differ significantly from a residential facility for seriously disturbed children who cannot function in their community of origin. The differences do not necessarily relate to the quality of instruction or to the caliber of student. There is, however, a distinctly different culture relating to these educational settings that will invariably determine, to a large degree, the focus of your social emotional learning prevention work.

Stage of Development:

Just as one evaluates the stage of their group in its life cycle, this type of assessment can be brought to bear on the entire school community. Is your agency hierarchical in its administrative structure with a top down management style that allows for little meaningful input from line staff? Is the organization more collegially based, where teachers have an authentic voice in the governance and direction of the district? Is there harmony between the local bargaining unit, administration, and the board of education? How are students perceived? Are they seen as partners in the learning process, or blank slates to be filled with information from expert instructors? Again, all of these determinants must be considered when involved in program design and ongoing program management. Is there awareness in the school district of the value of social-emotional learning and, in particular, the modality you are proposing? Is there openness to innovation?

Some Thoughts About High School Programs

We have found that high schools present unique challenges regarding implementation. There is an assumption on the part of some high school administrations that social emotional learning should be relegated to the lower grades. They feel that high school is for the serious business of academic mastery and preparing for post-secondary education or careers. Therefore, there is little time for exploring feelings and relationships. This is an unfortunate mindset, and the negative consequences of this thinking are reflected in outcome studies.

In a report titled, *Respected, Perspectives of Youth on High School and Social Emotional Learning (SEL)* issued by Civic with Hart Research Associates (November, 2018)[40] for the Collaborative for Academic, Social and Emotional Learning (CASEL) the following key themes were presented:

- Students and young adults from strong SEL schools report a more positive social climate and learning environment, doing better academically, and being better prepared for life than those in weak SEL schools.

- Schools that emphasize social and emotional skill development are broadly appealing to students across background, race, ethnicity, income, geography, and type of school attended, and students see the benefits of such schools, but fewer than half believe their high schools are doing a good job of helping them develop SEL skills; and

- Students, particularly some of the most vulnerable, cite social and emotional problems as significant barriers to learning, doing their best, and fulfilling their potential. (pg. 3)

Confirmation that schools with vital social emotional learning programs report a better social climate and improved academic performance is not surprising and should send a message to those with a focus that is primarily academic or vocational. This monocular vision is not thoroughly preparing students for success with their families, communities, and workplaces.

Survey results indicate:

Fifty-two percent of current high school students believe at least some changes need to be undertaken to make their school a better place for students to learn and do their best, though just nine percent believe many changes need to be made (pg. 13). Of greater significance is the finding that positive perceptions tend to weaken post-graduation.

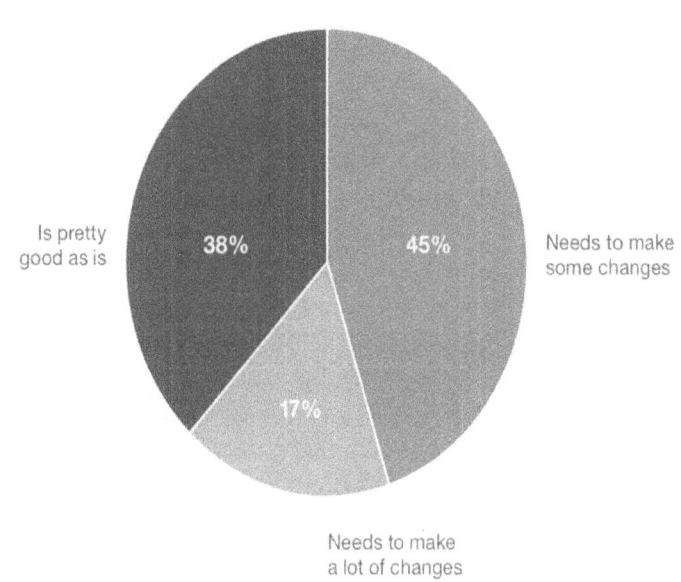

Top changes needed	
Better teachers	8%
More caring teachers	8%
Prevent bullying	7%
Better classes, diverse	6%

Needs to make a lot/some changes	
All post-HS young adults	62%
In four-year college	64%
In voc/community college	63%
Not enrolled	60%
Regular public school	63%
Other school	58%
Whites	62%
African Americans	66%
Hispanics	57%
City	57%
Suburb	65%
Small town/rural area	69%
Below average income	66%
Average income	59%
Above average income	64%
One/both parents college grads	59%
Neither parent college grad	68%

Recommendations moving forward include the following:

- Tight integration between SEL and academic content areas

- Ensuring student participation in crafting and monitoring SEL interventions

- Encouraging the participation of more marginalized and less participatory students in program development and implementation

- Clearly defining SEL goals and objectives by grade level

- Providing comprehensive training and support in SEL for all staff members

- Developing state benchmarks for SEL, integrated into the curriculum

These recommendations, among others, are referenced throughout the body of this text and supported by Full Value interventions. The report is a must read, as are a number of other comprehensive studies referenced in the description (pgs. 25-26). We are gratified that a focus is being brought to bear on high school programs and the critical need for integrating SEL primary prevention programs into the fabric of school life. High schools should be embracing this need with the same fervor as elementary, primary, and middle schools. To not do so does a serious disservice to students.

One thousand three hundred students participated in this study, encompassing diverse demographics. The population included 800 current and 500 recent graduates.

Summing Up

Out of necessity, the implementation guide for many programs is somewhat generic in nature. One of the many unique characteristics of building a Full Value School is that while templates are provided (i.e., Full Value Commitment, SMART Goals), students and teachers co-create their own amazing community. The structure for defining the Commitment is provided, but not the associated behaviors. These are brainstormed, debated, and defined by students in their own classroom and school. They are not universal or prescribed, nor should they be. Once they are prescribed, students view them as externally imposed rules. These prescriptions are just more of the same and make the students' commitment to them marginal at best. With this in mind we provide the following areas where information needs to be generated to ensure that a program unique to your school will be successfully implemented and sustained:

- Accurate assessment of need

- Determination of administration and board of education support

- Articulation of realistic program goals given the nature of the school(s)

- Building of program advocacy through education and demonstration of effectiveness

- Ongoing inclusion of gatekeepers

- Public relations that enhance the reputation of the school as a function of its support of Full Value School programming

- Inclusion of parents and, where possible, extension of Full Value into the home

- Adequate staffing and the provision of ongoing training opportunities

- Building in sustainability

- Linking staff with other like-minded practitioners through a collegial support network

- Rigorous qualitative or quantitative evaluative model to demonstrate ongoing effectiveness

- Ability to adjust program design on the run

- An ongoing and frequent public relations campaign through the use of various media and staff outreach to keep the program visible to the larger community

Reflection Practices

There are many resources available in the professional literature that guide discussions of experiences with groups. They may be labeled as debriefing, processing, closure, or exploration skills. We have chosen the term *reflection*, as it represents a more contemplative approach. Reflection means to connect not only to the experience of the group but also to how the individual has been affected as a result of their participation. Further, we have chosen strategies that will directly impact the understanding and practice of Full Value. These strategies can either be for post activity reflection or to encourage conversation during the Calling Group process. For the sake of clarity, we have established reflective categories. Where specific commercial products are recommended, their availability will be listed in Chapter 15, Odds & Ends. We have noted in the text that, depending on how an activity is presented to students, it can be used multiple times for different purposes. Additionally, activities used to teach specific Full Values can also be used to promote reflection. After each activity, you will note a Reflection header with suggested guided questions to help initiate conversations.

<u>Object Reflection</u>

Please see Chapter 15 for information on purchasing commercial (C) material.

- I Am About Cards © – Photographs of people and places. The people are often interacting with each other. All of the people photos depict various emotional states. Landscapes and buildings often represent a mood or feeling. At the end of an activity, cards can be laid out on a table, and students asked to choose one that reflects a connection to whatever Full Value Behavioral Norm is being learned or practiced. For example, if discussing Be Safe, the framing for card selection could be, "Choose a card representing how you felt about being safe during the activity. Be prepared to share your thoughts about the card with the group." It is okay for two or more students to choose the same card.

- Beanie Babies: When creating a Full Value Commitment with young students, Beanie Babies easily connect to specific behavioral norms. In Chapter 3, Beanie Babies are used with preschoolers to develop their Full Value Commitment. They can also be used as prompts for students to discuss thoughts, feelings, and behaviors when reflecting on the outcomes of an activity.

- Nature Objects (sticks, leaves, etc.): Students can be sent on a scavenger hunt to find objects in nature to connect to their Full Value experience.

- Small Polished Stones: These can be found inexpensively at your local rock and gem shop (or on the beach). They are often multi-faceted and varied in color and shape. After scattering them inside the circle of students, ask them to choose a stone representing the connection to the norms or distractors present during either an activity or resulting from a classroom interaction.

- Paint Chips: Easily obtained from your local paint or hardware store. The colors and their names often provoke emotional connections for students to their Full Value experience.

- World Wisdom Cards ©: These cards contain proverbs from all over the world. An example would be, "Community is never created by force." This is a Chinese proverb that would work well with Care for Self & Others. "If we don't change our direction, we are likely to end up where we're headed." This connects nicely to Set Goals. "You must do your own growing, no matter how tall your grandfather was." This is a good fit with Let Go & Move On.

Kinesthetic Reflection

- Human Sculpture (Chapter 3): Students meet in their small groups to create a sculpture representing a key learning from a completed activity related to Full Value. This will usually require some negotiation and compromise. It is important to stress to students that all must agree upon the representation. This models for students that Full Value is a continual process, for coming to a consensus on their representation will likely involve Care for Self & Others and Let Go & Move On. If issues arise during this process, an additional reflection might be warranted, or there may be a need to call group.

- Human Camera (Chapter 8): This can provoke discussion no matter what the activity. The direction may be, "Take a picture of something or someone that represents your feelings about how the group worked together during our Be Here activity."

- Journal Writing: Provide students with a Full Value specific prompt, paper and pencil, and time to write or draw. Students may elect to share or not share what they have written in their journals. If you can afford it, give students a bound book with blank sheets. This becomes a beautiful source of reflective memories (and associated wisdom) accumulated over the course of the school year. In addition, journaling provides connections between Full Value and the literature, language arts, and the visual arts curricula.

- Sculptures and Drawings, Stonehenge Activity (Chapter 11): The stacking of stones and other readily available objects found in nature to form a sculpture is an excellent reflection method for those students who prefer non-verbal expression. Drawings and paintings can also represent a student's experience during a Full Value activity. This reflection tool can be utilized no matter which Full Value you are teaching or exploring. Connections to the visual arts curriculum are many.

- Story Line: This is a collective group story. The teacher can begin the story if a student does not volunteer. Each student contributes one line to the story and stands next to the person who created the previous line. The framing of the activity around which the reflection story is built will determine, to some degree, what each student contributes. For example, if the activity is entirely focused on one specific Full Value, students might be asked to create a story segment that illustrates either the positive practice or the witnessed distractor. The teacher might say, "Your contribution to the story should reflect how or when Let Go & Move On behaviors were witnessed during the activity."

Verbal Reflection

- Word Whip: Students are seated in a Calling Group circle. This is a quick engagement and low risk strategy. For example, ask each student to quickly call out the Full Value Behavioral Norm they saw practiced the most during the activity. If a student cannot respond immediately, they can always pass (Challenge of Choice), but the whip around the circle continues until every student has contributed.

- Pair-Share: Students are divided into self-selected pairs and given a reflective question to discuss. Their response will require some consensus to be achieved. Once the Pair-Share time period is over, students circle up and report their consensus response to the provided question. A Let Go & Move On question might be, "Identify and describe three times you observed students practicing Let Go & Move On. Rank order from most to least which had the most impact on the success of the group."

- Sound Whips: An example of a reflection question for this strategy is, "Create a unique sound that represents Let Go & Move On, when you experienced that Full Value in the activity we just completed." The follow-up question would be, "Why did you choose that sound?"

What – So What – Now What (Rolfe et al., 2001)[41]

This sequence is beneficial for Calling Group or reflection facilitation, whether by a teacher or student, as it organizes the overall flow of discussion. We have found that students find this sequence to be clear and accessible. Using this approach is not limited to activities that teach Full Value. It can be used for reflecting on academics, as well. It aligns nicely with Bloom's revised taxonomy.[42]

What, So What, Now What	Bloom's Revised Taxonomy
WHAT	Remember
	Understand
SO WHAT	Analyze
	Evaluate
NOW WHAT	Apply
	Create

Having an overarching reflection framework that students are familiar with supports project-based learning, understanding plot in literature, working through algebraic equations, and all manner of other academic content areas.

The What

At the end of an activity, there may be a difference of opinion as to what happened. The What of the discussion builds consensus as to what actually occurred during the activity process and interactions between students. Without clarity around What happened, it becomes very difficult to gain meaning from experience. Having a few students agree to act as process observers during an activity will help bring more objectivity to this discussion. Some reflection techniques to consider using with the group:

- As noted under Kinesthetic Reflection, ask students to tell the story of the activity. Each student, in turn, contributes one line of the story, starting with how the activity began (e.g., "Our teacher explained the rules of the game, we decided to take some time to plan"). If a student is not ready to contribute, allow them to pass for one round of storytelling. After the story has been completed, ask students if they would like to provide any clarifications or corrections. Then ask for a vote from the group when it feels like it has reached consensus.

- In the same vein, break students into three small groups and have them draw representations of the beginning, middle, and end of the activity. These are then presented to the large group. Again, clarification should be asked for and any potential corrections discussed.

Some What topics for students to consider:

- Describe each important step in the activity you just completed

- What did you personally contribute during the activity?

- Describe the most important contribution you feel you made

- Describe a contribution that you saw one of your classmates make

- Describe one distractor that you saw

So What

Once the group has agreed on the What of the experience, it is time to move on to its meaning. The meaning or outcome of the activity should connect to its original purpose as decided upon by the teacher or co-created with students. For example, let's say the focus of the activity was on goal setting, and further, the level of commitment required from each student in order for the task to be completed successfully. During the activity it was determined that some students were utterly engaged, some partially, and some not at all. The So What moves the discussion from the observed behaviors to the impact of those behaviors on group functioning and success. How the students felt, what they thought, and how they acted within the experience are all worthy of reflection. This will not be factual information (as discussed when agreeing on What happened), but will be of significant value in determining what to take away from the experience. Some questions to pose to the group:

- How did you feel about those who were partially participating or not at all?

- Did your individual behavior choices influence the group? And if so, how?

- Did you make some assumptions about their lack of participation? If you did, what were those assumptions?

- For those whose participation was limited, was that due to A) confusion around the instructions, B) feeling incapable of coordinating movements without time to practice, or C) trouble dealing with the noise and motion? Other issues?

- How did you determine what your role would be in the activity? Did you feel you practiced Challenge of Choice? If so, how?

- Why did you feel like you had a responsibility to participate? If you did not feel that way, why?

- How is this discussion connected to our Full Value Commitment?

- Did the group stay with the agreed upon goal(s) or did the focus shift?

- Did we discover a more important purpose than was originally decided upon? If so, what was it?

- How did your behavior influence the group?

- Describe your beliefs and feelings about responsibility and participation.

Now What

The questions asked and the focus of Now What is to use successes and difficulties experienced during an activity to continue to build positive capacity with students in all areas of social, emotional, and academic functioning. The Now What of the process focuses on what students have learned from the experience and how it will influence future work together. This is another excellent opportunity to use some of the processing tools outlined above. As described under Object Reflection, present a pack of paint chips to students and ask them to select a color that represents their feelings about the group's ability to achieve their goals.

Some Now What questions to consider are:

- For those who were focused on the activity what did you need to do to make that happen?

- How might we work better as a group to be more inclusive of people who felt they did not have a role or a voice?

- What can we add to our positive behaviors or celebrate existing behaviors in our Full Value Commitment?

- What distractors do we need to be more mindful of during future activities?

- What positive behaviors and outcomes can we take from this experience together to support our work on future activities?

Here is an example of how What, So What, Now What would be used during activity reflection from Grand Right and Left:

The Activity: Grand Right and Left

Square Dancing was a prevalent form of dance in rural America. The dancing took place with large groups and depended on a caller who gave out directions as the dance went on. The caller had to be very clear about directions, and the dancers needed to follow them. If the directions were clear and the group followed them, the dance would be smooth and coordinated. It was a way for people to socialize and get to know each other.

How you do it:

Everyone gets a partner. The partners then form two concentric circles with the other participants (one circle is inside the other). Partner A starts on the outside circle. Partner B begins on the inside circle. The outer circle participants will start facing clockwise. The inner circle participants will start facing counterclockwise. Partners will start next to each other, hooking elbows. The goal of the activity is to traverse all the way around the circle, going right-left-right-left with other partners, and return to one's original partner at precisely the same time everyone else returns to their partner.

A caller who knows what they are doing and can give directions guides the activity. But this is a goal-setting initiative, meaning that the group needs to generate ideas as to how best to solve the problem.

Reflection: The sheer energy associated with this activity, coupled with the exuberance of youth, can easily lead to a breakdown in focus. While the goal is clear, there are many opportunities for the process to unravel. Remember to always use the activity as the basis for discussion. Ask the group to report what they saw (The What of the experience). This would include students losing track of the progression, missing an offered hooked arm and not knowing what to do, breaking a rule and not reporting it to the group, or behaving in a way that was counterproductive to success. Positives can also be reported. A student who gave verbal prompts to support a peer's efforts, the look of concentration on someone's face, etc. The So What part of this reflection would focus on how students felt and what they thought about their own participation and their classmates' participation. What did the experience mean to them? The Now What moves students to a problem-solving phase. How do we use this experience to help us to become a high functioning team? What new individual and group goals do we need to consider to build our capacities as we work together on future activities and assignments in the classroom?

The Adventure illustrates co-author Jim Schoel's (1988)[43] conceptualization on how engaging in activities promotes reflection and new learning. The wave represents the idea that guided experience generates forceful, forward movement in the life of the individual and the group. Reflection on the What, Now What, and So What of the experience occurs after the completion of the activity, leading to more effective group and individual effort going forward.

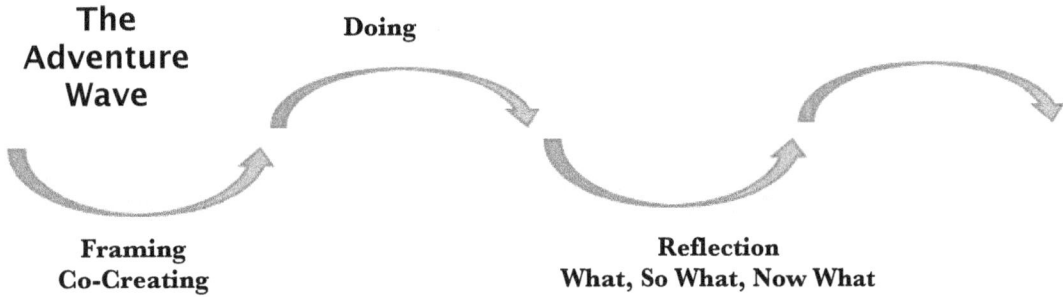

For a further list of Reflection ideas that can readily be adapted for use with public and private school students, please see *Exploring Islands of Healing*, pgs. 260-272.

CHAPTER 5

CALLING GROUP

"Belonging is the innate human desire to be part of something larger than us"[44]

-Brene Brown

The Why of Calling Group

Calling Group is one of the most effective methods of practicing Full Value Commitments and creating a safe and high functioning classroom environment. However, it can also be one of the most challenging processes to facilitate. Calling Group allows students to stop, gather, and explore what is happening in the moment. It helps students to find their voice and to practice the democratic process. The experience also builds student empowerment and the skills of empathy, communication, and problem-solving. Calling Group is a mutually developed skill that the teacher and students use to foster better relationships and a shared working practice. This chapter will provide some theoretical underpinnings for why Calling Group is effective and numerous strategies for implementation.

According to psychologist Carl Jung, "The circle is one of the great primordial images of mankind" (Moyers, 1988).[45] It is a symbol found throughout our history to represent several concepts in nature and human behavior. It is found throughout many cultures as an essential symbol that represents many deeply held beliefs about our existence and ourselves. Symbols like the wedding ring and the round table all represent the equality of relationships. Even the original flag of the thirteen colonies contained a circle. What has advanced us as a species is our innate desire to circle up and to develop collaborative communities. No other species other than humans has been able to cooperate so fully. It is essential to create and maintain a climate that promotes safety and security, thereby allowing this collaboration to flourish.

Many people mistakenly believe that life is still about the "survival of the fittest" (Keltner, 2014)[46] but current research, like that being done by U.C. Berkley's Greater Good, [47] and The Center for Compassion and Altruism Education and Research at Stanford Medical, debunks this belief. Their research reveals that as humans, we are social beings born to cooperate and support rather than compete with each other (Doty, 2015).[48] Studies have demonstrated that our nature is one of empathy and compassion.[49] Archeological digs of ancient cultures have turned up evidence that differently-abled people were well cared for by society. If only the fittest survived, why, as a species, would we care for the lame or ill? They would only impede our progress and risk our own survival. Steven Hawking would not have been considered physically fit, but no one would question his soaring intellectual capacities and contributions to society. The development of close communities where people are accepted, cared for, and valued enabled us to thrive as a species. Harvard researchers, currently completing the longest study on happiness, have shown that the number one factor identified for happiness is close, supportive relationships. They have also demonstrated that close relationships positively influence our physical, emotional, and intellectual health (Waldinger, 2015).[50]

It is also instructive review the most current research regarding the top skills needed in the workplace. Multiple studies list communication, teamwork, and problem-solving as the top three skills sought in this current job market. These are closely followed by various soft skills like interpersonal effectiveness, compassion, listening, leadership, and the ability to learn. In one list developed by the Opportunity Network[51], only two of the ten skills had anything to do with traditional academic subjects. So why have we created such a competitive school climate when so much of the corporate world realizes that all this competition is harmful? One of the reasons comes from Steven Covey's Scarcity Theory (2013)[52]. Where there is only a limited amount of anything, it promotes the survival of the fittest mentality. Covey also identified the Abundance Theory[53] that aligns with compassion, where there are many different avenues to success. These beliefs also connect well with the current work of Carol Dweck (2008) and the idea of a growth mindset[54] that is being taught in many schools today.

As demonstrated in the Project Aristotle study of group effectiveness by Google[55], the number one ingredient of an effective group is psychological safety. Calling Group allows this safety to take center stage in the classroom and school. This is a crucial area that may become the much-needed antidote to assist our students with their ever-increasing levels of anxiety and depression. Students feel disconnected due to a competitive and stress laden environment, causing mental health issues to have reached a crisis proportion. The Calling Group process offers a way to address this destructive environment and change it to a more collaborative and compassionate one. As mentioned in the mindfulness section of the book (Chapter 13), stress and its effects are very harmful to us. We need to offer students tangible survival skills that foster compassion, collaboration, and connection rather than competition, comparison, and isolation. Environments are required that go beyond the limits of just survival of the fittest to ones that promote and support thriving for all.

Types of Groups

Below are listed the types of groups we recommend students use as they begin this practice. Students may eventually add to this list or change the names to better meet their needs.

Information: This group is called for when there is a need for clarification. Information groups may be looking for an understanding of the actual problem that they are addressing. It may also be used to clarify who is taking on what roles to solve the problem. When there is some factual confusion, this group helps in developing a more straightforward path to understanding.

Celebration: This group is called to acknowledge the accomplishments of an individual, individuals, or the entire class. Many times, individual students have contributed to the group's goals and success without any acknowledgment. This group not only allows recognition but also encourages participation from all students.

Feelings: This group is called to check in on students' emotional needs and well-being. This is not a therapy or encounter group. Instead, it is a gathering that allows students to express their feelings and for the group to understand how everyone is faring. This expression develops empathy and compassion in students and helps them know how members may be impacted by the group's interactions.

Growth: This group is called to develop direction and to establish mutually agreed upon goals. SMART Goals or 4 Square may be utilized to assist in this process. It would also be helpful for educators to become familiar with the concept of a growth mindset to assist in this process. Both of these processes help develop more realistic and achievable goals that are growth oriented and not rigid.

Feedback: This group is called to provide students with an opportunity to provide growth-oriented feedback to each other. Feedback should be viewed as a way to assist the group and individual members in reaching their goals. This is not about constructive criticism or any type of criticism. Instead, the Full Value Commitment's behaviors and distractors should serve as a guide for delivering effective feedback.

Outcome: This group is called to come to a resolution around whatever issue the students are grappling with. Resolution usually results in action, which could mean a change in behavior, acceptance of responsibility, a new set of goals for individuals, a change in operating norms, or apologies.

How Calling Group Aligns with Full Value

Be Here: Make sure the feedback is as current as possible. The feedback should be about what is happening now with the person(s), not what occurred weeks or months ago. Is the feedback I am giving relevant to what is happening now?

Be Safe: The feedback should be delivered in a compassionate way to be heard rather than cause defensiveness. Is the feedback I am giving intended to help or hurt the person?

Be Honest: The feedback should be honest, but as mentioned above, delivered in a safe and caring manner. There is no reason for being brutally honest. This serves no purpose other than to shut down the listener. Is the feedback I am giving based on fact or opinion?

Set Goals: The person delivering the feedback should be aware of group and individual goals. Is the feedback assisting the person in reaching the group's goals or personal goals?

Let Go & Move On: The feedback should be delivered in a manner that can promote movement beyond the current situation. For example, is the feedback I am providing going to keep things in a chaotic or destructive state, or enable us to move forward?

Care for Self & Others: The feedback should be focused on the person receiving it and not on our own needs. Is the feedback I am giving intended to meet my needs or the receiver's needs?

Control to Empowerment in Calling Group

Before launching into how you do it, we would like to help you put your fears aside concerning the potential for students to call group because there is an ant on their desk, or someone accidentally stepped on their heel. When a group is called, its purpose is facilitated by the teacher (See Control to Empowerment, Chapter 1). Via modeling and coaching students begin to understand when Calling Group is appropriate and when it is not. Depending on the developmental maturity of your students this could take some time. There is no one magic month of the year for this to happen. It is essential to reflect on whether you are being over controlling or not controlling enough when evaluating whether students should or should not be given the authority to call group. It also could be that some students are ready while others are not. Empowering a student to call group should always be evaluated on an individual basis. Students who want to call group after every recess to avoid schoolwork need to be given boundaries and guidance. However, if students are dealing with interactions from recess that impedes learning, a group should be called to address this and find ways to move forward.

Facilitation of the group also falls along the control to empowerment continuum. Students may appropriately call a group, but it can then degenerate into name-calling, accusations, etc. Students will initially need help in maintaining focus on the group topic and the type of group being called. For example, if it is an information group, then feelings are not shared. The point is to build agreement on what happened.

The How of Calling Group

Step One: The person who wants to call the group announces, "I am Calling Group."

Step Two: The group circles up. Make sure the group is in a circle where all faces can be seen. No double-parking, meaning everyone needs to be in the circle.

Step Three: Determine who is leading this group. The person calling the group can take this role or ask someone else to lead.

Step Four: Announce what type of group you are calling. "I am calling a _____ group." The person then gives the reason for calling this type of group.

Step Five: Gather group content. This may be done with direct questions pertaining to the type of group called or facilitated with other resources (see below).

Step Six: Check in with group members and vote if needed.

Step Seven: End the group.

Calling Group Techniques

Knowing that both children and adults have difficulties expressing themselves, cards or objects can become part of the Calling Group process. Students can call a Feelings Group and utilize cards with feelings written on them, like the *I Am About Cards* (Schoel & Schoel, 2012).[56] As noted in Chapter 4, objects like polished stones, Beanie Babies, paint chip cards, or objects found in nature can also be used to assist in this process. The use of resources allows creative thinking and addresses the many different ways students prefer to express themselves. If carefully facilitated, this can smoothly transition into a reflection process for the group. It encourages and empowers the students to share in meaning making. This may allow students to develop more self-awareness and contemplative skills.

Co-creation between students and teachers allows the process of reflection to flow more naturally. For example, imagine a student calling an Information Group during a biology lab because he or she is unsure about the task and who is taking what responsibilities. This may lead to the group having strong feelings about what and how the roles are assigned. This may prompt a member to call a Feelings Group to hear from all members. A pattern of negative feelings may emerge that shows that most students are not happy with group assignments and responsibilities. This may then lead to a Feedback Group to address the bossiness of one of the members. The class may enter an outcome Group that defines new roles to be established and a more collaborative approach to the current lab. After the successful transition to this new way of being for the group, the reflection process becomes a natural discussion rather than a typical forced exercise. This specific group focus is unlikely to be repeated, as all students have had input into the problem and how to resolve it.

The When of Calling Group

The main goal of Calling Group in schools is to create a safe environment that supports learning. Groups are not for therapy and are designed to develop quick and effective resolution when problems arise. They should be primarily preventative in nature. This is where the control to empowerment model can assist the teacher. The teacher should model the appropriate use of Calling Group and be cognizant of time constraints. As mentioned, the goal of Calling Group is to support learning not to derail it. This is where the teacher's attunement to their students, awareness, and emotional intelligence is crucial.

Sequencing the Calling Group Process

"Circles create soothing space, where even reticent people can realize that their voice is welcome"[57]

-Margaret J. Wheatley

The following provides the teacher or student leader with a sequence to follow when introducing the concept of Calling Group:

- Circling Up

    Have the group circle up to create the 'perfect circle.' Once assembled, adjust with the no double-parking rule and ensure that all can be seen in the group. Next, instruct the group on creating the following circles.

    > Superman Circle: This circle has participants standing with everyone's elbows touching. Once all elbows are connected the group calls out, "Dun Da Duh."

Texas Big Foot: Start with a larger circle than you need with plenty of space in front and to either side of students. Have them take a Texas Big Foot step toward the center of the circle (just a really big step), then another until they form a reasonably tight circle for speaking with each other.

Velcro Circle: Have the members step forward until their shoulders are all touching. The group then makes scrunching sounds, like Velcro being taken apart.

Yoga Circle: This requires the members to step backward until they reach their arms out at shoulder height and touch opposing pointer fingers. Members then lean forward and lift one leg behind them (warrior 3 for you yogis), and once all connected, the group members call out, "Ommmmmmm."

Experiment with getting students to create these circles several times. The group can also begin to create their own circles with the appropriate motions and designs included.

There is also the option to say, "Let's gather round and circle up."

- Calling Group

Circling up allows members to enter into a community of different perspectives and equal voices. This democratic process allows the group to use the six Full Value Behavioral Norms effectively.

Variation 1: Calling Group Symbols

As a way of encouraging discussion about each group's purpose, have students create unique symbols for each. These can be used to focus students on the purpose of specific groups. Best practice is to have students envision their own representations of the groups. Some examples are provided:

Information: Students place their hands around their ears in a listening pose with elbows touching on each side of them.

Celebration: Students reach up and high five members on each side of them.

Feelings: Students place their hands on their hearts and touch elbows with people on each side of them.

Feedback: Students extend their hands in a giving gesture and touch thumbs with people on each side of them.

Growth: Students place their hands on the shoulders of the person on each side of them.

Outcome: Students cross their arms and shake the hand of the person on either side of them.

Once the group symbols are established, the following activity can be used to teach and reinforce them.

Activity Name: Rapid Groups

How you do it:
Students should play Zip Zap (Chapter 6) and Full Value Speed Rabbit (Chapter 3) before playing Rapid Groups. This will build familiarity with the activity.

A student stands in the middle and points to any person in the circle. The people immediately on the person's left and right join that person to make a sculpture. The person in the middle does one action while the people on the outside complete a different action that mirrors each other. The trios will create the group types in this variation instead of animals (Full Value Speed Rabbit). Have the students first decide how each trio will represent group types. The person in the middle should say, "I am calling a _____ group." This will assist in getting students used to leading groups.

Variation 2: Calling Group Charades: Split students into equal teams and play charades using the group types as the charade that needs to be acted out.

Calling Group & Trauma Work

Calling Group provides the opportunity for students to have a voice without the fear of emotional or physical consequences. It is a safe space. Students may contribute as an injured party, a supporter, a celebrant, or an observer. The classroom Full Value Commitment governs the Calling Group process. Students have agreed to be present with each other, maintain emotional safety in their interactions, offer honesty with compassion and empathy, care for each other (and for self), and agree to let go of toxic interactions and associated feelings. Forgiveness is practiced. Students who have experienced trauma (and all students) may choose their level of participation and their degree of emotional risk during Calling Group. Having a meaningful voice without negative consequences brings predictability and builds feelings of empowerment within children whose life experience can feel dangerously out of control.

CHAPTER 6

BE HERE

Activities in this section have been selected for their ability to connect and engage students with each other. To participate students must attend to the demands of the activity. They must be present. Additionally, these activities are rich with opportunities for students to learn about each other. We have found that when you know more about a person, the more likely it is that meaningful relationships will develop. Knowledge and awareness build closeness, caring, and empathy. Each activity provides an opportunity for students to explore the importance of being present and how that contributes to success. As noted in the introduction, suggestions for reflecting on activities will be provided as a way to energize your thinking. From these conversations will come specific behaviors that can be integrated into the classes' Full Value Commitment and the distractors that can get in the way. Activities are listed alphabetically.

Outcomes of Be Here

- Active Listening
- Becoming Comfortable in One's Skin
- Building Relationships
- Self-Reflection

Specific to Mindfulness

- Attunement
- Awareness of Slipping into the Past and Future
- Emotional Self-Awareness
- Integration
- Optimism
- Organizational Awareness

ACTIVITIES

Activity Difficulty Scale

1 (Easy) ------- 2 (A bit harder) -------- 3 (Pretty complicated) --------- 4 (Difficult)

The Activity: Blob or Add-on Tag   Time: 40 minutes

Materials: Boundary markers   Difficulty: 1

How you do it:
        These early experiential tag games can be traced back thirty plus years. Its

name originated with a fifty's movie, *The Blob*. An amoeba like structure, it absorbed everything it came in contact with. The purpose is to tag everyone, creating a long line of blobbed participants.

In a large play area (a field preferably or gymnasium) ask students to find a partner. The pairs should then spread out so they are not immediately tagged. The game can start with one pair being "it" and then chasing and tagging another couple. Once tagged, those two pairs link up by holding hands, and then attempt to tag more pairs. The game is over when the blob is complete, and everyone has been tagged (joyously, of course).

Rules:

- Contact between the taggers must be maintained. If any of the held hands separate, a tag has not happened. If hand holding is an issue, a two-foot length of ¼ inch rope (laundry line) will keep pairs close together but not touching. If one person lets go of the buddy rope, a tag has not happened.

- The pairs being chased must also keep holding hands. If a pair breaks hands while being chased, they must link up to the Blob.

- Only the end people on the Blob can do the tagging

- Escape from the Blob can only take place at each end of the line

- Running through or under the line is not permitted

The Blob is allowed to suddenly change direction by releasing hands, all individuals turning 180 degrees, and then taking hold of hands again. This is often a discovery, a problem-solving item for the group, but the teacher can suggest that strategy if they feel it necessary to help the Blob along. Space is also a consideration. Too much or too little can hinder the game. We find it is better to start with a smaller well-defined space while the game is being learned and expand it as you see fit.

Reflection: There is a logical consequence for either pairs or the Blob letting go of hands.

This happens if pairs are not cooperating fully and communicating about speed and direction. For the pairs that remained free the longest, what was their strategy? For pairs easily caught, what about their communication caused that to happen? The focus should always be on strategies for improving listening and cooperation rather than finger pointing. What is learned can be applied to round two.

Cross Categories: Be Safe, Set Goals

The Activity: Chicken Tag Time: 15 minutes

Materials: Rubber chicken, boundary markers Difficulty: 1

How you do it:
> The goal is to have everyone in the group tagged by the chicken. Starting with one "it" person, that person takes the chicken. When the leader says, "go," the chicken holder attempts to tag another person with the chicken. Once a student is tagged, they become an ally with the initial "it" person. They can then begin to throw the chicken to each other to tag more players. Each tagged person becomes an ally until there is only one person left. "Chicken check" can be called by anyone at any time to identify those people who have been tagged and are allies. Clear, narrow boundaries are necessary otherwise participants can range too far afield. However, it may be the purpose of the teacher to have this happen, which allows for more running, with the group benefiting from increased aerobics and strategizing.

Reflection: Identifying commonalities is a powerful way to connect us. The more connected we are the more powerful we can become. What commonalities does the chicken represent? Have the group identify and list as many things that they all have in common within three minutes. Are any of these a surprise?

Cross Categories: Be Honest, Set Goals

The Activity: Claytionary Time: 30-45 minutes

Materials: Sculpting clay Difficulty: 3

How you do it:
> If a picture is worth a thousand words, how about a sculpture? Two thousand, three thousand? Here's a chance for your students to find out. Take a trip to the local toy or department store and look for those classic yellow cylindrical storage cans with the colored tops filled with Play-Doh. If more permanent keepsakes are desired, buy Polymer clay that hardens into permanence when oven-baked.

Form a bunch of subgroups and have each choose a Sculpting Representative (SR). They will come to you and form a Clayhuddle (CH). In the CH you will give them a Sculpting Directive (SD), that is, tell each to go back to their groups and sculpt a specific object out of clay. Off they will go to their groups to begin sculpting while the rest of their group tries to guess what they are creating. The first group to guess correctly wins the round. Another sculptor is chosen and the game continues. Sculpting ideas can include well-known monuments, objects around the home, and, at a more symbolic level, representations of concepts, such as honesty, faith, truth, and love, all potential components of Full Value. Ask participants to sculpt their thoughts as a springboard to conversation. Again, the creations are guided by your imagination and the purpose and needs of the group you are facilitating.

Reflection: When using this activity under Be Here give a directive that represents this Full Value Commitment (e.g., an ear, a pair of glasses, an open hand). Once the small group guesses the item, ask them to share how the representation connects to Be Here.

Cross Categories: Be safe, Set Goals, Let Go & Move On

The Activity: Coming and Going of the Rain

Time: 10 minutes

Difficulty: 3

How you do it:

There are few natural occurrences more spectacular and humbling than a powerful thunderstorm. It provides a vivid reminder of our relatively small place in the cosmos, our fragility and vulnerability. Yet, there is also a beauty and power to the storm that connects us to the random majesty of the natural world.

This activity requires accepting and participating in the metaphor of creating a storm. If a student is not present (e.g., creating distractions, not paying attention to the instructions and process), the activity will fail. It is for these reasons that this activity resides in Be Here. A more profound lesson is that only as interdependent beings can we most successfully weather the storm.

Form your group into a circle that will allow for a comfortable reach between hands and the next person's back in the loop. This will necessitate students standing sideways, facing the back of the person in front of them. A quick but essential aside: this activity can be moving and very connecting for students.

However, it can also devolve into discounting behavior, with students hitting each other inappropriately rather than being gentle. Make sure that students have the readiness to make this a positive experience. Ask them to close their eyes.

Say to them (or however you would like to frame it):

> Have you ever really listened to a thunderstorm? It begins way before the coming of the rain. First, there is a dead calm, a still so quiet that it seems like the air cannot lift itself. Then comes a slight whisper of a wind which builds into a flag snapping blast of air that, when gusting, can knock you off your feet. A rumble of thunder is heard to the west. It rolls again, closer now. Then lightning flashes. It makes everyone's face light up. You begin to automatically count between the booms and blasts, calculating the distance of the storm. Suddenly it is upon you; trees twist in on themselves, whipped by the wind; rain slices in rigid sheets across the grass and pavement; thunder and lightning collapse into one continuous rage of fire and sound. Then, as the power seems like it will overwhelm us all, we sense a change. The rain starts to make more individual pats on the pavement; the wind allows the trees to unwind; the thunder rolls, but less often, and the lightning lights up a far-off place. It smells fresh and green. The sun takes a run at breaking through the departing storm.
>
> As a group we are going to create a thunderstorm together. As we go through the experience, think about the importance of maintaining our togetherness in weathering the storms that will seek to overwhelm our group as we continue this journey.

Explain to the group that they will feel the hands of the person directly behind them on their backs, and that they should transfer what they <u>feel</u>, using their hands, onto the back in front of them. It is important to stress that during the activity they will hear different sounds from different parts of the group, as the hand motions move around the group from one person to the next, <u>but they should only do to the person in front of them what they feel on their own backs.</u>

- Sound 1: Wind – Rotate your hands, palms open, to produce swishing sounds

- Sound 2: Light Rain – Pat your fingers in random taps on shoulders

- Sound 3: Heavier Rain – Increase the frequency of the taps, making them a bit harder, as well

- Sound 4: Pounding Rain – Slap the back rapidly with open hands

- Return to Sounds 3, 2, and 1 to make the storm depart

    As you control the change in sounds, you may continue each for as long as you'd like. When you stop your final sound, the wind will slowly recede around the group until there is silence, signifying the storm's passage and the end of the activity.

Reflection: There are several elements to this activity that connect to Be Here. Students sometimes mimic what they hear instead of what they feel on their backs. The Wind and Rain activity starts to fall apart if some people pass along what they <u>feel</u> on their backs while others pass along what they <u>hear</u> from somewhere across the circle. This can lead to an interesting conversation around the inability to truly split concentration between two competing sources. A classroom example would be the student who is talking to their neighbor while the teacher is delivering assignment information.

This is also a great activity that teaches about the present moment and how we can only experience it through our senses. You cannot hear in the future or the past. You can do practice rounds with just sounds: rubbing hands, snapping fingers, and clapping before attempting The Coming and Going of the Rain.

Cross Categories: Be Safe

The Activity: Everybody's It　　　　　　　　　　Time: 10 minutes (or more!)

Materials: Boundary cones or markers　　　　　　Difficulty: 2

How you do it:

There is no one "it" person, which immediately levels the playing field. However, you still have to be shifty and quick. With Everybody's It, everybody is free to tag everyone else. Once a student is tagged, the tagged person must go down on one knee. The last student who avoids being tagged is the one left standing. The game can be over quickly, laying the groundwork for starting again, and again. Establish boundaries, the size relative to the number of players and their physical ability. You will need a minimum of eight students, although with certain populations the game can be adapted by reducing it down to slow motion, with a smaller number participating. Having students frozen but still able to tag can increase the challenge. Or, people can be brought back to life by giving each other low fives.

Reflection: This is a great activity to teach participants about multitasking and attention. Research has shown that we can multitask (run and tag) but we cannot multi-attention. Attention can only be on one subject at a time. Participants get tagged more easily when their attention is on tagging someone rather than keeping themselves safe. Have participants identify the obstacles that compete for their attention at school when trying to get their work done.

Cross Categories: Be Safe, Be Honest, Let Go & Move On, Care for Self & Others

---

The Activity: Fire in the Hole   Time: 30 minutes

Materials: Bag of 9-inch to 12-inch balloons   Difficulty: 2

How you do it:

There is a high action, bodies squeezed close together, and numerous rapid-fire explosions activity. Dig into your balloon supply and ask the group to blow up a bunch of them, half the number as there are group members, with a few to spare. Now have the group pair off and offer each twosome a balloon.

The instructions are simple. Students must explode the balloon by pressing it between their bodies. No finger pinching or foot stomping is allowed to expedite the explosion. It must be two body parts pressing together to pop the balloons. Once a pair has popped their balloon, they must go off and seek another pair who has been woefully unsuccessful in exploding their spherical air sack. This ultimately leads to a bevy of balloon breakers in a large clump, laughing a great deal!

As for the name of the game, it's what the miners used to yell before setting off dynamite. So, offer them that tidbit at the outset of the game and have pairs yell it out before the popping begins.

Reflection: Ask students to focus on the strategies and behaviors they used to successfully break the balloon. What happened when they lost focus? How does being here in this activity connect to the Full Value Commitment and working together in small groups in the classroom?

Cross Categories: Set Goals, Let Go & Move On

The Activity: Flungee   Time: 45 minutes

Material: ½ inch thick length of bungee cord, rubber chickens   Difficulty: 3

How you do it:

Tie a piece of ½ inch bungee cord between two stout trees or posts with a secure knot. Conduct a few adult test pulls to make sure it is secure. You will have immediately created a giant slingshot. Now for the ammo! Pull out a batch of your much maligned, often ridiculed rubber chickens. Do you see where this is heading? The chickens certainly do. The options become almost too many to name, but here are a few.

Flungee for Distance: Bend your chicken around the bungee cord and haul back as far as your group can pull and let go in unison. You may be rewarded by seeing your chicken disappear over the horizon.

Chicken in a Basket Flungee: Get another chicken and launch it toward four group members who are carrying a crate or tarp between them. They must catch the hurdling chicken in their crate or tarp before it hits the ground.

Target Flungee: Draw a circular target on the ground with point totals set up like a dart board.

High Altitude Flungee: Keeping in mind the geometry formula that allows for measuring flagpoles without a ruler, launch a chicken straight up and measure the height at the apogee of its flight.

Now that you're cooking, don't just stop with chickens. Try rubber pigs, lobsters, and any other launchable objects that you might own. Some technical terms include the *Chicken Slip,* which occurs when a chicken, like a misaligned arrow, falls feebly off the slingshot after a mighty group pull. Then there is the *Poultry Plant,* a chicken mistakenly catapulted straight down and embedded in the ground. But as to the more profound implications of this experience, well, we are still cogitating on that. As a Be Here activity to suck students into a connected and joyous frame of mind, it's a sure crowd pleaser.

Reflection: Being connected is the basis for a group to be present with each other, no matter what the activity or initiative. The releasing and catching of the chicken are synchronized events. Both require clear and precise communication and agreement regarding the timing of the release and catch. Help the students connect this to the need for all members to agree to their developing norms. Have students identify how poor timing in their groups led to misunderstanding and confusion. Be Here questions can connect to how performance is affected by students' ability to stay focused on the task.

Cross Categories: Set Goals

The Activity: Gotcha or Finger Tag Time: 10 minutes

Difficulty: 1

How you do it:

Multi-tasking is a sign of our age. Gotcha underscores the challenge and absurdities of trying to do two things simultaneously (multi-tasking). Ask students to stand in a circle, and have them place their left hand in front of the person to their left, flat and palm up. Next ask them to take their right index or forefinger and put it straight down into the person's palm to their right. Everyone should have a left palm out and up and in front of the person to the left, and a right forefinger facing down into the palm of the person to the right. Now the challenge is presented. The task is to grab the forefinger of the person to the left while removing your forefinger from the palm of the person to the right. It is the mutual goal for all members of the group to do this at the same time! After this explanation, the teacher can say, "On three, try to grab and escape." Of course, if the teacher wants to count, "one, two, four," that could result in chaos, while providing an example of how listening (or not) is a vital aspect of being here.

Start with the left hand flat then switch so that the right hand is out, and so forth. Finally, a cross over grab can be put into play by pulling the pointed right hand free and grabbing the pointed right hand of the neighbor to the left. Now, that's not only double but triple tasking.

Reflection: This is another activity that lends itself to talking about how splitting one's focus or concentration is tough to do and often results in missing out on what either person is saying. This is also thinking about one thing while trying to do another. As with all of the activities in this book, this activity stimulates genuine feelings, thoughts, and behaviors that provide opportunities for linkage to what happens in the classroom.

Cross Categories: Be Honest

The Activity: Help Me Tag   Time: 30 minutes

Materials: Rubber chicken, fleece ball   Difficulty: 1+

How you do it:

> This game is focused on getting tagged participants freed and back into the game, the opposite of run of the mill tag games where you're "it" or you're out just sitting around. The freeing activity can take a variety of forms. First, the "it" person needs to volunteer. They are given a fleece ball and asked to tag everyone they can. Next, another person gets a rubber chicken. Once a person has been tagged, they are now frozen and cannot move. They will shout out, plaintively, "Help me, help me." The person who has the chicken can then throw it to the frozen person, thus freeing him. They are now free to run, throw the chicken to someone else who has been tagged, and become frozen. That person is also free to run and attempt escape from the "it" person. If the "it" person tags everyone before the rubber chicken gets passed, then the game is over.

> Another form of freeing takes the shape of two participants who have not been tagged, surrounding a frozen participant, and while holding hands, shouting out, "You're free, you're free!" If this is accomplished before being tagged, liberation has been achieved. However, if the "it" person gets there first and tags the two people trying to free up the frozen person, then they become frozen themselves. In this iteration, the chicken is superfluous.

Reflection: This activity is rich with opportunities for students to be present for each other. It is the only way to stay in the game. A student can choose to free a frozen classmate or not. A pair of students can choose to cooperate to free a classmate. The degree to which this happens, which is correlated to the length of each round, becomes the basis for discussion. What commitments did you make to help other students; to be present for them? If you chose not to rescue a student, why did you make that decision? How did the decision to assist or not assist affect participation in the activity? How does this discussion inform our Full Value Commitment?

Cross Categories: Be Safe, Let Go & Move On

The Activity: HI, LO, YO!   Time: 30 minutes

                                                            Difficulty: 3

How you do it:

> There can be no doubt about it; this is an elimination game. Since elimination is quick and nearly universal, the stigma associated with being thrown out is

significantly decreased. First, students must memorize three gestures. Once the gestures are taught, with everyone in a tight circle (there is no movement into or from the circle, except when a participant is eliminated), the game can begin. First, the gestures:

- "HI" is represented by placing your hand on top of your head. If the right hand is used, it will point to the person on the left. If the left hand is used, it will point to the person on the right. Hands must not point forward or backward when resting on the head.

- "LO" is represented by placing your hand at the waist, belly button height. Again, it is important that the hand is pointing either right or left.

- "YO" is represented by placing both hands together and pointing to someone across the circle.

- "NO" is represented by crossing both arms against your chest, thereby rejecting the "YO" gesture.

These gestures must be made correctly, or they are grounds for elimination. For example, if a participant says "HI" and at the same time places a hand on their belly, then that person is eliminated. When a person is eliminated the entire group (if they have a sense of humor) swing their thumbs vertically in the air and shout, "You're out of the game."

When played, the gestures go in sequence, with a random person starting. We go "HI," pointing at the person to the left or the right with our hand on our head; We go "LO," pointing at the person to the left or the right with our hand at our waist; We go "YO" by pointing both hands at someone across the circle. Finally, we go "NO" by crossing our arms, thereby rejecting the "YO" being aimed at us.

Upon receiving a "YO," that person starts the sequence over again, saying "HI" to either right or left, and so on. If a "YO" is rejected by a "NO," then the person who signaled a "YO" will start the sequence again, saying "HI."

Those who have been eliminated have a role, and that is of "heckler." Hecklers can distract the remaining players by having conversations with them. However, they cannot utilize any outside props like blankets, ropes, rubber chickens, etc. And, hecklers cannot touch the players. Only conversation is allowed.

<u>Reflection</u>: Post-activity discussion can focus on what it took to maintain focus despite the heckling, and how there are equivalents to heckling or bullying in the classroom that can distract students from being present with their work. What did it feel like to be a heckler or to be mocked? How did either role affect being present during the activity?

Note: If certain participants find elimination difficult, the game can be played without it. Mistakes are made and play goes on, without anyone being removed. The teacher can also sequence it, using GRABBSS (Chapter 4), to assess the group for its abilities and readiness. For example, introduce it first through non-elimination, and then take the risk of elimination as a more intense level of play.

Cross Categories: Be Safe, Be Honest, Let Go & Move On

The Activity: Hoop Relay   Time: 35 minutes

Materials: Two Sectioned Hula Hoops, timer   Difficulty: 2

How you do it:

It is preferable to have hoops that can be assembled in pieces so that you can make them bigger or smaller according to body size. Start with one hoop, placing the other in an innocuous place behind you so that students do not suspect that the second hoop can and will be utilized. The element of surprise is important.

Have your group stand in a circle and hold hands. Remember that buddy ropes can be used in lieu of holding hands. Once connected, the circle cannot break, or the activity needs to start over. One pair places a hoop between them. This becomes the starting point. The circled group is then asked to pass the hoop around, getting it back to the starting point as soon as possible. Powerful synchronicity is created, a truly fabulous thing until, of course, hands get separated, or one pair can't seem to get the hoop over each other's heads, or the sectioned hoop breaks at a joint, or an un-sectioned hoop gets crushed or broken.

The second hoop can be introduced when the first has been passed several times successfully. The group members will look at you like you are crazy. Have the two hoops start across the circle in opposite directions, and then converge toward each other. They will pass over and through each other with surprising ease, a lesson in prejudgments.

Reflection: The point of confusion often occurs when the hoops cross going in opposite directions. In the follow-up discussion ask how this activity connects to focus and concentration issues in the classroom, and how it is reflected in potential distractors within their Full Value Commitment?

Cross Categories: Set Goals, Care for Self & Others, Let Go & Move On

---

The Activity: Hustle Handle Time: 30 minutes

Materials: Timer Difficulty: 2

How you do it:

    Form the group into a circle. Have everyone say their first name, *clearly and distinctly*, starting with the teacher and going around the circle. Once accomplished, ask students to do it timed. A race with the clock ensues. The challenge is to maintain the 'clearly and distinctly' rule. You can stop the group and ask whether members are adhering to it. A reverse hustle handle can also be attempted: After one go-around, the teacher shouts, "Reverse!" This can go on until it is evident that the idea has been appropriately understood. Finally, to compound the overall confusion, start the name passing in clockwise and counterclockwise directions simultaneously. The teacher looks to their left and "passes" a name, then looks to the right and does the same. Students then pass their names along in each direction.

Reflection: Ask for volunteers (only) willing to try to remember each person's name (if this is a new group introductory activity). People have different short-term and working memory capacities, and those who are good at memorization apply a set of either intuitive or practiced skills to be successful. Have students share their strategies. Learning names and retaining them is a good Be Here skill to be practiced. Knowing a classmate's name is where it all begins.

Cross Categories: Set Goals

The Activity: Impulse Time: 20 minutes

Materials: Timer Difficulty: 1

How you do it:

    The purpose is to have the group pass an *impulse* around a circle (everyone holding hands). The impulse is generally a squeeze, one that cannot readily be seen. A way to keep the impulse from being detected is, of course, to have everyone close their eyes. One or several squeezes can be passed. With several squeezes the challenge is increased, for although it seems like a simple task, getting the correct number of squeezes to come back to the start point is often difficult. Impulses can go both clockwise and counterclockwise at the same time, increasing the potential for confusion, i.e., they need to pass through someone at a certain point, causing that person to handle two impulses at once. The impulse can be done for speed, using a stopwatch.

Reflection: The present moment is only experienced through our senses. This activity allows the sense of touch to be the focal point. For the activity to be successful, students must be very focused on the squeeze. This is like a non-verbal game of telephone. If students are not paying careful attention, the communication gets lost. Discuss with students how attending is essential to understanding. What Be Here behaviors support attention and concentration? How do these behaviors contribute to positive academic and social experiences in the classroom? Have them name the behaviors (and distractors) for their Full Value Commitment.

Cross Categories: Set Goals

The Activity: Island of Healing Circle   Time: 10-15 minutes

Materials: Rope to form a circle   Difficulty: 2

How you do it:

> Imagine a place where you most like to be. It may be on a beach surrounded by friends watching the moonrise. It could be an early morning run, dogs barking behind still dark windows. It might be in your bed on a rain-swept night. It could very well be inside your imagination. Wherever it is, it should be a safe place. This activity will take your students to their safe spaces individually and collectively. Make sure to stress when presenting the activity that the Challenge of Choice is to try to go to and stay in your safe space, but not feel pressure to share information about it with classmates. Make sure to participate. This sends the message that you are committed to being a partner in their work to establish and maintain behavioral norms. It also allows you to break the ice and share your safe space first, which often encourages students to do the same. Take a long piece of rope and knot it to form a continuous loop. Lay it on the ground or grass to form a circle, not so large as to allow for large distances between people, not so close that the claustrophobic refuse to enter.

> Now, walk your group through a brief visual imagery exercise that might go something like this:

>> I'd like you to get comfortable sitting around the outside of this rope circle. Anyone ever heard of visual imagery? Well, it is a way of going someplace else without physically leaving where you are. Sounds a bit weird, but it can be done if you are up for giving it a try. So, I'd like to ask you to close your eyes and imagine a special place, a place where you feel most

at peace, a place where you go to get back your strength after a difficult day or a challenging experience. This space might be your bedroom, on a beach, on a mountaintop, on your bike, wherever you wish it to be. Now, once you've found that place, try to bring all of your senses into your picturing of it. See, hear, smell, taste, and touch it until the feeling that safe space brings starts to fill you up inside. When you have got it, it will be time to enter the circle and find a place to sit, bringing your safe space with you. OK? Let's take a few minutes and give this a try.

After all individual group members have entered the circle, ask people to talk about their spaces. As students share, they are learning a great deal about each other, for along with the safe space there is often a personal story. The rope circle becomes a metaphor for an island to which the group can always return to and recapture the spirit of their safe space together. It also holds out the possibility of a harmony that the group will continually strive to achieve and maintain.

Reflection: This activity connects to our work with mindfulness. It provides students with a technique to be in the moment and to then reflect on that moment and the positive emotions associated with it. It is an exercise in being present within oneself. Some questions for students to consider:

- How does knowing something personal change how you feel about people in your class?

- Were you able to go to and stay in your safe space? What process did you go through in your mind to get there?

- How does this connect to being present? How can the thoughts, behaviors, and feelings that you used to go to your safe space contribute to developing Be Here behavioral norms and distractors?

- How did it feel for you to be in your safe space, and why?

- Why did you choose that particular place to go?

Variation: Islands of Healing Circle can be used to model the distractors and behavioral norms of the Full Value Commitment. Before beginning the visual imagery process to help students get to their safe spaces ask them, while they are still outside of the circle, to think about something in their school or home life that gets in the way of their goals and aspirations. Where students are willing to share, have them describe these impediments to their classmates. Then ask them to deliberately turn their thoughts away from the distractor(s) and instead focus on finding their safe space using the visual imagery prompts provided above.

Reflection: The Full Value Commitment at its core is a living process to support an optimal environment for growth while leaving behind negative thoughts, feelings, and behaviors that work against creating and maintaining this positive culture and climate. Using The Island of Healing Circle in this way vividly contrasts the difference between negative impediments and an ideal place for students to be together. Some questions to consider:

- How did thinking about distractors and your safe space feel different?

- How does this connect to creating our classroom Full Value Commitment?

- Does thinking about your distractors help you think about how to move away from them? In what way?

- How do the Full Value Behavioral Norms help to sort out our distractors?

Cross Categories: Be Safe: Helps participants get in touch with their *safe space* to be used as a technique for finding strength, clarity, and comfort during difficult times

---

The Activity: Knee Tap Time: 20 minutes

Difficulty Level: 2

How you do it:

> An alternative school in New Jersey used this as a convening activity at the start of school each day. The principal reported that it gave students the chance to focus on one thing and to truly be in the present. Have students sit on the floor, in a circle, with legs crossed (if possible). Have each person place a hand on the person's knee next to him or herself, left hand on the person's knee to the left, right hand on the person's knee on the right. This will create an interlocking series of hands where arms are crossed as each person reaches to the right and left, all around the circle. The task is to tap the adjacent person's knee in sequence. The in-sequence rule is crucial, for if a person taps

before you do, then the consequence is that you must start over. Students should be encouraged to either admit their error or point out when they have seen a problem with a tapping sequence. If students do not initially feel comfortable with this, the teacher can take on the responsibility. Working toward student self-regulation is the goal (and the goal of much of this work). If a person slaps twice, it can be reversed, but don't invoke that rule until the group has mastered getting around the circle at least several times without making a mistake. It can be done timed, as well.

Touching can be an issue, especially in a sensitive area like the knee. If this presents a problem, then shift to the lower leg, or even the foot.

Reflection: Some questions to raise with students:

- What was needed from each of you to make this activity successful?

- How did it feel to be the person to break up the tapping sequence?

- If any of you made the deliberate choice to break the tapping sequence, why?

- What feelings did you have when the group was successful?

- Did reversing direction add an additional challenge? Why?

- When you lost track of the sequence causing an error, can you recall the thoughts you were having at the time?

- What Be Here behavioral norms and distractors can we generate from this activity for our Full Value Commitment?

Cross Categories: Be Safe, Set Goals

The Activity: Look Up – Look Down! Time: 15 minutes

Difficulty: 1

How you do it:

An excellent place to begin Be Here is to make eye contact. This can be surprisingly difficult for some people to do. When in conversation, they tend to stare at your left ear or off into space, with an occasional furtive glance in the direction of your retina. Once mutual eye contact is made, however, it seems to begin to break down some barriers.

Let's have your students give it a go! Form into the obligatory experiential circle, not too close, but not too far. Have students cast their eyes downward. When you, or some other volunteer, issues the command "Look up," each group member tries to make immediate eye contact with another person in the circle. If eye contact is made, then the pair leaves the circle. This goes on until only two people are left, who can't help but make eye contact. You might offer couples some direction as to how to spend their time once united. A conversation could occur around sharing some personal information, goal setting, construction of a Full Value Commitment, or how awful the weather has been around here lately. The nature of the directive will be framed in the context of your perception of what the group needs. It may just be a nifty way to form pairs for the next activity you've chosen, which may happen to require partners.

As a follow on activity, pair up students and have one stare at the other's ear while having a conversation. Ask students to talk about how the deliberate avoidance of eye contact affects the conversation.

Reflection: Ask students to describe the different feelings associated with making eye contact versus avoiding a person's eyes. How does making eye contact change the relationship between two people? How does this connect to Be Here? Offer small index cards and ask students to write down their feelings. Collect them and tape them to the wall. Students can do a gallery walk to review them. Ask students to reflect on the commonalities and differences of the feelings represented on the cards and how that connects to Be Here.

Cross Categories: Be Honest, Set Goals

The Activity: Meteors Time: 20 to 30 minutes

Materials: Fleece balls, twice the number as there are members in your group Difficulty: 2

How you do it:

This highly aerobic activity is another sure bet for engaging recalcitrant participants in the spirit of the group; this is a stellar Be Here activity. It also contains an important lesson about when participants cross the line between playing hard to have fun and playing too hard to be hurtful. Make sure to have a sack full of fleece balls on hand, and be prepared to lose a few, especially if you are playing outside in a field that borders the woods.

To begin the game, students must throw their meteor (fleece ball) up over their heads as high as possible. When it comes back down to earth as a meteorite, players scoop up the closest one and start running and throwing.

Hand each group member a fleece ball, hereafter known as a meteor. The object is simple -- to hit any students who run by with your meteor by throwing it at them. If a meteor strikes you, the outcome is fatal. You must fall to the ground where you've been hit and go through as elaborate or as simple a dying scene as you wish. However, in actuality, you are mostly dead, not completely dead. If a meteor happens to roll by, either by accident or by the design of a temporary ally who tosses a ball near you, and you can reach it from your prone, mostly dead position, then you are back in the game. The altruistic rejuvenation of a mostly dead player is where the game moves from competition to cooperation. This is a game that only ends through mutual consensus or exhaustion. The object is to be the last meteor chucker still standing; an improbable outcome.

Reflection: This activity can help explain how our thoughts emerge from our minds. We are bombarded by thousands of thoughts a day. Most we can just let go of, and we are not impacted by them. However, we get stuck in some thoughts and become immobilized. Have students identify thoughts that stop them in their tracks instead of being energizing, healthy, and productive.

Cross Categories: Be Safe, Care for Self & others

The Activity: Near – Far Time: 20 minutes

Difficulty: 2

How you do it:

Sesame Street is ingrained in our psyches the same way Father Knows Best and Leave It to Beaver were the programs du jour of the 50s. One of our favorite characters is Grover, a long-necked, blue, furry critter with very lanky arms. Grover seems able to move in all directions at once while standing still, with all appendages flapping at once in disjointed directions. Grover's main educational purpose is to teach the concept of Near and Far to children all over the planet.

He does this by running up to a camera, getting eyeball to eyeball with the lens and announcing, "Near," then dashing off in reverse, receding in the distance as if sucked back by a wave while yelling, "Far." He does this in a voice that is difficult to describe, sounding somewhat like a gruff alto squeak buffed with sandpaper. Come to think of it, he sounds a lot like Yoda of Star Wars, which makes sense, as Frank Oz was the man behind both characters. If you still can't confidently sound like a Grover and move like a Grover, tune into Sesame Street for a bit to see him in action. Once mastered, it is easy to teach doing a Grover to your group members.

Divide your group in half, forming two lines with approximately thirty feet between them, facing each other. Have the lines approach each other in a Grover-esque fashion, arms flailing, high stepping, neck bouncing as if just ejected from a Jack in the Box while yelling, "Near." As the lines approach, each participant finds a Grover partner (most likely the person opposite them in the approaching line).

A friendly conversation ensues. Grover is known for his engaging personality. After a brief exchange, the tide moves away, and all the Grovers are sucked backward to their original positions. This backward movement is accomplished while still facing forward, arms continuing to flail, neck bouncing, legs going in all different directions. Repeat as often as necessary.

Reflection: The Be Here element to this activity is to have students each share a sentence's worth of information when they come together (this could be personal or related to an academic content area) and then see how well the information is retained during reflection.

Cross Categories: Set Goals, Be Honest, Let go & Move On

The Activity: Pairs Tag   Time: 20 minutes

Material: Rope for making a circular play area   Difficulty: 3

How you do it:

Pick a partner. When everyone has one, the game begins. First, there is a preparation session. This is only necessary if the singing option is chosen. With the singing option, the tagged person sings the first line of a song that the partners have agreed upon in the partner preparation session. Each time a partner is tagged, they sing their first line. This results in a discordant and funny song being sung throughout the tag game.

When the game is over (usually by mutual agreement and exhaustion), gather everyone together as if they were in a chorus. By having them sing their first lines at the same time (with you, the leader playing the part of a maestro, directing with tremendous and dramatic flourishes), you will have created a truly disjointed piece of music.

However, singing is not necessary to play the game!

Stress that the only task is to tag one's partner, and tag back and forth, ignoring everyone else within the defined circular play area. The one who is tagged first must spin around in place for a count of three, then walk toward their partner to tag him or her back. This goes back and forth until it is clear that it is time for the game to be over. If the student being chased steps outside of the circle, they become the tagger. To make it more interesting the teacher makes the boundary smaller as the game goes on, until there is very little room to move. Caution students that walking is essential and that tagging is important, but not so important that it comes at a physical risk of someone becoming injured.

Reflection: The walking commitment and how well it is adhered to form an excellent opportunity to review Be Here and Be Safe issues with students. The simple goals are to tag or not get tagged by just your partner. What makes this difficult is the many people who can get in your way. This is also an opportunity to help students look at the obstacles that block their attention/goals and to identify strategies to get this attention back. The spinning can represent a way to get refocused/let go and to change the goal.

Cross Categories: Be Safe, Care for Self & Others, Let Go & Move On

---

The Activity: Peek A Who   Time: 30 minutes

Materials: Tarp or blanket   Difficulty: 1

How you do it:

Here is another minimal prop and engaging activity for learning names. Split the group in half, and ask one of the halves to separate from the other by ten to fifteen feet. Then, ask the students to kneel. Take a blanket and, either with a student volunteer or a co-leader, hold it up so that it divides the group, your partner on one end, and you on the other. The blanket should be held so that members in one group cannot see any members in the other group. Each group is then asked to send a representative up to the blanket barrier. Students then face each other with the blanket held up between them. On the count of three, the holders drop the veil, and the first student to say the other's name wins the round. The loser must join the group on the winner's side. This excellent name game can go on for quite some time with each group getting larger, only to shrink in the subsequent rounds. Everyone knows when it is time to end it. It is a joyful game, full of laughter and goodwill.

Reflection: The ancient word for mindfulness means *to remember*. This activity allows students to work on their open awareness. Have students identify what stressors interfere with their memory. It is also an activity that can focus on the importance of connecting through awareness. How many times do you meet someone and you forget their name instantly? This is due to us being more distracted by our thoughts and feelings. Have the students identify the many factors that may interfere with a personal connection. These may be concerns about being liked, judged negatively, or not fitting in.

Cross Categories: (See Chapter 12 for application to academic content areas)

The Activity: People to People Time: 30 minutes

Difficulty: 2+

How you do it:

This is a soulful activity that calls for gettin' down with your students. It is especially effective with large groups of twenty or more. Ask students to pair up in whatever creative way you choose to make that happen. Start clapping your hands together while rhythmically repeating the phrase, "people to people," syncopating your claps with whoops, uh-huhs, and other sounds suggestive of soul music. Invite the

group to join you in your a cappella riff. Pretty soon everyone is clapping, snapping, singing and saying, "people to people."

While the group continues to chant, tell them that you will change people to people to the name of a body part, like "elbow to elbow." When you call out the change, also say you'd like partners to start touching elbows together while also changing their call to the body parts they are touching. After a few minutes of bumping elbows, you'll call out "people to people," which signifies that everyone should find a new partner. This will create a few moments of rushing around while the hand clapping continues, as does the "people to people" refrain.

Once everyone is set and still clapping, ask for a volunteer to suggest another appendage connection. The worst it usually gets is "butt to butt," but be on the alert for someone capable of testing the limits. It is important to assess for readiness before choosing this activity. Some students may just be too immature to maintain appropriate boundaries. Other good touchable options are cheek to cheek, nose to nose, eyeball to eyeball, toe to toe, hip to hip, and a whole host of other non-sexual options. The game continues with pairs having an opportunity to suggest a different connection, separated by "people to people," which gets students connecting with a different partner.

Reflection: There are many connections to Full Value in this activity. The Be Here aspect is the social interactions that can't help but occur as students rhythmically and physically interact. If you can sell this activity well, there is a lighthearted sense of fun and community that begins to build. You'll find that people just don't want to stop playing People to People.

Cross Categories: Be Safe, Care for Self & Others

The Activity: Robot Tag Time: 30 minutes

Materials: Boundary cones or markers Difficulty: 2

How you do it:

Each participant becomes a robot with an on and off switch, activated and deactivated by tagging one another. Using four cones to mark the boundaries, explain to students that they are going to be robots with an on and off switch on their backs, represented by placing an open hand, palm facing out, on their backs. Explain to the group that this is a tag game where the object is to tag people on their switch, thus freezing them. Frozen robots can tag active robots, but only within reach. The game ends when one or two robots are left still moving. Rules can be modified so that robots can also unfreeze each other throughout the game. While frozen, ask students to concentrate on one thought and hold that thought exclusively until they are unfrozen.

Reflection: Focus on a discussion of how easy it is to become distracted. Ask students to share if they could focus on only one thought while frozen and, if not, what other ideas occurred to them. This can lead to a conversation concerning attention and focus as elements of Be Here with a classmate, the teacher, or lesson material.

Cross Categories: Be Safe, Let Go & Move On

The Activity: Speed Snap (or Whistle) Time: 30 minutes

Materials: Timer Difficulty: 3

How you do it:
>Getting around a circle as fast as you can while passing something has fostered a whole genre of activities. With Speed Snap, the something to be passed requires only the snap of a finger. The activity ends when the passed snap returns to the person who volunteers to start the activity. Circle up the group. Have a student yell, "go," and the finger snap gets passed around the circle. It becomes a problem to be solved, and therefore has the cross-category of Set Goals. The penalty for a failed attempt requires a restart. An example of failure is two participants snapping at the same time. An added and more complex addition is the two handed, two snap variation. The starter person starts the snap, moving clockwise and counterclockwise at the same time. As the snaps cross, it becomes aurally and motorically challenging.

Reflection: Setting a speed record for this activity requires a laser focus on when the person before you snaps. Timing is everything. If you snap too soon, it will result in the aforementioned unison snap, which causes a start over. If you hesitate, precious time is lost and the possibility of a world record is compromised. Get feedback from students as to how they worked on their focus, and how that can contribute to their Full Value Commitment under Be Here. Also discuss distractors.

Cross Categories: Set Goals, Be Honest

The Activity: Surf's up! Time: 30 minutes

  Difficulty: 2

How you do it:
>Imagine an ocean. See the waves smacking onto the sand. Now imagine an ocean on dry land, with people as the waves and the sand, well, there is no sand. This activity allows for much non-self-conscious contact and some conscious crushing. Get your group to form a tight line facing you. Have them lie <u>face down</u> with their bodies as close together as possible. Starting from the

end of the now horizontal line, have the first student begin rolling like a rolling pin over the rest of the group. After two or three people have been rolled over, start the next person going. When a roller reaches the end of the line, they should resume a prone position, squeezed tightly against the person next to them. Punctuated by groans and laughter, the surf will slowly move along, ever changing, never quite the same, and perhaps a bit blacker and bluer as the journey progresses. This activity should operate in a jewelry-free zone to avoid unfortunate skewering of surfers.

A fair amount of good-natured self-sacrifice is involved with Surf's Up as people get rolled on, elbowed, and mushed. This is a non-verbal Be Here experience that helps students engage with the group and the activity process.

Reflection: This activity can be done as a moving body scan. In a traditional body scan meditation, a person uses any sensations felt throughout the body as the focus of awareness. Using the terms *pleasant*, *unpleasant*, and *neutral* helps identify these sensations. Students can become aware of these sensations as they roll and call them out. Lay out several paint swatches (chips). After the activity, have students select a paint chip that represents their experience.

Cross Categories: Let go & Move on

The Activity: Toss a Name Game   Time: 30 minutes

Materials: Fleece Balls, and other tossable items   Difficulty: 1-4

How you do it:

It cannot be overly stressed that essential to Be Here is to connect with people by their first names. Here is a simple game to make that happen. With five or six tossable and soft items (they have to be soft enough to hit someone in the eye and not cause damage), take one of the items and pass it around the circle. Initially begin with fleece balls, as they are easy to catch and very soft, so as not to cause any injury. Sillier items can be introduced later, such as rubber noses, Beanie Babies, and rubber chickens or fish. Introducing these additional items surreptitiously, while students are focusing on the demands of the activity, tests how focused they are, while adding a level of whimsy and fun. Non-spherical items also add challenge to completing a successful catch. As the fleece balls are passed along, each student introduces themself to the adjoining person. Students are asked to remember each other's names.

Once an object has been passed around the circle a few times, establish a throwing and catching pattern using one fleece ball only. The ball is tossed from one person to the next with each student catching and throwing it once, until it traverses entirely around the circle and returns to the first person who threw it (usually the teacher). The only rule is that you cannot throw the fleece ball to the person directly on either side of you. As each student catches the ball, they say their name. Then, before tossing it, they say the student's name, receiving that throw. Politeness points are earned by thanking the person by name who throws you the fleece ball. Occasionally, asking if anyone is willing to name everyone provides an additional challenge and name reinforcement.

Reflection: Paying attention is essential to the success of this activity. The thrower must make sure that the catcher is ready and the catcher must be focused on the thrower. Finally, there is paying attention to each member of the group in case you ask a volunteer to name each person. A discussion involving all of these elements will provide behavioral norms and distractors to add to the class Full Value Commitment.

Cross Categories: Set Goals (See Group Juggling)

The Activity: Ultimate Zombie (12 years old and up)   Time: 40 minutes

Difficulty: 4

How you do it:

Sometimes to support students' work at Be Here, you need to help them along by grabbing their interest. This is particularly true when working with a group of disaffected adolescents who can find many things very dull and stupid. Ultimate Zombie is an activity that is so out there that it tends to motivate kids to come on down off the bleachers and check it out.

Zombies are ugly, decaying creatures of the night whose sole mission is to seek out hapless humans and make them members of the undead fraternity. Have your group <u>close their eyes</u> and get into the bumpers up position (arms extended with palms facing away from the body). Anoint one of the unsuspecting humans as the Ultimate Zombie (UZ) by squeezing their arm twice. Allow the squeezed person to whisper, "pass," should they object to UZ status. Once the Ultimate Zombie is chosen, the game begins. The UZ and humans shuffle about.

When the UZ bumps into a human, it screams a horrific Zombie scream right in the human's face, immediately converting the human to a co-Zombie. The UZ then continues on its way, immensely satisfied that there is one less human to muck things up.

This new Zombie disciple is now empowered to convert humans using the same simple and effective technique of shrieking into the face of anyone it encounters. Could this be the end of humanity as we know it? The one small ray of hope is that when two Zombie disciples encounter each other and shriek, they become converted back to humans.

So, there you have it, an activity that has everything an adolescent could want: the undead, screaming, shock, and surprise. What more could you ask for?

Reflection: This activity can teach about being open and aware rather than tense and worried. Help students realize that being more present, rather than focusing on being tagged, better prepares them for the tag and allows them to be less startled. Have students use I Am About Cards to identify feelings before and after being tagged. Have students identify when being loose is better than being tight. When is it better to be tight rather than loose? When is it better to be prepared as opposed to feeling uncertain?

Cross Categories: Be Safe

The Activity: Zip Zap   Time: 30 minutes

                                        Difficulty Level: 2

How you do it:

With the group standing in a circle, introduce the activity to them while standing in the center yourself. First, form them into groups of three. The person in the middle of the circle will point at the center person of the threesome and say, "Zip." They must then immediately duck while the two other students on either side of the student must immediately point at each other (over the top of the ducking student) and say, "Zap." If there are not enough students to form threesomes and have a person in the middle, the teacher can play. Otherwise ask for a volunteer to be "it" to start the game moving.

If the center person of the threesome fails to duck, that person becomes "it" and goes to the center of the circle, where they point at the center person of another threesome. If any one of the side persons fails to "Zap" correctly, that person goes to the center, and so forth. You will find people zipping, zapping, and ducking at the wrong time and in the wrong way. Of course, when the group gets good at the game it is more challenging to get them to make mistakes. Other forms of chicanery then need to be employed: speed, point behind, down through your legs, or any method that will get students to finally make a mistake.

Reflection: Focus, attention, and commitment are prerequisites for the group to experience

Success in this activity. Anxiety can also be a component. Some questions to pose to the group:

- When you did not duck when "Zipped" or point when "Zapped," what were you thinking and feeling?

- Did you feel a commitment to this activity? If not, why?

- How do you think that focus and attention contributed to success?

- Did you learn from mistakes and, if so, how did the learning contribute to better performance?

- What did you notice about other members of your group of three and other participants? How did their behavior support or detract from success?

- Did you feel any performance stress, and if so, how did you manage it?

- What can we take from this activity to support either developing or improving our Full Value Commitment?

Teach that relaxed alertness is a state that helps us to be focused but not overly anxious. Have students either close their eyes or look down and take ten, slow, five-second inhales and a five-second exhale breath between each round. Ask students to split into pairs and discuss the differences when breathing is used or not used.

Cross Categories: Let Go & Move On

CHAPTER 7

BE SAFE

Establishing and maintaining student physical and emotional safety is at the core of a positive school environment. Students must feel free of the fear that they might be physically or emotionally harmed during their school day. Unfortunately, negative student interactions have become a significant distraction in schools. In response, several states have enacted legislation stipulating a reporting and investigation process for harassment, intimidation, and bullying (HIB) and mandating primary prevention programs that seek to reduce HIB. Full Value Schools was approved as a primary prevention model in a number of school districts in New Jersey.

Statistics from a 2016 study conducted by the Centers for Disease Control, entitled, *Indicators of School Crime and Safety*, while offering positive trends in reducing verbal and physical assaults, are still chilling in terms of the number of incidents reported at all grade levels. The following key findings were connected to specific study indicators that reveal a significant number of threats to safety:

> Preliminary data show that there were 48 school-associated violent deaths[1] from July 1, 2013, through June 30, 2014 (Indicator 1). In 2015, among students ages 12–18, there were about 841,100 nonfatal victimizations (theft[2] and violent victimization[3]) at school[4] and 545,100 nonfatal victimizations away from school (Indicator 2). In 2015, about 21 percent of students ages 12–18 reported being bullied at school during the school year (Indicator 11). Ten percent of elementary teachers and 9 percent of secondary teachers reported being threatened by a student from their school in 2011–12. The percentage of elementary teachers who reported being physically attacked by a student was higher than the percentage of secondary teachers (8 vs. 3 percent; Indicator 5).[58]

Keeping students safe is a core responsibility for educators and a pressing issue in our schools. However, this can only be accomplished if we teach students to self-regulate. The activities in this section will help students better understand and practice the skill of being safe. These activities will then guide students to select appropriate behaviors for their classroom Full Value Commitment as a direct result of their experiences together.

Outcomes of Be Safe

- Trust/Mistrust
- Feeling Secure
- Responding Rather Than Reacting
- Self-Regulation
- Welcoming Authentic Interaction

ACTIVITIES

Activity Difficulty Scale

1 (Easy) ------- 2 (A bit harder) --------3 (Pretty complicated) ---------4 (Difficult)

The Activity: Air Traffic Controller   Time: 45 minutes

Materials: Cones, ropes, or paper plates for runway markers   Difficulty: 2+

How you do it:

Newark, Burlington, LAX, O'Hare, Logan. Nine A.M. Winds are light and variable out of the north-northwest. Skies have broken clouds at 15,000 feet.

It's a perfect day for flying. This is a pairs activity, with the usual role reversal to allow each partner to turn either flying or guiding. The responsibility of the Air Traffic Controller (ATC) is to choose and guide the pilot along a flight path while avoiding other airplanes in flight. This is done through voice commands only as the ATC runs alongside the plane. The pilot, who has decided for some peculiar reason to fly blindfolded (or with eyes closed), must listen intently to the voice commands of their ATC to maintain operational safety, like not crashing into a wall, a tree, or a set of bleachers.

Establish a runway using cones, ropes, or the group's imagination. Each pair taxis to the head of the runway, then takes off into the wild blue yonder. For the teacher, the sight of ten pairs of pilots completing loops, barrel rolls, banks, and dives is enough to bring a smile to even the most jaded adventurer. Encourage sound effects and elaborate maneuvers (loops and barrel rolls permitted), while stressing the need to avoid mid-air collisions or impact against immovable objects. Flight insurance is optional.

Reflection: Within the category of Be Safe there are many lessons to be learned from this experience. The flying blind status of the pilot requires the placing of great faith in the spotter (ATC). The nature of the relationship can be the basis for creating a robust metaphorical scenario. When is it wise to put your faith in another? What are some of the consequences, positive or negative? The activity is there for the framing, depending on needs and imagination.

Cross Categories: Care for Self & Others

Activity Name: Blindfold Walk (Sherpa Walk)   Time: 45 minutes

Materials: (Optional) Objects for students to pass over or under   Difficulty: 3

How you do it:

When you think your life is tough, just reflect on the Sherpa. While westerners hike up the Himalayas in designer outerwear, the Sherpa lug everything from satellite receivers to the celebratory dinner for two on the summit up to impossible heights. That being said, this activity really has very little to do with the Sherpa at all, but provides you, as the facilitator, with a jumping off point for a group lecture on the decline of physical fitness in American society.

The story goes that your group has suffered a plane crash by taking an unfortunate turn left instead of right that brings you into intimate contact with the side of Mount Everest. Miraculously all survive but are temporarily suffering from snow blindness. Along comes the Sherpa (ah, now you see where they fit), who, being kindly people who pity hapless westerners and coincidentally need them to generate future climbing income, decide to lead the group to safety.

The Sherpa does speak a consistent language, but it is totally unfamiliar to the group. The group must decipher the Sherpa's language, ultimately guiding them to move up, down, left, right, stop, or go. The task of the blindfolded group is to stay together while following the Sherpa down off the mountain. The Sherpa may only speak but not touch any group members.

Before commencing the journey, you, as the teacher, need to plot a course of travel and review it with group members who have volunteered to be the Sherpa guides. The route can be geared to the level of challenge you wish to provide, keeping in mind students' physical fitness, or lack thereof, and age. Appealing to all of the senses when planning your route will add significantly to the experience. For example, hanging fake hair, moistened rope, or other slimy objects that students must pass under will certainly fire their imaginations. Passing over and under objects, such as tables or large tubes, also adds to the adventure.

Spotting by the teacher is essential to maintain a safe rescue environment. The crash victims should also be encouraged to move slowly and deliberately as they clamber down the mountain. After all, few plane crash survivors are in the mood to jog. When working with blindfolds keep in mind that not all people tolerate them well. Offer the option to keep eyes closed should some object to blindfolds. Always remind them of the Full Value Behavioral Norm of Be Honest to cut down on peeking.

The Sherpa story is a playful example of how to generate and maintain enthusiasm for an activity and help the group fall into the experience, suspending their disbelief.

Reflection: This activity creates a feeling of vulnerability for the students being guided without the advantage of sight and deep responsibility for students who are facilitating the rescue. The opportunity to connect this experience with behaviors that ensure the physical and emotional safety of the group will become readily apparent during the post activity reflection. Some questions might include:

- How did it feel to be deprived of your sight, relying on your classmates to guide you?

- As a guide, what responsibility did you have?

- What did you have to concentrate on to keep your classmate safe?

- How does this activity connect to practicing safe behavior in our school?

- Who is your Sherpa in our school?

- How is emotional safety different than physical safety?

- What words or phrases can we come up with that describe behaviors that support physical and emotional safety?

Cross Categories: Set Goals, Care for Self & Others

The Activity: Cross the Mall

Time: 40 minutes

Difficulty: 3 - depends on the age of students)

How you do it:
Have the group circle up. The task is to cross the circle in four ways: the first, as quickly as possible, head down, not engaging anyone; the second, somewhat slower, but still determined, looking at people but not connecting; the third, slowly, seeing people, and making sure to shake hands with some of them, saying hello. The fourth (if the group is ready) is greeting each other like long lost friends or loving relatives separated for a long time. After each crossing, students are asked to stop and reflect upon how it felt and to hold those thoughts until after the four crossings have been accomplished.

This crossing activity seeks to simulate group experiences in public spaces where participants are required to move physically. The movement can come from small groups, as in a crowded elevator. The elevator has reached the desired floor, and some of the participants need to get off, some need to get on, and some stay while waiting for their floor. The same is true for a bus or subway stop. Similar experiences can be had in the mall, when a person coming in can meet a phalanx of exiting shoppers. These meetings, crossings, comings and goings, can have a range of effects on one's well-being, depending on the nature of the experience, i.e., whether one is rammed, squeezed, butted, elbowed, tossed, pilfered, causing one to drop their package or briefcase, lose their glasses, and in the end, their composure. Conversely, the crowd could magically open itself to your movement, with admiring and sympathetic fellow travelers helping you on your way. Or the experience could be something in between.

These meetings are excellent common ground for participants to reflect upon. Everyone has had similar experiences unless they have lived a life like the poet Emily Dickinson, called the "Recluse of Northampton." But even Emily would have understood because she seemed to know everything about the human spirit in spite of her isolation.

The main idea here is the mode of travel we desire. As Harry Chapin said, "It's not the getting there, but the going that's good." It presents an opportunity for the group to make choices and describe what this mode of travel will be. The teacher can say, "We are going to be together as a group for a period of time. How do you want to be with each other? How do your three (or four) crossing experiences represent how you want to be with each other?"

Note: During the fourth crossing a student may wish to greet another with a hug. This may or may not be OK with the potential recipient. It is advisable to work out a signal or verbal exchange between people on the fourth crossing for Challenge of Choice to be exercised. The question could be asked, "Is it OK for me to give you a hug?" It should be made clear that the student being touched has the choice to agree or disagree. This is an opportunity for both students to find a way to greet each other warmly that is mutually acceptable.

<u>Reflection:</u> The connection to trust is the establishment of the depth of the relationship. The deeper the relationship, the more connected we are. While there is increased risk in this choice, the rewards are also profoundly richer. A post activity group reflection concerning the importance of building trust as the foundation for establishing, maintaining, and deepening relationships will certainly inform the creation of Be Safe behaviors and distractors for the classroom Full Value Commitment.

Cross Categories: Be Here, Care for Self & Others

The Activity: Evolution Time: 30 minutes

Difficulty: 2

How you do it:

All of us either voluntarily or involuntarily take on certain roles in life. Our sense of values, i.e., our ideas of who we are, tend to be projected into these roles and associated responsibilities. Behavior is inseparable from our character. "He's a devoted husband." "She's a loving mother." "He's a wastrel" (well, no one really uses the word "wastrel" anymore). "She's a real leader in this company." In groups, students also take on different roles, reflecting a self-assessment of strengths and deficits. In groups there are leaders, followers, agitators, enablers, isolates, critics, helpers, caregivers; the list goes on and on. Some of these roles are healthy and some are not. Students quite often take on multiple roles over the life of a group.

But whoa, hold on there, let's just wait a minute; you're serving up pretty heady stuff here. This game is supposed to be about eggs, chickens, monkeys, and humans. True, but it's also about giving groups of all compositions and intentions a chance to self-assess the roles of its members, and how it feels to try one of those roles on for size.

There are four groups in Evolution: Eggs, Chickens, Monkeys, Humans:

- Eggs are mute (not having mouths) and walk around with their arms over their heads, with their hands touching.

- Chickens, who are skimpy on brains, strut around flapping their wings while making chicken noises. That's about it for the chickens.

- The monkeys, who are a bit more upscale on the ladder, swing their arms in an ape-like fashion while alternating between screeching (when offended) and grunting. They also occasionally groom other monkeys by picking nits out of their hair. Nits are apparently quite a delicacy among monkeys.

- Finally, we have the humans, who sashay about uttering expressions like, "I'm cool, I'm a human." "Ugh, monkeys, chickens, and eggs, who threw this party?" and other similar but no less condescending remarks.

All players quite naturally begin as eggs. As with most hierarchical systems, eggs yearn to be chickens, chickens ache to be monkeys, and monkeys, being somewhat ill-advised, would almost die to be humans. This transition is inevitable and often rapid in Evolution. The transformation occurs when two members of a similar caste, i.e., two eggs, meet as they wander about. The old reliable odds or evens fingers' shoot-out occurs between them. The winner moves up to the status of a chicken, while the other remains a lowly egg. Now let's say that a newly anointed chicken meets another chicken. The winner of their odds/even shootout moves up the ladder to monkey-dom, while the loser returns to lowly egg status. You can see how quickly one's fame, fortune, and intellectual capacity can rise, fall, and rise again.

While there is a significant amount of hilarity associated with Evolution, people also experience real feelings about their rapidly shifting roles as the game progresses. While eggs, chickens, monkeys, and humans are the generic roles we have defined, the possible assignations are endless, limited only by the role issues you wish to look at in your group (See a different use of Evolution in Chapter 13). Aside from this activity's great metaphorical potential, it is also a heck of a lot of fun.

Reflection: When the laughter has died down, the serious implications of this activity can be drawn from the students. There are often different social groups within schools, each with its own status. Those relegated to what are perceived to be the lower castes can feel resentful, isolated, and marginalized. Like an egg, having no voice. This activity highlights those castes and often provokes genuine feelings associated with either remaining an egg or rising to human, only to fall back down the popularity ladder. While reflecting, help guide students to think about these hierarchies, the feelings they might engender, and the potential consequences that flow from those feelings. How does belonging or longing to belong connect to physical and emotional safety? The activity can help students to identify and talk about the social group(s) they are affiliated with, and how that impacts their sense of belonging and self-esteem. This also offers students with no affiliation the opportunity to reflect on their status and share their feelings with the group.

Cross Categories: Be Here, Be Honest, Set Goals, Let Go & Move On, Care For Self & Others

---

Activity Name: The Gauntlet Time: 30 minutes

Difficulty: 3+

How you do it:
Some of you may have had the fortune or misfortune to attend a

performance of Medieval Times Dinner & Tournament; a staged series of sword fights, jousts, and acts of knightly courage that may include running the gauntlet, that is running between pairs of stout nasties with evil grins just waiting to smack you with a broadsword or mace as you dash through, hoping to make it to the other side with life and limb intact. Our experiential Gauntlet is much friendlier and more supportive.

Create two lines of students facing across from each other, leaving a corridor between them for a student to travel. The two lines of students are the catchers who will stop the student walking between them (on an imaginary wire) from falling through the line. When the activity begins, they must be in a spotting position with one leg back, knee bent to provide support when the walker leans into them. The walker may choose to travel between the lines without leaning, or lean into the line several times. The walker may also choose to lean forward or backward, causing the line's members closest to the lean to provide spotting either in front or behind the walker. Once the walker leans, the students in the line must help him or her return to

a vertical position and make sure they are stable before walking can continue.

Before entering the Gauntlet, the group should go through the important safety calls. If during the calling sequence, the teacher (or the student) feels that people are not focused (being here), the calls start again. This is relatively easy to determine: Students not responding in unison, students not focusing their attention on the walker, students engaged in side conversations, etc.

Calls:

Participant asks the group, "Spotters ready?"
Group responds in unison, "Ready."

Participant says, "Ready to walk?"
Group responds in unison, "Walk away!"

Note: The Gauntlet can serve many purposes, including practicing spotting under unpredictable conditions as the walker leans forward, backward, or into the line of spotters, and as a group-trust activity. A good training option for students to understand the spotting requirements (and for you to assess their readiness) is for you to do the initial Gauntlet walk. Make sure not to over commit to a lean in any direction until good spotting is demonstrated.

As for Medieval Times, it is splendid. Always bet on the Red Knight and take your earplugs!

Reflection: There are two different trust experiences in play during this activity:

1) Surrendering your safety to the group as a walker balancing on an imaginary wire.

2) Students providing active and attentive spotting support.

Ask students to share their thoughts and feelings on these very different roles as they relate to establishing their behavioral norms and distractors under Be Safe.

Cross Categories: Be Here, Care for Self & Others

Activity Name: Hands Up! Time: 20 minutes

Difficulty: 3+

How you do it:

This activity does not require a Western Motif, six shooters, or participants with an ancestral lineage stretching back to the Urps, the Dillons, Bonnies and Clydes. However, it does require the rapid upward lifting of hands to allow the unimpeded passage of a participant as they first walk, and then ultimately jog through a line. Like the structure of The Gauntlet, form a line facing each other, very close together, with space between students for a participant to traverse. Pairs then extend their hands horizontally outward to form a zipper with palms down, adjusted to be at approximately the shoulder height of the walker or runner.

As the walker or jogger enters the line, hands are raised out of the way, not unlike the fan wave at a ball game. Increasing the traversing speed increases the visual tour de force of watching arms whip upward out of your line of travel. If a participant insists on wearing a hat, this is one of few instances where flipping the brim into the rear position makes sense. Forward-facing brims often result in a Hands Up! hat flip, causing the hat to sail off into the stratosphere. Spotting calls (see above) should be used to focus everyone's attention on the activity. As noted, if there is no clear evidence of a focus on the walker/jogger, the calling sequence begins again. The teacher or an observant student should initiate this.

While the run through is visually and motorically spectacular, each participant should walk through once before attempting the Hands Up jog! Have walkers and joggers begin their jaunts at least ten feet from the beginning of the first pair of students to allow spotters to adjust to their speeds.

Reflection: Hands Up can be used as a wonderful metaphor for life in school. As students walk or run through their day, what are some of the barriers to success? What are the risks, and how does the focused support of a trusted group assist in the journey? What behavioral norms and distractors can come from this experience?

Cross Categories: Be Here, Care for Self & Others

The Activity: Mine Field Time: 1 hour

Materials: See object list below Difficulty: 2

How you do it:

This activity allows for the creation of a relatively benevolent Mine Field using fleece balls, rubber chickens, chairs, sprung or set mousetraps, plastic squids, and other creatures, hanging crepe paper streamers, and any other non-lethal objects you might have handy lying around your house or classroom. First, mark off a large rectangular boundary area, say twenty feet wide and forty feet long. The dimensions of the Mine Field can be varied to increase or reduce the challenge or adjust to group size. Now take your explosive items and scatter them about the Field, making a straight-line path through the exploding debris impossible to travel.

Divide students into pairs. One strategy is to pair students who either do not know each other well or are having some issues with each other. One member of each pair is sightless, either by keeping eyes tightly squeezed shut or using a blindfold. The partner must guide their companion through the objects while remaining <u>outside</u> of the boundary area. A suggested planning session is essential to reduce the risk of going "boom." Completion may mean reaching the other side, only setting off a certain number of mines (objects), or any other definition of success that the group of students wishes to establish.

Sending more than one student into the field at a time from opposite ends adds to the explosive potential. Know what your group is capable of here. There is a difference between challenge and chaos. A variety of successes can be had, from a simple traverse to one where no objects are touched at all, to competition between travelers for the least number of touches. Switching guides midfield is another delightful variation. Ask the group to think metaphorically about the exploding objects. What might they represent as impediments to reaching individual and group goals? Label them using the group's ideas.

Another option is to add objects, each labeled with a Full Value (Be Here, Be Safe, etc.). Picking up one or more of these provides immunity from touching objects that are strewn about the field that, when bumped into, would send the traveler back to the starting line. If two travelers link up while holding a Full Value object, they are both granted immunity. This is another terrific place for provoking group thinking about detractors within the Full Value Commitment.

Before beginning this activity decide what the objects in the Mine Field represent in terms of Be Safe behavioral norms and distractors that students feel are important to include in their Full Value Commitment. As part of the task, students can be guided to protect the Norms, and avoid distractors. If a distractor is bumped, it can also be picked up and saved for further reflection when the group talks about the experience.

<u>Reflection:</u> Perhaps the place to begin is to check with student pairs how it felt to be guided without sight and serve as a guide. The terms trust, vulnerability, and safety come to mind when thinking about being guided sightlessly through a series of obstacles. The words responsibility, caring, protection, and anticipation (among many others) connect to serving as the guide. Identifying the feelings associated with the experience can then lead to a discussion about how this relates to Be Safe. What behavioral norms are essential? What are the distractors that can get in the way?

If at all possible, Mine Field should be included when selecting a Be Safe activity. It involves all members of the class, is always intriguing to students, and provides opportunities to integrate numerous Full Value norms simultaneously, even when the primary focus is on only one of them. Here are some suggested questions for students to reflect on that illustrate the cross-norm connections:

- When being guided through the Mine Field, how did trust factor into your success? How is trust related to the successful completion of a goal?

- To be truly successful, honesty is required when there is the potential for touching an object and having to start again. If you were to have a touch or two that you did not report, how would that affect your feelings concerning the success or failure of completing the goal?

- There are times during the pursuit of a goal that you experience roadblocks and associated feelings of disappointment. This may have happened in the Mine Field when you touched an object and had to start all over again. How did you make use of that experience? Were you able to Let Go & Move On and learn from the experience? If so, what did you learn? If not, how do you think mistakes could inform future progress?

- Not being mindful of the task of getting through the Mine Field can lead to distractions and a collision with an exploding object. How did being present contribute to your success?

- As a guide partner, how did Care for Self & Others contribute to the success of the journey through the Mine Field?

Cross Categories: Be Here, Be Safe, Be Honest, Care for Self & Others, Let Go & Move On

---

The Activity: Star Wars Time: 30 minutes

Materials: Various lengths of rope for creating different sized circles Difficulty: 2

How you do it:

The activity presents the problem of diminishing safe spaces for an entire group. Offer each student a piece of rope of varying lengths and ask him or her to assist you by tying off the ends to form a circle. Rope lengths need to be pre-determined by the teacher after surveying the group size, to make sure that at the end of the activity there is one circle large enough to hold the feet of all group members.

To start things rolling have the group scatter around a large play area. Ask them to stand in their rope circle. Tell them that only their feet, both of them, must reside within a circle. Choose a word that directs them to leave their safe space and find another. The word should reflect the metaphorical experience that you have created or co-created with the group. This could be as non-symbolic as "switch" or "change" to a specific Be Safe distractor that students need to understand and avoid to maintain a healthy balance in their lives. On command, they must depart their safe harbor, travel through unknown seas, and dock at a new circle.

On the fourth switch, using great stealth, remove one of the circles, and for each subsequent turn, remove another one. You can tell students notice as their movements toward the remaining circles become more purposeful, rapid, and panicked. Allow everyone to get settled, issue the command, and continue removing circles. Eventually the entire group will have their feet squeezed into one surprisingly small safe place. If everyone can see each other, this is a terrific time to hold your group reflection of the activity.

An interesting reframe of safe spaces is stuck spaces. During the initial activity description raise the issue of how we can become too comfortable with the knowns in our lives, causing us to stagnate. These spaces might include not taking a leadership role during group work in class, a predictable but unhealthy friendship, or just a way of thinking that is so rigid as to avoid entertaining the opportunities that other ideas might have to offer. Asking participants to offer examples of their stuck places (if appropriate for your students) will undoubtedly lead to a thought-provoking group reflection time at the other end of the activity.

Reflection: If students view the goal as being to keep themselves personally in a safe space, this will become a competitive activity. Often this is the form it will initially take. Raise the question with students as to how the activity might have been different if they planned a more cooperative strategy to solve it. Some related questions:

- How did it feel to see circles (safe spaces) being removed?

- What was more important, to find a safe space for yourself, or assist another student in getting to a space? Why?

- How can you connect the idea of emotional safety to this activity?

Cross Categories: Be Here, Set Goals, Let Go & Move On, Care for Self & Others

*   *   *   *   *   *   *   *   *   *   *

The Trust Sequence

Note: Instructions for facilitating the following trust activities with students are provided with the understanding that formal training must occur before their use. Without training provided by experienced staff from Full Value Communities or other credentialed organizations, these activities should not be attempted.

An assessment of readiness is essential. The teacher must be very confident that students understand their responsibility for protecting the physical safety of their classmates, demonstrate spotting proficiency, and are willing to commit to doing so. Assessing for physical condition, coordination, etc., is also essential. If a student can't participate in catching, they may be able to fall. If they can't, or do not wish to do either, then use

Challenge of Choice to assist them in finding positive ways to participate. To establish and maintain trust is a most fragile and challenging process. We know from countless experiences in many settings that trust activities can provide a powerful shortcut to fostering feelings of emotional and physical safety in a group. It is common after a well-constructed trust sequence to hear comments from group members like, "I feel so much better about everyone here," and, "We're much closer as a group than we were a few hours ago." However, what is so quickly established can be just as easily torn down. A joking comment from a participant, like, "Hey, wouldn't it be funny if we pretended to drop her," can cause almost irreversible harm. So, we are asking, for the sake of your group's physical and emotional safety, that you be acutely aware of their readiness to take on the fundamental responsibility of protecting each other during the following trust activities.

> I remember standing at the top of a rock face holding the safety line for a student. All of the mechanics had been scrupulously attended to. The ropes were tied off properly, knots checked, etc. As I took rope in while the student climbed, I chatted casually with a staff member standing next to me. When my student arrived at the top of the climb, he was furious. He yelled at me about not feeling safe during the climb because I was chatting with someone. And he was absolutely right to be angry. While I knew he was never physically at risk, he experienced my conversation as a lack of focus and concern for his safety. His perceived risk was the critical element, not my sense of how safe he was. Lesson learned. - Richard

If you plug trust activities in at the right time and place in the life of the group, your students will be richly rewarded, as they become more able to support each other in pursuit of group and individual growth. One final important note: success has many faces. For some students catching may demand more courage than for a student who falls. This is a critical lesson for students to integrate. We ask students to stretch past their comfort zone, and when that occurs, no matter what the degree of completion, it should be celebrated.

Note: We have named this "The Trust Sequence" as it is common nomenclature in the field of experiential learning. However, feel free to rename the process with your students. Their choice may depend on how they wish to frame the experience based on the needs of the group. This is the beauty of co-creation and student ownership of their Full Value process.

Activity name: Two Person Trust Fall   Time: 50 minutes +

Difficulty: 3

How you do it:

As long as there have been flat surfaces and two people willing to catch each other, there have been Trust Falls. To get started, have your group members pair up, creatively trying to avoid matching a Lilliputian with a giant. We have found that group members often intuitively avoid pairs of unequal

height and weight as they size up the possible negative momentum-generating consequences. Each pair initially designates a spotter (the person catching the faller) and a faller (the one who falls). Roles are switched to give each person a chance to do one or the other. The spotter assumes the classic position: one leg back, for bracing the impact of the faller, hands up and aligned to the faller's back. The faller, as the name implies, has a more straightforward but no less noble task, that is, to fall stiff as a board backward with hands folded across the chest to be caught by their loyal and committed companion. To gain some initial confidence and catching skill, it is wise to start with a minimalist fall, starting with hands on the faller's back, then with one foot of distance between the faller's back and the spotter's hand brakes. As pairs improve their catching and falling abilities, greater falling distances can be tried, the ultimate being the fire-person's catch, wherein the spotter forms upward-facing arm hooks. The faller spreads their arms so that they are fully extended perpendicular to the body (see picture). This configuration offers an extended and thrilling fall with a safe and reliable catch. What it has to do with firefighting escapes us, but perhaps further research will provide a sensible answer.

When demonstrating Trust Falls, it is important to stress that protection of the head and upper body of the faller is the primary goal, not making a classy-looking catch.

When demonstrating a fall with either a co-facilitator or a volunteer participant, lower them all the way to the ground on one catch, perhaps even collapsing in a heap beneath the faller. This helps to debunk the notion that anything but a perfect catch is not OK.

As described during the activity, Hands Up!, we have found that establishing a series of basic voice communications between the spotter and faller helps to focus both on the activity. For this activity, the calls are slightly different from those for Hands Up! as the demands are different. The communication begun by the faller, intoned with great solemnity and commitment are as follows:

Calls:

    Faller: Spotter Ready?
    Spotter: Ready!
    Faller: Ready to Fall.
    Spotter: Fall Away!
    Faller: Falling

Experiential groups in 4-H Camp from Washington State practice an additional call. Prefacing the five calls, the faller announces, "My name is _____ and I choose to do this Trust Fall. Will you support me?" This clarifies the purpose of the experience, which is to state who you are, what you are doing, and to feel safe in asking for and receiving support.

The faller controls the call sequence. If at any point during the exchange the faller feels that the catcher is not paying attention, they start the call sequence again from the beginning.

Activity name: Three-Person Trust Fall   Time: 50 minutes +

        Difficulty: 3

How you do it:

This ménage-a-fall introduces the face-first fall and an additional spotter. The setup is basically the same as the backward Trust Fall, with the added spotter assuming a position directly in front of the faller, one leg back with

knee bent for bracing and hands up ready to catch. For obvious reasons, there is a greater necessity during a fall forward for the faller to fold their arms across their chest. The forward spotter should catch the faller on either elbows or upper shoulders.

Another hand positioning option for the forward fall is to have the faller extend their arms and place hands so they are crossed, one wrist over the other, with palms facing each other. Fingers should be intertwined. Then the hands are rotated down, then up into the chest (see next page).

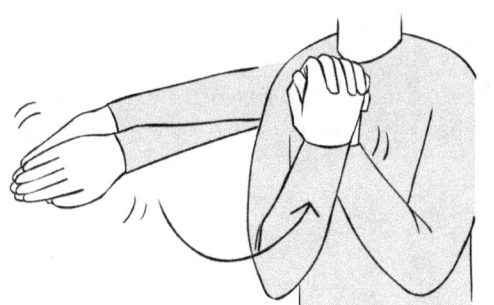

An even more foolproof suggestion is to have the faller slip their hands into either a single or a crossed set of six-inch rubber gym rings, then placed up against the chest. These can't be escaped between the fall and the catch.

The mantra of the safety calls is precisely the same, initiated by the faller and responded to by the spotters.

We have noticed that there seems to be an almost genetic propensity to slip into the venerable game of Ping-Pong during this activity, with spotters serving as paddles and the faller as the little white ball. This can result in the faller being projected backward and forward, with little cause for trust found in either direction. Instead, suggest to your triads 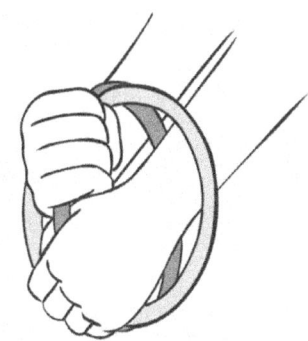 that the faller be returned to an upright position between spotters. The slight momentum is generated from the return to vertical, serving to move them forward or backward.

Cross Categories: Set Goals; Let Go & Move On; Care for Self & Others

---

Activity Name: Wind in the Willows   Time: 50 minutes +

Difficulty: 3

How you do it:

If you've ever climbed to the top of a willow tree on a windy day, you'll know why this activity is so unique and so powerful. There are fathers who used to climb willow trees early in the morning and, swaying like mad ship captains, called to wake their sons. But that is another story. If you haven't been blessed with a climb up into a willow, well, here is a chance to allow your group to have a very similar experience without ever leaving the ground.

Get your students in a tight shoulder-to-shoulder circle. Ask them to "assume the spotting position!" A flurry of hands should leap to the ready, palms out and facing the middle of the circle. One leg should be set back for bracing. A volunteer should be invited to be the faller. Standing in the center of the circle with arms folded across the chest (or using methods outlined in the Three Person Trust Fall, above), the faller must keep their body ramrod stiff while falling into the group. The group receives the faller and moves them across and around the circle. The requisite and hopefully now familiar calling sequence is used, begun by the faller. It is helpful to add the faller's list of key words the phrase, "I'm done." This is uttered when the faller becomes Willowed Out and wishes to be returned to a vertical position in the center of the circle.

The "I'm done" command eliminates the possibility that the spotting stops before the activity is over. Should the faller's movement across the circle begin to accelerate, remind the group of the no Ping-Pong rule. Suggest to the faller that an eyes-closed experience is much more transcendental. And the next time you pass by a willow tree waving in the wind, and its branches do beckon, give yourself a treat and go for a climb.

Cross Categories: Be Here, Care for Self & Others

Activity Name: Levitation　　　　　　　　　　Time: 45 minutes

　　　　　　　　　　　　　　　　　　　　　　　Difficulty: 2-3

How you do it:
Bearing little resemblance to Amazing Randy's effortless lifting of an able assistant within a Hula Hoop, this activity nonetheless can provide each group member with a feeling of floating through space. It can be built into the Wind in the Willow activity as Part B of the total package. After Winding and Willowing for a time, the person in the middle is allowed to settle into a prone position (head even with feet) while the group rushes in to form a cradle of hands underneath them. The levitee is gently borne upward with spiritual and mystical or perhaps life ending thoughts rushing through their head. Once reaching the top of the lift, the student is rocked back and forth with long sweeping motions while slowly being lowered back down to the ground.

Safety caveats include assigning one spotter to the student's head, keeping the person relatively parallel to the ground during the lift, not overreaching the shortest lifter, and making sure that all group members are carrying weight. Spotters should also be given the ole lift with your legs, not with your back rule to avoid a strained back. Interesting variations include spotter-generated whooshing sounds, absolute silence (punctuated by the grunts and groans of committed lifters), and spotters gently pressing down on the person's body for a silent count of three after being lowered to the ground.

This last option should be discussed and agreed upon by the participant before being used, as there may be an issue with this type of touching. The age of students should also be taken into consideration when adding this last variation.

Cross Categories: Let Go & Move On, Care for Self & Others

Trust Sequence Reflection: As noted at the top of this section, while great benefit can be gained from student participation in the trust sequence, the need for an absolute commitment to safety requires a careful assessment by the teacher of student readiness. A fundamental maxim is that if in doubt, don't. This reinforced caveat aside, profound changes can occur in individual students and the group as a result of experiencing success with these activities.

While the faller must commit to letting go of control and surrendering their safety to the group, the true responsibility lies with the spotter. The activity connections to developing material for a Full Value Commitment can be easily drawn out from the group. Some questions to consider:

- What was it like to fall into the arms of the group?

- What thoughts and feelings did you have before, during, and after the experience?

- If you had trouble making any commitment, why? What do you need from the group to try to participate in the activity?

- How did it feel to be a spotter? What thoughts and feelings did you have before, during, and after a catch?

- Did you have to make any adjustments during your spotting?

- What can we take from this experience to add to our Full Value Commitment?

Cross Categories: Let Go & Move On, Care for Self & Others

CHAPTER 8

BE HONEST

Lacking honesty, all forms of cooperative activities will fail. There are times when focusing on honesty with a group becomes most important. Being honest requires tempering courage with kindness. An open exchange always holds the potential for conflict, which is something we all tend to avoid. A common consequence of withholding feedback, particularly when it involves the violation of feelings or strong beliefs, is hurt feelings that fester. Small slights can rapidly become magnified, often resulting in a response that has little to do with the initial concern and more to do with the feelings that build up over time.

Being honest requires a certain amount of vulnerability. It can mean admitting mistakes, owning failures, and letting other people down. Dishonesty can then be rationalized. When, for example, a student violates the rule of an activity (e.g., stepping out of bounds), which can cause the whole group to start over again, a choice needs to be made. Taking ownership of the mistake could cause the wrath of the group to descend upon them, causing one to feel inadequate. Conversely, if the group has decided to accept and live by certain rules of honesty as their yardstick for success, not reporting a violation diminishes the group's goal. The individual must decide to either take what may seem like the easy way out by pretending the breach did not happen or by reporting what actually occurred. The same can be said of a student who has witnessed an infraction. They are faced with the choice of notifying the group or becoming complicit by remaining silent.

Honesty can also involve courage and risk. There may be times when a student needs to bear witness to the transgressions of another student, such as a bullying, harassment, or intimidation incident that has occurred out of sight of an adult. There are times when a student knows of a peer who has spoken openly of suicide. Telling an adult takes courage and could risk at least temporarily compromising a friendship. Co-creating desirable Be Honest behaviors and encouraging an environment where they are valued support the practice of courageous honesty.

The activities below provide all sorts of opportunities for identifying elements of Be Honest. They offer experiences to engage students in conversation about developing behavioral norms and distractors. It is important to keep in mind that most of the activities in this book require honesty for the group to accomplish them with fidelity. Be Honest can always be part of the post activity reflection, no matter what value is being focused on.

Outcomes of Be Honest

- Exploring the truth
- Integrating Feedback
- Practicing an Ethical Code of Behavior
- Values

ACTIVITIES

Activity Difficulty Scale

1 (Easy) ------- 2 (A bit harder) -------- 3 (Pretty complicated) --------- 4 (Difficult)

The Activity: Back-Stabbers Time: 30 minutes

Materials: Large clothespins (if possible), thin markers, and boundary rope Difficulty: 2

How you do it:

Although this tag activity has a catchy name, perhaps it does not fully capture the Be Honest intention of this chapter. You are welcome to come up with a different name for this or any other activity in the book. Each student is given three clothespins and a marker and asked to write a word or sentence on each pin reflecting a Be Honest behavior, such as "tell the truth" or "admit mistakes." Color-coding each student's clips will facilitate identifying the owner at the end of the round. Students then spread out within a boundary area. The chase begins with the object being to clip three clothespins on the back of other students. Students cannot use more than one of their clips per person. Once a student has been fully clipped, they are out of the round. This is announced by the student attaching the last of three clips and shouting, "I win, I win, I win!" The round ends when one student remains with fewer than three clothespins on their back. Students then circle up and read from their clips. The author of the clip that was attached is identified and has the opportunity to share why they chose a particular Be Honest behavior. Some repetition will likely emerge during the group's reflection, which is fine. This will model for the group a commonality of thinking; what is most important to them. This activity provides a way for students to identify behavioral elements of the Full Value of Be Honest. And, it is fun.

Reflection: The discussion can focus on each student's choice for describing a Be Honest behavior. Often the choice is connected to personal experience, either positive or negative. If the Be Honest behavior comes from a negative experience, this will provide an opportunity to begin developing a list of distractors for this Full Value.

Cross Categories: This activity can be used to identify behaviors from any of the Full Values simply by changing what students write about on their clothespins

The Activity: Blindfold Square   Time: 60 minutes +

Materials: Long length of rope   Difficulty: 3

How you do it:

> This is another low prop, unpredictable problem-solving initiative (the root of all goal setting) that will either be solved quickly or not at all, depending on the group's mindset. Reach down into your activity kit bag for a rope anywhere from 100 to 200 feet in length. Find the ends of the rope and tie them together. The rope length will ultimately determine the dimensions of the square. The larger the square, the more difficult communication becomes, which certainly raises the challenge quotient. Do a quick line up by height, date of birth, length of shoelaces, or the birth date of each person's maiden aunt. Once the group has formed up in a line, by any means you choose, spread them out along the closed rope as you hand it to them.
>
> Once rope-equipped, the group members put on blindfolds (or keep their eyes closed). Invite the group to form the rope into a square, and to not open their eyes until there is a consensus that the task has been accomplished. It is important to have some spotters on hand to protect group members from

> wandering into trees, bushes, highway Impact Attenuators (did you know that's what those big yellow sand filled barrels are called?), and other human impediments. Groups will tend to drift about while holding the rope, so be prepared for active spotting.

<u>Reflection:</u> As we all strive for success, this activity often provokes a fair amount of surreptitious rule violations, particularly when it comes to peeking. As the facilitator, you

will observe students opening their eyes to check the status of the square. This is a 100 percent certainty. Ask students to reflect on and respond to the following questions:

- Why did you choose to open your eyes during this activity?

- Were you concerned about your physical safety? Why?

- Did you feel it was necessary to be successful? Why?

- Did you notice anyone else opening their eyes? How did you feel about that?

- If you did, why did you choose not to say anything?

- Did you feel frustrated during this activity? What was frustrating to you?

- If you did and remained silent, why?

- While you were successful in forming a square, how did peeking affect your feelings of success? Was forming the square more important than honoring the agreed upon rules, and if so, why?

Cross Categories: Be Here, Be Safe, Set Goals

The Activity: Compass Walk   Time: 60 minutes +

Difficulty: 2

How you do it:

If you have ever had the misfortune of being lost in the woods, this activity will resonate, but hopefully not create too much anxiety. Compasses were invented because we have a tough time walking in a straight line, even with our eyes wide open. Perhaps it is because one leg is shorter than the other, or our heads are slightly tilted. This tendency to walk in circles when we have no frame of reference creates the opportunity for this surprising activity. A large open space is required, such as a soccer field. Form your students into partners and have them line up at one end of the field. Keep each pair well-spaced apart. Have them identify a point at the far end of the area that they will walk to. This could be a soccer net, a foul pole—anything that is of a decent size and in a specific spot. Within each pair, one person will be sightless, either by closing their eyes or by wearing a blindfold, and the other will be there to provide protection from running into other people or objects along the journey. The sightless person decides when they think they have reached the targeted goal and opens their eyes. Success is often elusive.

These roles will switch for the return journey. After round one, call group to talk about the experience, with a focus on being honest about staying sightless and what it felt like to get or not get to the selected goal. Having the group come up with strategies for the return trip is also a good topic. If the group is feeling competitive, come up with a time goal for all pairs to complete the trip from point A to B. The entire group against some arbitrary record continues the process of building cohesiveness at no one's expense. Here are some additional variations:

- Have both students in a pair close their eyes and walk arm in arm.

- Have them jog toward the goal (make sure the traversing space is very flat and clear of obstacles.

- Try solo or paired walking backward.

- Crawl solo or paired instead of walking (make sure you pick a dry day).

Reflection: This activity provides an opportunity to talk about the idea of mistrust as a healthy response in some situations. We all seem to have fears of being sightless. It can have to do with a feeling of loss of control, a legitimate concern about injury, or a lack of confidence in the person who is guiding us. The honesty within this activity can be to accept the lack of trust as a reasonable response.

When connecting this activity to academic content, two areas come to mind: science and history. How would early navigators have fared if there were no sextants? Would it have been possible to sail out of sight of land and find their way from one place to another without some sort of tool to calculate direction? There is really little difference between being successful (or unsuccessful) at navigating across a soccer field or the ocean.

Cross Categories: Be Here, Be Safe, Set Goals, Care for Self & Others, Let Go & Move On

---

The Activity: Human Camera Time: 40 minutes

Difficulty: 2

How you do it:

While we have placed Human Camera within the category of Be Honest, this is but one example of many equally weighted uses. Pair up your group and explain that one person will be the camera (35 mm, single lens reflex), while the other will be the photographer. The photographer will lead the eyes closed (shutter closed) student, who is serving as the camera, to take a picture that represents a contribution that they (the photographer) have made to the group during a day of being together. The image is taken after the photographer has lined up the camera in the correct position, usually accomplished by gently tugging on the camera's ear or touching a shoulder (know your group) while making a shutter noise. Roles are reversed with the camera becoming the photographer and vice versa.

This can be a difficult task for some groups, as it requires symbolic

reasoning. Give them some examples that may, in fact, reflect behaviors that you witnessed that were helpful. For example, you might say, "I noticed one group member practicing being calm during an argument today, which could have otherwise led to a major confrontation. That pond over there, with the still water and the sun bouncing off of it, would make a great picture of calm. And remember when we did The Electric Fence (Chapter 9), and how some people were strong helpers and patient with each other? Well, that big rock behind us has a feeling of strength and patience about it." In all but the most challenged of groups, these suggestions will get the metaphorical ball rolling.

While this is an excellent way of getting people to offer self-affirmations and think about each other's positive role in the group, there is also a colossal trust component implicit in being led around blindfolded or with eyes closed. The Human Camera can be used to develop Full Value Behavioral Norms for Beings and Villages (Chapter 3) to identify past thoughts, behaviors, and feelings that you want to let go of, and certainly for goal-setting. All one needs is creativity and a willing camera!

Reflection: While we have placed this in Be Honest, the narrative above has wandered through several Full Values. How you reflect on this activity will be determined by its introduction to students and what norm(s) you are teaching or reinforcing. For example, during small group work on a project, some students may be taking on more responsibilities than others, but no one wants to disclose this, ratting out a peer. Yet there is legitimate resentment associated with having to carry more than one's fair share, particularly when the group may be graded on outcomes as a team. Human Camera can be used to promote a climate within small groups where offering honest feedback becomes more permissible. To build skills in this area, recognizing that it is acceptable to have these feelings and to express them, is a place to begin. A Be Honest focused introduction can go like this:

> To the photographer: Think about a time when you had feelings about your participation in a group project. You may have felt that you were doing all the work, or did not have enough say in what part of the project was to be your responsibility. You may have felt that others were not taking the assignment seriously. Or you may have felt distracted and not want to participate yourself for some reason. Guide your camera and take a picture of something that represents one of those circumstances. We will talk about what your picture means when we reflect on this activity later.

The pictures students take provide opportunities for engaging in a meaningful reflective conversation on giving and receiving honest feedback about small group participation.

Cross Categories: Be Safe, Be Honest, Let Go & Move On

The Activity: Have You Ever?   Time: 45 minutes

Materials: Spot markers, paper plates   Difficulty: 1

How you do it:

Form another one of those large circles, using spot markers or some other designation to indicate a station where each person will stand. Ask for a volunteer to come into the circle, removing the marker they were standing on. Now we have one more person than spots, a critical element of this initiative. Explain that the volunteer is to ask the group a question employing a "have you ever" format (see below). You might want to offer a few tame examples, such as:

- Have you ever worn polka dot underwear?

- Have you ever ripped that tag off the pillow that says, "Do not remove under penalty of law?"

- Have you ever gone swimming with your clothes on?

- Have you ever sneaked into a ballgame, concert, or movie without a ticket?

- Have you ever had a pet?

Once the question has been asked, those who have must leave the spot where they were standing and find another spot to occupy other than one directly adjacent to their original spot. Meanwhile, the person in the middle is also gunning for a spot. The situation of having too few spots produces the inevitable new person in the middle, who then asks a Have You Ever question.

OK, you say, this sounds pretty much like the game you have known and loved for years. Ah, but here is the wrinkle. Did we forget to mention this is an important activity for you to participate in? You will somehow not make it back to a safe spot at some point in the game and find yourself in the middle. You can initiate a quantum shift in the level of content within this activity by asking any one of the following questions:

- Have you ever made fun of someone with a group of people?

- Have you ever violated someone's trust?

- Have you ever taken something from someone that didn't belong to you?

- Have you ever thought about really hurting someone?

- Have you ever felt sad and alone and not known where to turn?

- Have you ever been let down by a good friend?

- Have you ever felt like an outsider looking in?

- Have you ever felt misunderstood or not heard?

As you intersperse these questions, group members will have the freedom to move to another spot, a silent indicator of identification, and ask similar questions when they are at center stage. The questions from participants will become very telling. The intensity level of your questions has to be carefully geared to the purposes and age level of the group. We have found that people often find it easier to disclose behaviors and feelings in this format, particularly after initial disclosure around less charged topics gets them moving. Sequence it right, take the risk, and you will be richly rewarded with grist for the reflection mill.

Interesting variations include using pairs instead of individuals. When a Have You Ever question is asked, pairs need to check whether they have shared the experience before moving off their spots.

Asking, "Will you ever?" is another option, particularly as it relates to goal setting.

Reflection: This activity can be useful in bringing to the surface honest disclosure and conversation around behaviors that are difficult to talk about, particularly when dealing with how people relate to each other in family, work, and social situations.

Cross Categories: Be here, Set Goals, Let Go & Move On

The Activity: Moving Without Touching Time: 25 minutes

Materials: Masking tape Difficulty: 2

How you do it:
> Moving without touching anyone else is the goal of this activity. The whole group gathers in the middle of the room. When the teacher says, "everyone moves," everyone in the group works at coming as close to each other as they can without touching. You can act like cars on the highway, or birds in a tree or at a feeder, or airplanes in the sky. Students will find out that it is easy to come close to someone when that person is standing still, but another thing altogether is to have that person try to come close to you at the same time you are moving. The Be Honest aspect of this activity is people acknowledging they have touched while passing. Once a touch has occurred the closeness of the group is marked with tape on the floor, and the group tries again until there is a consensus that they can get no closer without touching.

Reflection: The ethical dilemma in this and many other Be Honest activities is admitting to a rule violation with the real possibility of impacting the group's success. A focus of the conversation needs to be: Is succeeding with a rule violation truly a success? Is the process as important as the outcome?

Cross Categories: Be Here, Set Goals, Let Go & Move On

The Activity: Spin the Yarn Time: 60 minutes

Materials: A ball of brightly colored yarn Difficulty: 2

How you do it:
> Form the group into a circle within easy tossing distance with a ball of yarn. With you starting the process, share some positive feedback to a student across from you and toss them the ball of yarn. The student calls out another student's name before launching the yarn and shares a positive asset or strength about that person. This continues until the ball of yarn comes back to you and a lovely web is woven across the circle, linking all of the students together.

Reflection: Prompt for a discussion with students as to what the web represents for the group and how positive, honest feedback can contribute to their Full Value Commitment.

Cross Categories: This activity can be used to develop behavioral norms for each Full Value, depending on how it is introduced

---

The Activity: Scavenger Hunt　　　　　　　　　　　　　Time: 60 minutes+

Materials: Various objects found outside the classroom, 　　Difficulty: 2
glue guns (may require supervision)

How you do it:
Bring the students outside to an area where there are lots of small objects that can be gathered. These might include pinecones, small rocks, bottle tops, bark, small tree sprigs, and scraps of paper; whatever students can find in the space of twenty minutes. You can provide some information about the purpose of the gathering or just ask students to find small objects for use in a classroom activity. Have them bring their unique treasure trove back into the classroom. Using their assembled materials, have them each construct a sculpture that reflects an interaction they had with someone that involved giving or receiving feedback (positive or negative), or taking responsibility for an action or event, or holding someone else responsible for a behavior. How you frame this will depend on the age of your students. An interesting and informing variation is to have students gather materials and create their sculptures in pairs or groups of three.

Reflection: After allowing sufficient time for construction, ask students to describe their sculptures. Encourage each artist to share the interaction, the feelings involved, and if and how the situation was resolved. Ask students to develop a list of strategies associated with a positive outcome, as well as distractors that got in the way.

Cross Categories: This activity can be used to develop behavioral norms for each Full Value, depending on how it is introduced.

The Activity: Sweet & Salty　　　　　　　　　　　　　Time: 40 minutes

Materials: Pretzel sticks & M & M's (Check for food allergies　Difficulty: 1
and alter foods as needed. The main criteria are
one being sweet and the other salty)

How you do it:
Circle up the group and give each student a sweet and salty item. Explain that the salty item represents a problematic experience they may have had

over the past week, while the sweet item represents a positive experience. Ask each student to share their experience as a way of modeling honest feedback. After each contribution, the student gets to eat their sweet or salty item.

Reflection: Ask students to reflect on how the taste of their respective items connects to the experiences they have shared. Make sure to allow students to pass if they are not comfortable sharing (they can still eat their treats). Assess the group's readiness before trying this, so you are not faced with only a few contributors. As always, if you find that students are reticent, you can always participate and go first!

Cross Categories: This activity can be used to develop behavioral norms for each Full Value, depending on how it is introduced.

The Activity: Truth Drawings Time: 40 minutes

Materials: Crayons, markers, paper Difficulty: 2

How you do it:

Ask students to think about a circumstance with a friend, school peer, teacher, or family member that required being honest. This might involve giving and receiving feedback or an admission of a mistake. Distribute paper and crayons, and ask the students to draw the scenes.

Reflection: Once completed, circle up and ask for volunteers to share their scenes. An effective way to break the ice for this type of activity is to complete a drawing of your own and go first. This also communicates the message that you are with them in this process, not standing above and apart from them. An important component of sharing is to have students discuss how to put the outcome of each depiction into a few words to add to their Full Value Commitment under Be Honest. Behaviors like telling the truth, accepting responsibility, and offering feedback in a gentle way can all be discussed. Coaching may be necessary here to parse the drawing descriptions down to a few words. How these behaviors are framed will always depend on the age of your students. The drawings will serve as evocative prompts for provoking a meaningful conversation. Another option for displaying work would be to hang the pictures around the classroom and have a gallery walk, moving from one to the next with each artist describing their creation.

Cross Categories: This activity can be used to develop behavioral norms for each Full Value, depending on how it is introduced.

CHAPTER 9

SET GOALS

So much of our lives is focused on setting goals. In organizations, strategic planning (a fancy title for setting multi-year goals) is a significant task. Businesses set production, sales, and expansion goals. For educators, goal setting has become a preoccupation, often directly linked to employment. In New Jersey, for example, to set and meet Student Growth Objectives is a component of teacher total evaluation scores, which is ultimately a component of earning tenure.

However, very little time is dedicated to how we achieve goals; the process of getting from point A to point B. Instead, there is a huge focus on The What (the objective) but not on carefully defining the goal, assessing its personal importance, and marshaling the necessary internal and external resources. We are good at defining where we want to go, but less able to determine how we get there and when we have arrived, an example of negative design. For it can be the case that an established goal may be antithetical to the person being asked to achieve it. It would pass the common sense test for the goal setter to have a hand in defining their commitment to a goal, which should be at the beginning of the process. But even the most well-intentioned advocates often get caught up in what is important to *them* as a goal, rather than establishing whether the goal setter has the same level of interest and commitment.

> Recently I met with the director of a non-profit whose mission is to pressure school districts to ensure that students with learning disabilities attend college. The program advocates for starting students down this track in junior high school. When I suggested that very few students know whether they want to go to college in junior high school, the response was defensive. This is an example of setting a goal *for* a student as opposed to the goal being created with the advice of a teacher or counselor without the imposition of what could be an inappropriate projection. Junior high school students might end up in a college prep program but there are so many other options including trade schools, the military, or going directly into the labor market. - Richard

Our review of the syllabi for K-12 schools, colleges, and universities reveals that little to no formal instruction is offered on setting goals or teaching goal setting. There just seems to be an assumption that we all know how to do it. However, if that were the case, we would all be much better at it. At a recent training we asked the question of fifty teachers, "How many of you participated in coursework specific to goal setting in your college courses?" Two teachers raised their hands.

Defining and working toward goals, whether personal or professional, is essential to teaching and living Full Value, which is why Set Goals is included as one of the six foundational concepts.

Set Goals & Full Value Commitment

In an earlier chapter, we introduced several options for developing a Full Value Commitment with students. This is where the goal-setting process begins. The Full Value Commitment is a dynamic representation of a group goal with defined behavioral objectives. If the teacher frames this as a goal-setting process, it will serve as an excellent jumping off point for further goal-setting work with students.

Aside from linking goal setting to the development of a classroom Full Value Commitment, goal setting can easily be connected to the instructional process. The teacher might conduct a whole class review of goal-setting with students as part of the lesson introduction. For example, students can work through all SMART Goals areas in a large group, establishing specific goals together as assignments. A conversation about goal setting can also be integrated into any activity used to teach Full Value. All of the activities have the potential for goal setting embedded within them. Process topics can be frontloaded into an introduction of the activity.

ACTIVITY EXAMPLE

The Activity: Helium Hoop   Time: 35 minutes

Materials: Hula Hoop   Difficulty: 1

In the Helium Hoop activity, the group holds up a Hula Hoop with their index fingers extended and lowers it from shoulder height to the ground without breaking contact. If contact is broken, the group resets the Hoop at shoulder height and tries again. Completing this task requires several individual and group commitments to be defined and agreed to.

- Agreeing on the objective (What are we trying to accomplish?)

- Making an individual commitment to participate fully (being here, self-monitoring)

- Contributing to the success of other participants (offering encouragement, feedback)

- Staying with the activity (managing frustration, finding humor and magic in it)

- Accepting failure as a learning tool (trying again, regrouping, avoiding blame)

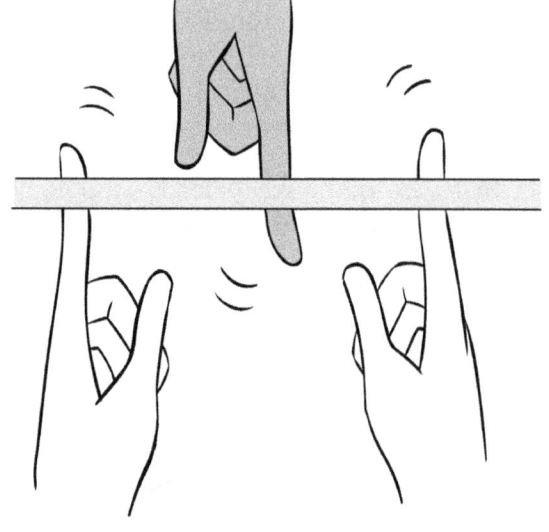

- Acknowledging participation (leadership, follow-ship)

Instead of simply relating the goal-setting process to completing a task, rich metaphorical activity structures can also be created. There may be an issue with students working cooperatively or not valuing each other's input during a class discussion. Interacting with classmates around the hoop takes on a specific focus. It represents the class working together, listening to each other, and valuing each contribution. These are all skills that need to be practiced and lived during their time together in the classroom.

The goals of this activity can be student or teacher-initiated. A student might call group and identify the problem that when they had something to contribute, other students were talking. The teacher can propose the Hoop as a goal-setting activity to address this. With teacher guidance, students brainstorm how the activity process connects to the student's concern. Students might agree to be silent and have the student who raised the complaint be the sole provider of instructions during the Hoop activity. Students might agree on a sound or word that indicates when one student distracts or interrupts another during the problem-solving process.

Whether the goal is achieved or not, the affective, cognitive, and behavioral outcomes can be reflected upon with specific connections resulting from participating in the Hoop experience.

The Focus of Goal Setting

We suggest that students set goals with a focus on academics and the school community. Academic goals can range from developing more effective study skills to becoming better organized around schoolwork. School community goals can run the gamut from working more cooperatively with peers to taking risks around sharing feelings with other students. Again, it becomes a collaborative effort between teacher and student, and between students, when a group goal is being developed.

Individual goal setting can be accomplished via student-teacher conferences. This provides a confidential opportunity to interact with students in defining goals. Parents can be looped into the process to provide support, encouragement, and resources. Families can also use goal-setting methods at home.

One of the most important lessons that students will learn is that getting to the outcome feels less daunting when you break down the goal-setting steps. It can be the case that when students are faced with the goal to do better on tests, it simply feels overwhelming. The goal is associated with negative feelings of repetitive failures. When a student sees that there is a way to get there using incremental steps and that interim successes are experienced along the way, the experience becomes much more positive.

Directed or Self-Directed Goal Setting

Goal setting is a personal journey that must be connected to one's aspirations. There is a visceral need to set goals, but the process is often not adequately taught, as noted in the introduction to this chapter. The following material helps to provide students with tools to fashion meaningful and relevant goals. Again, care should always be taken not to directly project one's perspectives and needs onto what the student should be working on. Guidance, gentle nudging, asking the right questions, and connecting students both to their aspirations and impediments to achieving those aspirations are part of the teacher's crucial role. But if a student does not take ownership of their goal, it is unlikely that it will be achieved. Taking ownership of goal setting builds the larger capacities of self-regulation and independence. Students who have successful outcomes from a goal-setting process they have defined, initiated, and completed experience positive empowerment and self-efficacy.

Goal Setting & Distractors

When creating a Full Value Commitment with associated goals to set our behavioral norms into motion, significant attention is given to defining distractors or impediments. This should also be included in the goal-setting process. The WOOP model of goal setting (see below) adds the important emphasis of looking at inner obstacles to offer better chances of success. The four steps are:

- What is your wish?

- What is the best outcome?

- What is your main inner obstacle?

- Make a plan

The alignment with SMART Goals is clear. Paying attention to inner obstacles adds an additional and essential dimension. WOOP (Penman & Vedantam, 2016) defines inner obstacles as "an emotion, an irrational belief, or a bad habit."[59] Research in this area over a period of twenty years would indicate that people who hold a Pollyannaish view of their ability to achieve goals without consideration of impediments do not experience the same frequency of sustainable success. Therefore, we suggest that this becomes integrated into your goal-setting work with students.

Goal Setting with Primary School Students

It is never too early to begin teaching students how to set and achieve goals. The student's developmental stage determines how complex the goal and the process to get there will be. For a preschool student, some behavioral goals might include taking turns, putting away toys, hanging up their coat, putting a backpack in a cubby, or using a tissue instead of a sleeve. All are simple but important skills to learn and practice. These goals can be represented in drawings or by creating a short video that students can refer to. Many helpful motivational templates exist online for free or low-cost use by teachers (Rycroft).[60] Our criteria for what to use are that it should be simple, it must be graphically attractive, and most importantly, it must be asset-based. A form that asks students to offer "What I wish for" and "What I would like to work on" is far better than "What do I need to learn that I don't know" and "What do I need to get better at?" The language is simple and positive. Students who are writing can fill them out either independently or with assistance.

 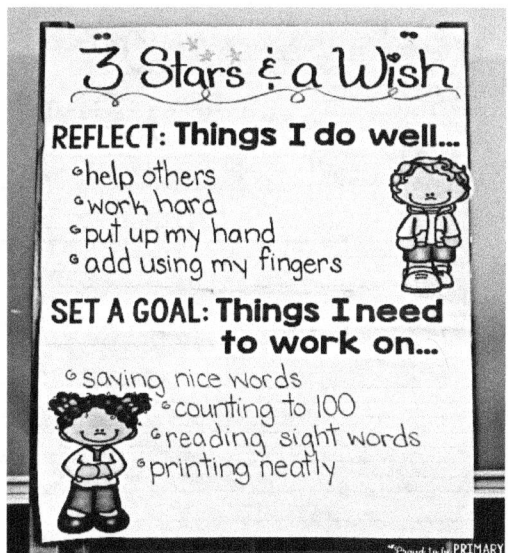

A discussion with the teacher can occur around the steps to accomplish the goal(s) with a simple sequence defined and practiced. Students can be encouraged to state where they need to ask for help and what they can do more independently along the way. And of course, success should always be celebrated.

Goal Setting with Elementary School Students

In an article published in Scholastic Magazine (January 16, 2016)[61] Gina Connell provides a very comprehensive process for creating SMART Goals with her students. She introduces the steps with a colorful and engaging poster. She then leads students in a discussion of specific and non-specific goals. This is a critical step, as all the rest of the work of goal setting flows from the defined goal. Students often have difficulty developing goals that are well defined and measurable. Ms. Connell reports that students enjoyed creating a list of vague goals, i.e., goals that do not have enough meat to them. Students then brainstorm specific goals and record them on a SMART Goals planner (See Chapter 16, Printable Materials).

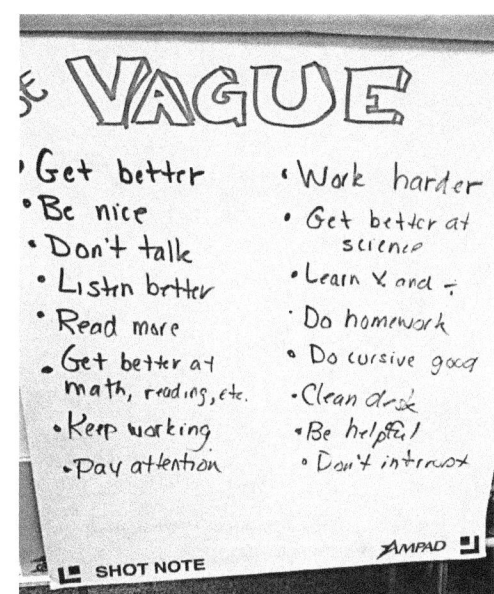

This is a draft copy of goals that will be transferred to individual Goal sheets (See Chapter 16, Printable Materials) as the final step in the process.

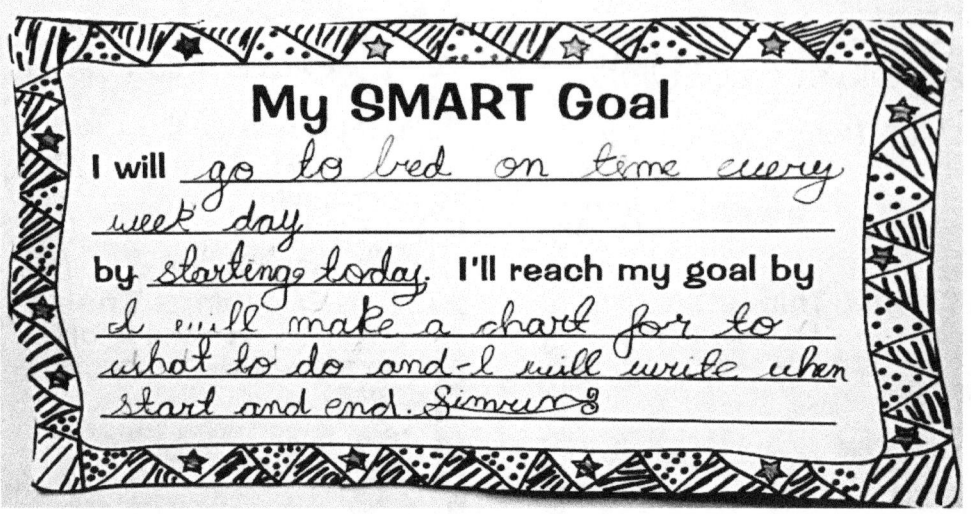

Goal Setting with Middle & High School Students

<u>The Ideal Self</u>

This is an exercise in self-reflection for middle and high school students developed from the work of Richard Boyatzis (2000).[62] Students examine who they want to be as a person and who they are now. This exploration is built around a drawing that each student creates, representing their strengths, gaps, and goals associated with those gaps they wish to work on to achieve an Ideal Self.

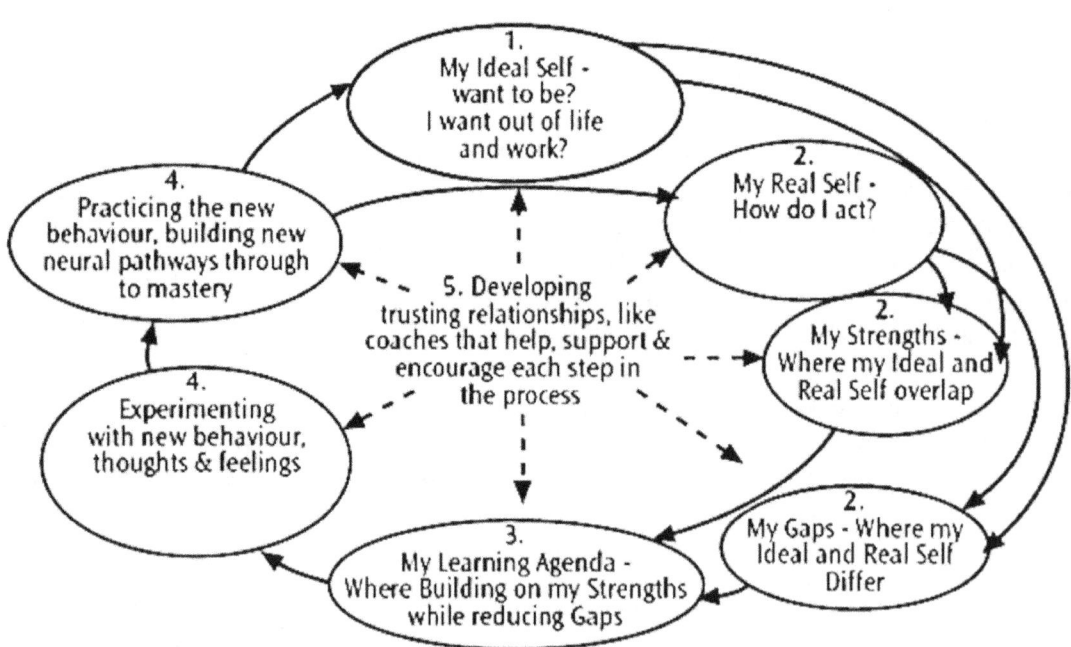

Using the above model, students individually reflect on the following questions:

- Ideal Self: Who do I want to be as a student?
- Real Self: Who am I as a student?

Students are then asked to identify three strengths that will help them get closer to their Ideal Self and three gaps that will potentially be impediments. This information is included in the visual representation of the Ideal Self. The student may draw him or herself or a symbolic representation and then write strengths and gaps within the drawing.

Goal Setting Templates

Two templates are provided below to assist in framing the goal-setting process for middle school and high school students. However, the components of defining goals and obstacles are the same across all age groups. It is the level of conceptualization, the sophistication of goals, and the language that differ.

SMART Goals[63]

To set effective goals, it is important set SMART ones!

S - SPECIFIC What is it you wish to accomplish? You should set one goal at a time, stating exactly what you are responsible for. Research has shown that a student who says they want to do one thing or another seldom progresses beyond the 'or.' The individual does neither. This does not mean you can't be flexible with your goal. Flexibility in action implies the ability to judge that some endeavor you are involved in is either inappropriate, unnecessary, or the result of a wrong decision. Even though you may set out for one goal, you can stop at any time and drop it for a new one. But when you change, you again need to state your goal without an alternative.

M - MEASURABLE How will you know when you have reached your goal? Your goal must be stated so that it is measurable in time and quantity. For example, suppose the goal is to finish writing a term paper in three weeks. You would specify your goal by saying, "I am going to complete the outline week 1, do my research week 2, and write the paper week 3." That way, the goal can be measured; at the end of each week, you know whether or not each of the benchmarks has been achieved.

A - ACHIEVABLE Is achieving this goal realistic with effort and commitment? Have you got the resources to accomplish this goal? If not, how will you get them? The goals you set must be accomplishable or reasonable with your given strengths and abilities. It is too easy to set impossible goals that are simply not realistic. While you want to stretch yourself, you do not want to set goals so difficult that they're unattainable and frustrate you.

R - RELEVANT Why is this goal significant and vital to your life? This element requires careful exploration with students. We sometimes set goals that are imposed, driven by the expectations of others. Conversely, there are instances where students do not see the big picture and have needs they wish to gratify that do not contribute to their growth in the school setting.

T – TIME-BOUND Ideally, you want to be able to monitor progress. To do that, you've got to be able to measure or count performance frequently, which means you need to put a record-keeping system in place to track performance. It is also important that timeframes are defined. Goals can be changed or wholly rewritten, but this should not lead to an indeterminate end date. If goal completion is drifting, attention needs to be brought to the SMART Goal area(s) that may be creating a problem.

Asking for Help

Another simpler graphic model for goal setting is provided below. A unique component of this model is the boxes that ask students to define what they are willing to commit in terms of personal resources, and determining what they will need from others. We feel that this second area of commitment is especially important.

Asking for help is often experienced as an admission of weakness. We would reframe that as the intelligent use of resources that others around you (teachers, students, family) may possess. Learning how to ask for help builds more highly functioning teams in the classroom, workplace, and the community. All of us have different capacities and strengths. This happens naturally in some situations, such as with team sports. Some people are better at fielding than pitching. Some people have great outside basketball shots, while others are better rebounders or passers. We never question these different capacities and how we value them.

The analogy to academic achievement would be that some students are better at visual-spatial reasoning and struggle more with verbal concepts. Some students are more random-abstract in their approach to tasks, while others are more concrete-sequential. Sometimes one method is more effective than another. Some students can work autonomously without much encouragement, while others require constant feedback and encouragement. When setting goals, assessing these internal competencies and asking for help from peers who possess them in a greater measure indicates wisdom, not weakness.

4 Square Goal Setting Worksheet

1) What do I want to accomplish?	2) What will I need from my classmates?

3) What personal resources/ strengths will I need?	4) How will I know that I've achieved my goal(s)?

Set Goals & Trauma Work

Set Goals provides a template for problem solving, asking for help (an area of critical need for students who are suffering), and for defining success. Unfortunately, the experiencing of trauma can throw the goal-setting process into the abyss. Often, those experiencing trauma live moment to moment, are in the fight, freeze, faint, or flight mode. The inability to engage in a process to set and achieve goals, and most importantly, to trust that those around you can provide compassionate and empathetic support, can block any movement forward. Drawing upon the behavioral norms within Full Value as the basis for planning and achieving goals supports the student who has or is experiencing trauma in moving forward toward positive change. Taking incremental and definable steps also assists in making the growth process less overwhelming.

Outcomes of Set Goals

- Achievement/Failure
- Accepting Help
- Brainstorm and Plan
- Cooperation Versus Competition
- Empowerment
- Growth Oriented
- Defining Clear Objectives
- Intelligent Risk Taking
- Independence
- Intention into Action

ACTIVITIES

Activity Difficulty Scale

1 (Easy) ------- 2 (A bit harder) -------- 3 (Pretty complicated) --------- 4 (Difficult)

The Activity: Balloon Trolley Time: 35 minutes

Materials: Bag of 12-inch balloons Difficulty: 2

How you do it:

In this activity you just pick a destination and go for it as a group. Sounds simple enough, but as you know, experiential activity appearances can be deceiving. Materials for this challenge include a bag of balloons and a group of people willing to go on a trip. Pick up balloons of some substance—at least twelve inches in diameter inflated is the minimal regulation size for this activity. Theme balloons can be fun, such as smiley faces or Star Wars. If you can find a bag of fat, elongated balloons, grab 'em. We once searched eight party stores in vain. They seemed to be discontinued as per a marketing genius who determined that round is in, elongated is out. Go figure! Anyway, here is the setup for Balloon Trolley.

Lay out a course of travel with a difficulty level that relates to your classroom goals at the moment and the nature of the group. One bunch of students may need to travel up and over boulders, while for another, the challenge of just getting there without committing homicide may suffice. The task is to have a line of students, with a balloon held between each of them, move from one place to another. Hands may not be used to hold the balloons in place; only bodies pressed together exerting pressure. The difficulty of this innocent task should now be coming readily apparent. As an initiative to illustrate the components of goal setting, this is a real winner.

Some thoughts around variations include allowing the group to determine what constitutes success. Does that mean no balloon drops, the fewest over three attempts, one or two? Empower students to assess the level of success they find acceptable. Now give them some planning time before the trolley leaves the station, and then let them have at it.

The balloons provide a terrific writing surface to get the group thinking about what they are transporting (and taking good care of). Full Value behaviors, individual or group goals, or just questions to consider may all be marked on the balloons.

Reflection: This activity and others that follow offer the opportunity for some students to serve as process recorders. The activity itself is very engaging, with participants who can become too caught up to keep an objective record of their process. Some initial conversation starters might include:

- What did you need to do to maintain contact with the balloons?

- How much of this depended on your commitment, or working out strategies with your partners in the line?

- If you were to use one of the goal-setting strategies we are learning, how would you connect this activity to a goal-setting component?

- What were some of the distractors that got in the way of a no balloon drop success?

Cross Categories: Be Here, Let Go & Move On

The Activity: Calculator or Key Punch Time: 45 minutes

Materials: 30-foot rope, 30 numbered rubber spot markers (paper plates will do), masking tape (if you are using paper plates), stopwatch Difficulty: 2

How you do it:
Tie the ends of the rope together to form a rope circle large enough to comfortably fit the spot markers. Inside the circle randomly place the thirty numbered spot markers. Explain to students that continuous improvement is the purpose of this activity. The object is to touch each spot in numbered order from one to thirty as quickly as possible.

Here are the rules:

- The group starts behind a line that is at least fifty feet from the circle.

- They are not to see the activity before their first attempt.

- A total of three attempts at improving performance time are allowed with a five-minute planning session before each try. The first planning session occurs before the class has seen the activity (but it has been described).

- Time is kept for each round and starts when the group congregates behind the starting line.

- Only one person is allowed inside the circle at a time. An arm or a leg intruding into the circle is included in this rule.

- The activity ends (for timing purposes) when all spots have been touched in sequence, and the group has returned to behind the starting line.

- After each round, the teacher informs the group of their time and the number of observed mistakes (e.g., multiple touching of the same number(s), more than one person inside the circle at a time).

Reflection: If using the 4 Square approach to goal setting, this activity helps to focus on boxes two and three. Ask students how they were willing to commit to making this activity successful. This could include concentration, focus, contributing ideas, and looking out for people, so they did not violate the boundary rule. Prompt students to explain what help they asked for from their classmates to be successful. As an observer during the activity, keep track of behaviors that were distracting, impeding success, or slowing the group down. Mention a few of your observations, ask students to add to your list, and brainstorm how improved performance can come from accepting and working through the distractors. Aside from informing the goal-setting process, all of this information contributes to the classroom Full Value Commitment.

Cross Categories: Be Here, Be Honest, Let Go & Move On

The Activity: Duct Tape   Time: 45 minutes

Materials: A roll of duct tape, two milk crates   Difficulty: 1

How you do it:

Here's a goal-setting activity that may raise a few eyebrows, if you haven't already taped them down. Bet you've found lots of uses for duct (duck) tape over the years. The stuff is amazing. It seals packages, fixes leaks in hoses, patches holes in sheetrock; just about anything that's broke it can fix, at least temporarily. But had you thought about using it to tape a human to a wall, suspended off the ground?

Offer students a roll of duct tape and a sturdy box to stand on. Borrowed milk crates labeled "Property of Ding-Dong Dairy" make excellent temporary stands. Make sure to pre-test the wall you are taping to for tape-fastness. This is equivalent to testing colored fabrics before throwing them into the laundry with the whites. Nothing irritates a building administrator more than finding a large strip of industrial paint torn off the wall.

The object of this activity is simple. The group must plan a strategy for duct taping a willing participant to a wall, so that when the temporary stand is removed, they remain hanging with only the support of the tape. Sounds nuts, well... it is. It is also a great visual, a ludicrously delicious proposition, a goal to achieve, and a real problem to solve. The tape job should be of sufficient quality to allow for at least a ten-second hang time.

A few minor caveats; tape to skin contact should be forbidden. Long sleeve shirts and pants, not shorts are required garb. Think of the application of duct tape to the skin as akin to a huge Band-Aid that would need to be rapidly torn off to make removal possible. Make sure to make that point clear to the tapers before commencing the activity (Be Safe, Care For Self & Others). Have spotters at the ready once the plastic milk carton is removed in the unlikely event that the tape job doesn't hold. Finally, the participant(s) should have the option of a face forward or cheeks forward position on the wall. Once the group has taped one person successfully, try for two people with one roll of tape!

<u>Reflection:</u> All kidding aside, this activity requires a significant amount of planning to be successful. It is essentially a physics problem. What is the most effective construction to support a certain amount of mass? Make sure to allow for significant planning. Listen carefully and record the group's process. In discussing the outcome, make sure to hit upon as many pieces of the goal-setting process as possible. Help students formalize this process into short phrases that can be added to their Full Value Commitment either as a behavioral norm or a distractor. Specific to this activity, probe how many students tuned out because of the initial perception that the idea seemed improbable. Help them connect these feelings to problems they face in their daily lives and with their own life goals. Seemingly impossible tasks can be managed with personal commitment and group support.

Cross Categories: Be Safe

The Activity: Electric Fence   Time: 45 minutes

Materials: A 15-foot piece of thin rope   Difficulty: 2

How you do it:

Find a piece of thin rope and stretch it between two fixed points at a height of approximately three to four feet (adjustments to be made dependent on the average height of your group). Haul out your virtual generator and extension cord, the one you once purchased along with dried food to weather the Y2K meltdown. Once the generator is fired up and the cord attached to your fence, the group is ready to proceed. The object is to get the entire group over the now sizzling bare wire fence without touching the wire or the area underneath it, which has also become positively charged with electrons smacking against each other. Breaking the plane beneath the fence or touching the wire temporarily incinerates the group. Everyone must return to the starting side to be regenerated. The reason all are toasted at once is that during the journey over the wire, the entire group must maintain physical contact at all times, ergo when touched by the wire or breaking the plane beneath, zzzzzzzzzzzt, the circuit is completed.

The interconnectedness required in this activity forms a metaphor around the importance of including others in your goal-setting process. One can set a goal, but it may be impossible to reach and difficult to know if you've gotten there without support and feedback from others. This activity can literally not be achieved without everyone being connected. It is a basic rule of this activity, and a pretty basic rule of life.

Reflection: During the discussion, focus on the interdependent nature of goal setting, as outlined above. Whether it is successfully educating children, reducing crime, or combating climate change, these goals will not be achieved without a community effort. A goal can rarely be achieved without at least a modicum of help. Some questions to consider:

- Why was it important to keep in contact with the people in front and behind you?

- What commitments did you need to make to stay connected?

- Did you discuss with the person next to you any strategies to stay connected?

- Did you let go during the activity but not let anyone know? Why?

- How do you feel the rule of staying connected in this activity relates to successfully achieving your own life goals?

- Who might be someone in our class, at home, or in the community you rely on to reach your goals? Give an example of how they helped you.

Cross Categories: Be Here, Be Safe, Let Go & Move On

The Activity: Goal Partners   Time: Ongoing

How you do it:

> A partnership is a basic structure for human relationships. Partnerships go to many levels of complexity, from friendship to marriage. In our lives, we have often found that developing a growth partnership with another person is extraordinarily helpful.
>
> By participating in a goal partnership, we connect with another person about specific areas in our lives we are choosing to work on. For example, a goal might be, "Developing and implementing a comprehensive plan for exam review." In sharing and during the check-in time with a student partner, we can break down what the goal looks, sounds, and feels like. We can begin to identify places where we lose the goal focus. We can make a deal with our partner that when they perceive we are losing focus, it is expected that there will be a reminder coming.
>
> The great thing about partnerships is that they are equal. No one is better than another. Each student has goals to work on, and hierarchies are not allowed. They are also confidential; goals may be announced to the whole group, but the specifics around monitoring and achievement are, for the most part, kept between the partners. Partnerships, in short, are safe and growth-enhancing.

Cross Categories: Be Safe, Be Here, Be Honest, Care for Self & Others

---

The Activity: Great Egg Drop   Time: 1 hour+

Materials: 2 eggs, 30 inches of tape,   Difficulty: 2-3
20 straws, 6-foot stepladder,
large plastic bags

How you do it:

> Like deliberately breaking eggs? Who doesn't? The anticipation and emotions generated from drop to impact can almost be tasted. Think back

to egg and spoon races, or the egg toss competitions of your camp days. Whenever there was implicit tension in a game, an egg could often be found lurking somewhere nearby. In the Great Egg Drop, as with most potential 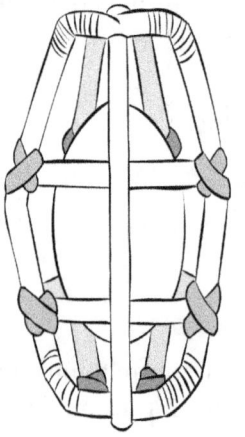 egg breaking activities, the point is to protect two eggs from their ultimate demise. Divide your students into smaller sub-groups. Four to six students is an optimum number. Offer them the following materials: two eggs, twenty straws, and thirty (not twenty-nine) inches of masking tape. Students must work together to design and build a deployment system that, when launched from a height of at least seven feet, will protect the eggs from attaining open gelatinous status. Beyond explaining what the term *deploy* means, do not offer any suggestions as to what the system should look like. Points can be awarded for advertising your deployment system to the other groups, parsimonious use of resources (i.e., the least amount of tape, fewest straws), dropping technique, the elegance of deployment system design, and egg survival. If you come up with enough point categories, there's bound to be a tie.

After the systems have been developed, the launch takes place from a stepladder surrounded at its base by a liberal number of plastic garbage bags. You can certainly use a bare floor, but don't count on any favors from your building custodian for the foreseeable future. On the count of three, drop!

A note about time—if your class periods are typically forty-five minutes to one hour, have students construct their deployment systems on one day and launch the eggs and reflect on activity outcomes the next.

Reflection: The goal is clear: to protect an egg from a fall from seven feet. However, how the group gets there is the stuff that reflections are made of. This activity is rich with metaphorical possibilities as long as you have set the stage before beginning the activity. Some questions to ask to encourage co-creation:

- Given what we would like to work on today as a group, what might our eggs represent or stand for?

- What does the deployment system represent?

- What elements of goal setting will be helpful to include to ensure a successful attempt?

- How will you decide who will do what in your group?

After the activity is complete, elements to process are how the students felt about working together including the sharing of responsibilities, the success or failure of their deployment system, and what was learned from the planning, construction, and outcomes.

Cross Categories: Be Here, Let Go & Move On, Care for Self & Others

---

The Activity: Group Juggling Time: 30-45 minutes

Materials: Soft throwable objects. Fleece balls are a must Difficulty: 2

How you do it:

Group juggling perhaps has more variations than most any other of our activities. Juggling is magic, and group juggling is even more magical. As a Set Goals activity, it is second to none, but there are certainly a bunch more applications. Here is the basic version with some variations to follow. Ask students to arrange themselves in a loose circle. Start with one fleece ball and set up a sequential throwing and catching pattern, with no one person getting the ball twice, until everyone in the circle has handled it. If you start the pattern, then the ball should return to you.

Have the group practice until they become comfortable with the catching and throwing order, making accurate throws and good catches. Now for the juggling part. Tell them that the Olympic juggling record for a group of their size is six balls going at once. Casually ask them if they are up to the challenge. Rarely will you get a negative response. Start the throwing sequence again, adding the additional balls at appropriate intervals. If you can get five or six balls going at once for even a minute, that's juggling! An interesting variation is to give each person an object to throw, and have them toss it to their designated catcher, all at the same time. This unison toss is challenging and visually spectacular.

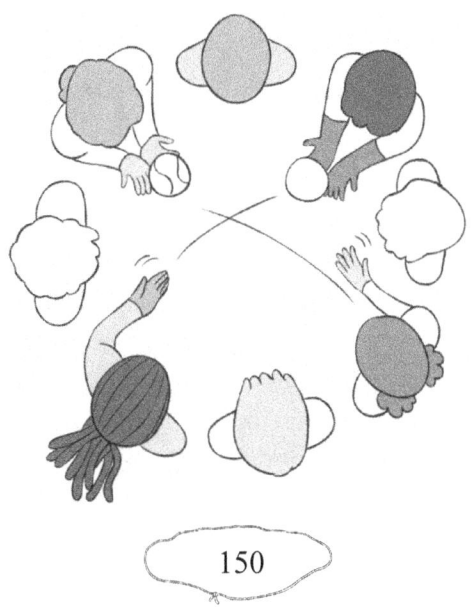

Reflection: There are many moving parts to this activity for fluid juggling to be achieved. There is the necessary commitment to throw with care and accuracy while also being ready to catch at the same time. Planning is critical. If groups devote time to working on strategies, they are much more assured of success. All of these elements can be reviewed during the reflection piece. A primary question is what the balls might represent in terms of the goal-setting process? This question provides the opportunity for students to repeat the activity with a different focus. For example, if there were distractors to success, they can be identified and the balls labeled with them (e.g., losing focus, fooling around). This brings attention to these distractors with the increased likelihood of avoiding them.

Cross Categories: Be Here, Be Safe, Care for Self & Others

The Activity: Human Knot (Tangle) Time: 30 minutes

Materials: 3-foot lengths of ¼ inch (or thereabouts) rope Difficulty: 2

How you do it:

The ground rules are simple: have the group bunch together as tightly as possible, all facing in, then reach out and take someone's hand. The only exception is that you can't hold both hands of another person, thus creating a square dance partner, but not much else.

We have noted, watching countless knots being untangled, that there is a tendency for people to get a death grip on each other's hands, which can lead to sprained fingers and wrists. A way to avoid this problem is to issue each participant a Buddy Rope, a three-foot piece of polypropylene. Now instead of grabbing another hand, you simply grab a free end of a Buddy Rope. Create Buddy Rope handles by tying an overhand knot at each end. Presto, no more twisted digits!

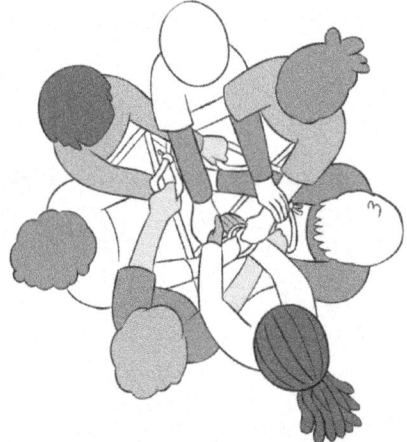

Once hands or Buddy Ropes are connected, you have one massive knot to untangle. Participants must untangle the knot, ultimately forming a circle, without letting go of the Buddy Ropes - simple, but devilishly difficult.

This activity is ripe for engaging in goal setting, working as a team, looking out for others, self-sacrifice, and fun. There is this tremendous sense of satisfaction as the tangle suddenly evaporates due to a series of movements, not unlike finally getting that valuable spool of kite string straightened out. The linguistic and metaphorical possibilities are also rich. Think about how we get "tied up in knots" with problems in our lives. Then there is the feeling of having a "knot in your stomach." What kind of proactive and cooperative work does it take within the classroom to untangle problems? Make the best fit with the needs of your students and get that group tangled up and ready to go.

Reflection: One of the attributes specific to this activity is patience. There may be a lot of standing quietly, while smaller segments of the knot work on getting untangled. This quiet time is often not passive, as those not directly engaged in the untangling process often have a better vantage point from which to offer suggestions. Therefore, a suggested focus for reflection can be to discuss how patience and observation contribute to successful goal completion. In goal setting, there are times when things are beyond one's control, such as relying on a goal partner or a member of a small group to get their piece of the project completed. How the student learns to address these outside elements are essential skills to build.

Cross Categories: Be Here, Be Safe, Be Honest, Care for Self & Others

The Activity: Leaning Tower of Feetza   Time: 45 minutes

Difficulty: 3 (or 2 if you just use a pile of sneakers-see below)

How you do it:

An important aspect of successful experiential activities is their ability to appeal to a sense of visual aesthetics. If it looks cool, then more than likely students will think it is fun to do. The Leaning Tower of Feetza is at the top of the charts when it comes to visual impact. Imagine yourself in Pisa, Italy, standing at the base of that improbable white tower. You turn to a man at one of the fifteen tourist kiosks surrounding the place. You reach into your pocket, ready to shell out some Euros for a plastic souvenir.

Freeze frame. The town is different, it's Galena, Illinois, and you are standing in a gym, staring up at an improbable tower of sneakers straining to touch a basketball hoop set at ten feet. The tower leans left, then right. There, it contacts the rim. Now that's a Leaning Tower of Feetza.

This is a high energy, spotting intensive, sweat-inducing, goal-setting activity. The goal is to build a tower of heel to toe touching feet (or hands), with no one person's feet placed consecutively to a height of ten feet (or whatever height you feel is appropriate for your group) in the air, and to hold that position for ten seconds (where H= height and FPS = feet per second). Good spotting is essential here to lift and protect the upper reaches of the tower while ensuring that it doesn't collapse in a heap onto the bottom participants. Any estimated height of ten feet (lower for a younger group) will do as long as there is no wall to lean against to support the group's efforts. It's hard not to get involved. It's hard not to be amazed at the sheer visual excitement! And it's darn hard to get it done.

This activity tends to involve fun, support, interdependence, problem solving, goal setting, balance, commitment, trust, journeying, and some small share of selflessness. Set aside time to brainstorm with students on how to best accomplish the task. If one were to use the 4 Square goal-setting worksheet, it might look like the sample below.

The contents of this sheet will be as varied as the nature of the group of students participating in the activity. The 4 Square process can be used to model all forms of goal setting for students, whether related to academic content or relationships with peers and family.

What do I want to accomplish	**What will I need from my classmates**
Build a tower of feet from the gym floor to the bottom of the basketball hoop and hold that position for 10 seconds.	The commitment to stay with the activity. Assuring safety by holding each other up and careful spotting. Listening to ideas and concerns. Trying out different options. Respecting different levels of participation.
What personal resources/strengths will I need	**How will I know that I've achieved my goal(s)**
Not giving up. Trying as hard as I can. Knowing my limits and sharing them with the group. Not being afraid to offer my ideas. Choosing a role in the activity for myself that I am OK with (Challenge of Choice). Pushing myself past my comfort zone.	The group has gotten as high as it could after three tries.

A less high thrill variation is to divide students into small groups and have them use their footwear to construct the tallest freestanding structure possible (see above). A time limit is set and precise measurements taken when the construction time is over.

Reflection: This is one of the best examples of a goal-setting activity that involves the need to maintain physical and emotional safety and Care for Self & Others. Setting and sharing goals and asking for help to accomplish goals can often cause students to feel vulnerable and embarrassed. What went into maintaining a feeling of safety during this activity? Did any students feel unsafe? How did this affect the level of commitment? Were students able to interrupt the activity and talk about their feelings? If not, why? These questions can be a place to begin as a suggested focus for reflection.

Cross Categories: Be Here, Be Safe, Care for Self & Others

The Activity: Moonball   Time: 30 minutes

Materials: Medium size beach ball(s)   Difficulty: 1

How you do it:

> This is a perennial favorite with most groups. The props and objectives are simple. Keep a ball of one description or another floating above the heads of the group for as many taps as possible (keeping in mind the numerous Olympic moonball records that have been set and broken). The only starting rule is that no person can tap the ball more than once without an intervening tapper hitting it. An urgency to keep the ball up develops, particularly as the number of successful taps begins to rise. There is also the uniquely distinct group sigh when a Moonball prematurely returns to

Earth. There is a bevy of ball variations to be had. Name the ball to be symbolic of something related to the group process, such as the Full Value Goal Setting Ball, then label it (using strips of masking tape) with positive behaviors related to setting goals, as suggested by students. Students have to work to keep them protected off the ground. Ask students to think about what it takes to make that happen. Get more than one ball going at once. Play traveling Moonball by setting a distant finish line as the group's objective. Have students alternate hands on each hit, or use their feet. As with most of these activities, the possibilities are endless.

If you have offered students planning time before beginning, this is a wonderful activity for the use of SMART Goals as a tool:

- Specific: What is the group goal for Moonball, and can it be stated clearly? Are students aware that the goal can be changed depending on the experience and that it is essential to say the goal without equivocation (keep <u>or</u> out of the goal statement)?

- Measurable: With Moonball this is easy. However, students will need to commit to honest reporting of double-taps to adhere to the rules of the game.

- Achievable: This connects back to specificity. For example, the group might set a goal of 100 consecutive taps but find, after many attempts and reformulated plans, that this number is unrealistic.

- Relevant: This component has to do with ensuring that the intention of any goal is to have a positive outcome and, further, that it has value to the person setting it.

- Time-bound: In Moonball, time can be an added element of the goal. Does the group want to complete 100 taps without time constraints or within ten minutes? The group's decision will dramatically affect planning and pacing.

<u>Reflection</u>: Focus on each SMART Goal element after the activity time is over. How realistic was the goal set by the group? Was the demonstrated commitment during the activity commensurate with the initially stated relevance? Was there a need to reformulate any elements of the SMART Goal plan? Going through this process using an actual activity helps students to visualize how this might work for them when developing their own SMART Goal(s).

Cross Categories: Be Here, Be Safe, Be Honest

The Activity: Phil Le Basquette (Fill the Basket)   Time: 45 minutes

Materials: A bunch of Whiffle or foam balls, 5-gallon bucket, 100-foot rope for boundary marker (clothesline is fine), 4 foam blocks or small carpet squares, masking tape, markers

Difficulty: 2

How you do it:

Fill the Basket involves throwing several balls into one container without being able to get close to it. The name and scenario for this activity relate back to a historical drama. Phillipe Le Basquette was a French Canadian. During the diaspora of the French from Nova Scotia (they were expelled by the English - the poem Evangeline by Longfellow commemorates the tragic event), Phillipe taught his people how to survive by setting a goal and then working continuously to achieve it. They soon spread into the Louisiana area, where they developed Cajun (Acadian) cooking and music. None of this would have happened without the foresight and leadership of Phillipe Le Basquette and his unique goal-setting work.

Drawing on those origins, this activity is often presented with a metaphor focused on goal setting. Students are encouraged to identify a goal and connect the goal to the balls that must be thrown into the container (sometimes the goals are written on tape and attached to the balls – be aware that if you use foam balls, the tape may pull the foam apart over time). If the balls have been aptly taped and goaled, the activity can be reflected on in connection to the goal work (sharing of goals, support for goal work, necessary resources, goal partnerships).

Form a large circle with the boundary marker. Place the container in the middle of the circle. Make the circle as large as necessary to provide a challenge for the group. The circle may need to be larger or smaller depending on the size of the bucket and the throwing skills of the students. Place all the balls on the outside of the circle boundary. Ask students to stand around the outside of the circle.

Each person is issued a ball. Then have the group pair up. Ask each person to generate a goal they are working on or want to begin. Give the pairs ten minutes to talk, five for one, five for the other. At the end of the time, ask them to reduce the goal language to three words or fewer. Then, place the goal on the ball: One person, one ball, and one goal. At the beginning of Filling the Basket, you might share that for Phil Le Basquette goal setting was a survival skill and helped his people prosper. It was true in his day; it is true today.

Here are the rules:

- The goal is to throw all the balls into the container in the middle of the circle in the shortest possible time.

- At no time may anyone touch the ground inside the boundary marker or the boundary itself.

- Any balls that do not make it into the container must be retrieved and thrown again until they are in the container.

- To retrieve a ball on the ground inside the circle, the group may use the foam blocks or another ball to knock the stuck ball close enough to the edge to be retrieved. Or a person may lean into the circle to grab a ball - without touching the ground. Students can offer counter-balance support when someone leans in to get a ball.

- The foam blocks or carpet squares can also be used as stepping stones (i.e., students can walk into the center of the circle if they stay on the blocks or squares without touching the floor). Students must be in constant contact with the blocks while inside the circle, or they are lost. Objects may not be thrown into the bucket while someone is inside the circle.

- If anyone touches the ground inside the circle or the boundary rope, three balls must be removed from the container and thrown again.

- The timing starts when the first ball is thrown. It stops when the last ball is in the container.

- The group may have several rounds to achieve its best performance.

- No other items may be used to assist in either throwing balls into the container or retrieving balls from inside the circle.

The larger the circle boundary, the more complex the challenge becomes. The distance from the edge of the circle to the container should prevent any group member from leaning in and dropping the balls into the container. Using a smaller container also increases the challenge. Be sure the container can hold all the balls. Adding other objects (rubber chickens, fleece balls, bean bag animals, etc.) can inject both humor and more challenge.

Allowing the group to use the foam blocks or carpet squares as stepping stones provides a safe method for retrieving objects. However, this option may not always be necessary or appropriate depending on the group's skills. If people cannot use them, they may have to make decisions about intentionally touching the floor to retrieve an object, knowing it will also cause them to have to re-throw three other objects.

Another method for setting up this activity is to give a specified time limit. The goal is to see how many objects the group can get into the bucket before time runs out. This option allows for the group to experience success no matter how many objects are in or out of the bucket at the end.

Reflection: During this reflection ask student pairs what their goal-setting process was like.

- Did they set goals together or work independently?

- Were any impediments to the goal identified? What were they?

- What goal-setting strategy did they use, and why was it selected?

- How did the pairs interact with the larger group? Was that important in solving the problem? If so, why?

Ask them to briefly review each element of their goal-setting process (i.e., state the goal, what were they willing to personally do to assure success, what did they need from others, and how did they measure success).

Cross Categories: Be Here, Let Go & Move On

The Activity: Pipeline Time: 45 minutes

Materials: See description below Difficulty: 3

How you do it:
    If you've ever played the game Mousetrap or been interested in Rube Goldberg devices, this will become a favorite activity. Some construction is required, as well as a short list of supplies. Take a trip to the local plumbing supply, hardware store, or lumber yard and purchase two, eight to ten-foot sections of white PVC water pipe. 1¼ inch diameter pipe should do nicely.

Now, find a friend who owns a table saw and have the pipe ripped lengthwise into two pieces. This will leave you with four lengths of track that objects can be rolled down. Using a hacksaw cut these tracks into smaller lengths of various sizes, the smallest being a foot in length, the largest, two feet.

Prefabricated pipeline kits can also be purchased at Training Wheels, a go-to company for all sorts of experiential learning equipment, including our Full Value Activity Bag, containing most of the materials and props listed in this text that you may not want to find or make on your own.

Now get yourself a bag of nicely colored regulation size marbles (ones that will fit in your tracks), and you are ready to play Pipeline. Starting from one end, the generic objective is for the group to move a set of marbles, two being a nice challenge to begin with, from one place to another, using the pipe tracks to get them there. <u>The marbles must always be in motion</u>. Students may move the tracks to get them in position, but once a marble enters a track section, it (the track section) must be held stationary until the marble exits onto the next track. The more marbles in the Pipeline, the more difficult the challenge. Other rolling objects can be used to slow down the action, such as golf or small rubber bouncy balls. Chances for success are increased if students are encouraged to take some time for planning before beginning this activity. On the other hand, if they wish to just launch into it, that will also yield some excellent experiential outcomes.

<u>Reflection:</u> Depending on how the purpose of this activity is co-created with students or framed by the teacher, many different elements of goal setting can be discussed. For this reflection, let's focus on the need to make an intense individual and group commitment to be successful. If we were looking at the 4 Square model, this would fall under "What will I need from my classmates" and "What personal resources/strengths will I need." If using WOOP, the focus might be on "What is your main inner obstacle?" A SMART Goal focus would be on the sections Achievable and Relevant. Pipeline will not work if everyone is not fully committed to being where they need to be to move the ball(s) forward. This is both an individual and group commitment. Keeping an individual marble or ball rolling in your pipe section requires a total personal commitment.

Cross Categories: Let go & Move

The Activity: Star Gate   Time: 45 minutes

Materials: Length of 1/8 inch bungee cord   Difficulty: 2
or a Hula Hoop (or both)

How you do it:

There is no question that the whole class will be involved while doing Star Gate. That is one of its major appeals, that, and its portability. Star Gate can be used almost everywhere. All you need is a space ample enough for your group to stand in a circle and stretch a bungee (tied into a circle), to such a degree that the largest person in the group can go through it without touching. Going through, incidentally, means entirely over the body, not simply stepping into and then out of it.

Here are the rules:

- Each person holding the Star Gate must remain physically in contact with the rest of the group via at least one other person. The cord holders must be in contact with both the group and the cord.

- There can be as many cord holders as you would like. However, the person going through the cord cannot touch it. In terms of difficulty, you can decide whether hands are part of the cord (i.e., if the person passing through touches a hand holding the cord, the whole group needs to start over). You can also decide about the penalty for touching: that person goes back through, or the group starts over.

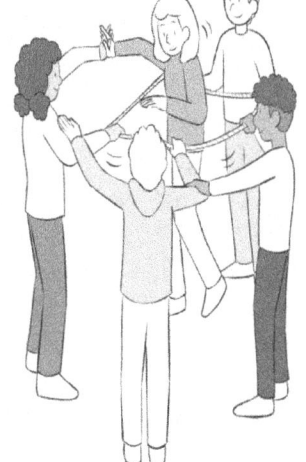

- Each cord holder can only hold the Star Gate with one hand. This rule can also be adjusted according to the needs and abilities of the group.

- Subsequent rounds can be played by asking the group to set time goals.

Critical to the activity is how long the bungee is. If it is too short, the activity becomes impossible. If too long, the challenge is limited. Gather several lengths of bungee, and then you'll be ready for small, medium, and large size groups. Hardware stores carry bungee cord for fastening tarps to cars and boats, etc. 1/8 inch will work just fine. The knot is the difficult part.

The best choice is a triple fisherman (or barrel, or stopper, or jam, or lover's) knot. What is a fisherman's knot, you may ask? It is two configurations exactly the same that, once tied, can be pulled tight into each other. The harder the pull, the tighter the knot becomes. Overlap the ends of the cord, and make certain that there is a foot of working cord at each end.

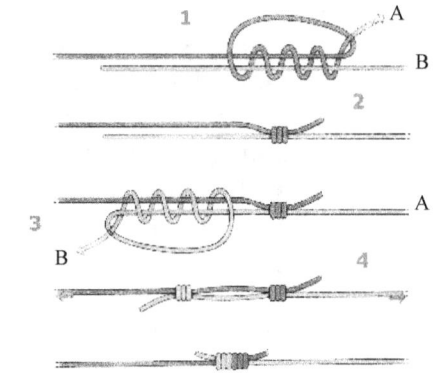

1. Wrap end A around B loosely, three times.

2. Take the end of A and bring it back along the wrap, and tuck it completely under that wrap. After the tuck under its own wrap, it must come out facing in the same direction it was in originally (that is, in the opposite direction of B). You will need to have approximately four to five inches remaining. The wrap you have constructed with A around B should slide loosely over the B end.

3. Turn the whole configuration 180 degrees. Cord end A should face in the opposite direction from where it faced when you first started.

4. Next, take cord end B and wrap it around A in the same manner. Now, you have the same knot tied in the same way on both ends of your rope. And, you have a perfect circle in the rope.

5. Finally, pull the two knots together so that they jam, or wed. Do not pull the knots together before you have checked out the size of the bungee circle you have created. You may need to adjust the knots to make them smaller or larger.

A simpler version (no knots to be tied) of Star Gate can be practiced using a Hula Hoop. Once accomplished, a group can come back and try the Bungee Challenge version.

Reflection: Star Gate offers similar opportunities to many of the other activities in terms of reflection. A unique aspect, similar to the Electric Fence, is the requirement that students stay connected throughout the activity. Among other reflection topics, this can highlight the importance of focusing on a goal and asking for help as an element of goal achievement. Invariably, contact between students holding the bungee cord or Hula Hoop will break. Some processing questions for students:

- What strategies did you use to successfully get through the Star Gate without touching?

- What did you need from the Gate holders? How did they support your success?

- For those of you who were able to maintain contact, what did it take?

- If you lost contact with a classmate, what were some of the distractions?

- What positive behaviors can we add to our Full Value Commitment?

- What distractors do we need to be mindful of?

Cross Categories: Be Here, Be Safe, Be Honest, Care for Self & Others, Let Go & Move On

---

The Activity: Team A Vs Team B   Time: 30 minutes

Materials: 2 objects of your choice for passing   Difficulty: 2-3

How you do it:

Healthy competition can be a good thing, except when it goes against a group working together as a unit to achieve a common goal. Here is a way to get a group to look at the negative impact of competition when trying to keep all of their oars in the water rowing with synchronicity.

Grab a fleece ball (or an old sneaker) and circle up your students. Ask them, while being timed, to pass the fleece ball from person to person around the circle. After establishing a speed benchmark, have them attempt a faster and faster time. Once they have reached an Olympic number, explain that you will divide them up into two teams, A and B. Team A will continue to pass the ball in a clockwise direction, while Team B will try to beat their time in a counterclockwise direction. Now it's time to really heat up the competition.

Get two fleece balls (or two other objects) going at the same time in opposite directions. Where they cross always provides a delicious moment of confusion. Now wait, you say, that's ridiculous, it is one and the same team. It seems implausible, but the singular group does start to compete with itself, sometimes dissing the other team even as it realizes on another level the absurdity of the competition. Another interesting variation is passing first names at high velocity first clockwise (Team A), counterclockwise (Team B), then in both directions simultaneously. Try it, playing your presentation as straight as possible. You won't believe how people get sucked into the competition.

Reflection: This activity is a metaphor for individuals and groups working at cross-purposes while stating that they are working toward the same goal. Covert competition and sabotage can be witnessed in any classroom or school activity. This activity can be used to demonstrate how pointless competition can become, particularly if everyone is actually on the same team. Labeling both positive and distracting behaviors always contributes to the formation or tweaking of the class Full Value Commitment.

Cross Categories: Be Here

The Activity: The Flying V   Time: 20 minutes

Difficulty: 2

How you do it:

There is an exquisite Joni Mitchell song called *Urge for Going* released initially on the back of the single Big Yellow Taxi until recently only to be found in England. There is one verse particularly evocative verse. The winter is coming in, and she sings, "See the geese in chevron flight, laughing and a racing on before the snow. They get the urge for going, and I guess they have to go."

And so, it can be said for goal setting, as our urge or instinct to experience a more fulfilled life pushes us forward. The title and demands of this activity speak to the intensity of the commitment involved in goal attainment, and the planning and pitfalls that one encounters along the way.

Begin by posting the students' goals and behavioral norms on a tree or other stationary object some sixty yards from the group. The group may eyeball the route from their position, but not conduct a survey walk to their goals. Have them shut their eyes and begin to navigate toward their destination. They may hold hands or use buddy ropes, as a variation. Along the way, the group may ask three agreed upon questions of their teacher regarding the journey. Interestingly, the group quite naturally moves into the shape of a chevron, with one leader guiding the flock. The activity ends when the group agrees that they have reached their destination, which may or may not be the case.

Reflection: Once the exact destination has been reached (or not), the group can reflect on what it took to get there and how the work they did together applies to the goal-setting process. How did the group's questions help or hinder progress? Were the posted behavioral norms used during the journey? What distractors emerged? How does a journey involving unknowns connect to setting, working toward, and achieving goals?

Cross Categories: Be Here, Be Safe, Be Honest, Care for Self & Others

---

The Activity: Traffic Jam Time: 60 minutes +

Materials: Paper plates to use as spot markers, masking tape Difficulty: 3
to hold down the plates, or rubber spot markers
that the physical education teacher is sure to have,
small pads and pencils

How you do it:

This activity presents with an innocent simplicity that can devolve into frustrating complexity. Lay out the plates or rubber markers in a line with one more marker than there are students in the class. Find or select twelve volunteers (any even number will do, between eight and twelve students). Divide this group in half, facing each other, standing on spot markers, with the empty spot marker between them. The object is for students to change places using a set of legal moves to pass each other. Successful completion will result in both groups facing away from each other with an empty spot marker in the middle. While engaged in figuring out the correct sequence of moves, the rest of the class will be acting as traffic officers, carefully observing and recording what is occurring within the Traffic Jam.

Here are the rules:

- You may step onto an empty spot marker in front of you.

- You may go forward and around a person if there is an empty spot marker in front of them.

- You may not go backward.

How might this activity help a class of students struggling to work cooperatively toward a common goal?

The introduction might go something like this:

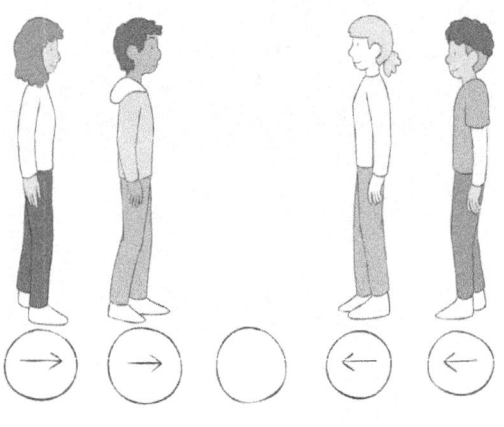

"We seem to be having difficulty working together in groups on projects in class. Although your teacher is obviously brilliant, I am still having a hard time understanding what is getting in the way of you working together. So, I thought we could do an activity to see if we can figure out what we need to work on to improve our group performance. The activity is called Traffic Jam. The reason I picked this is that sometimes working together can feel like a four-lane highway with cars just zipping along, no problem, and sometimes working together can feel like New York City at rush hour, with all of the traffic lights broken. Ever been stuck in a traffic jam? (The class responds with numerous horror stories). Well, good, then you know what I'm talking about. The object of this activity is for two groups of people to change places with each other by using the spot markers in a row in front of them. There are certain rules for movement (you go over the rules). Meanwhile, the rest of the class will be traffic officers. I would like you to write down on your ticket pads each time something happens that prevents the group from solving the problem. What are some things that might happen to interfere with the traffic moving right along? (Prompt students to offer examples that begin to get them thinking about behavior and the connection to working together). OK now, let's get started."

Reflection: Predictably, the task can become stressful and even unsolved. During the group's post activity reflection all kinds of negatives will come spilling out. You must model appropriate feedback and control the flow of comments so that the group does not deteriorate into apportioning blame. Out of this dialogue will emerge the already identified distractors, and a series of positive operating behaviors.

The flip side of the negatives is reviewed:

- If not listening was a problem, what might be a good behavior for groups to work better?

- If impatience were a problem, what might be a good behavior for groups to work better?

- If not everybody participating was a problem, what might be good behaviors for groups to work better?

Why use an activity, given the dynamics of an uncooperative group that will often lead to conflicts? Two reasons are offered:

1. If the focus is on provoking negative behaviors typical of the group, a frustrating activity will accomplish that. Forget about the outcome (they didn't solve it) and focus on the process (they were really on each other during the entire activity).

2. The use of paradox is a potent tool in experiential learning. Introducing an activity that provokes some conflict allows students to develop insight into the necessary steps to complete it the next time around. There can then be transference to the classroom setting.

Cross Categories: Be Here, Be Safe, Be Honest, Let Go & Move On

---

The Activity: Warp Speed Time: 30-45 minutes

Materials: Soft throwable objects (fleece balls) Difficulty: 1-4

How you do it:

Warp Speed builds off of Group Juggling skills. With a similar structure, we tap into the juggling magic of moving balls around within a set pattern. But we are no longer simply moving the balls, making certain that none hit the ground. With Warp Speed we are adding the element of time. The skill element of throwing and catching is moved into the realm of how fast we can do it. The relaxed atmosphere of balls flying about in a pattern is replaced by the tension of goal setting and problem solving. Best results come from a group of ten to fifteen participants.

Limit the balls to four while doing Warp Speed, because it makes the activity more doable. Try to utilize balls of a different size, color, and shape, although that is not necessary.
Here are the rules:

- The balls must go around in sequence, meaning that they cannot be placed in a hat or scarf and passed as a bunch.

- Each ball must leave and arrive as a discrete entity.

- No ball can touch the ground.

- All students must come in contact with each ball.

- Balls cannot be passed through an external object.

- These rules can be modified when necessary for physically challenged students. For example, balls can be rolled across a table for those unable to throw or catch.

Out of the box brainstorming is the hope of this activity. Because of the patterned throwing and catching sequence students start with, only a certain amount of speed can initially be achieved. However, nothing in the rules precludes students from changing the location of throwers and catchers, and forming chutes or cylinders out of their arms and hands, increasing the speed of completion dramatically. We've actually seen it done in 4 seconds!

Reflection: The discussion around this activity can focus on the press of time. How does the rule of completing the throwing and catching pattern as quickly as possible change the dynamics of the group? Are shortcuts taken? Are rules more easily violated? Do leaders become more strident and demanding? Is there an increase in stress, and how does that affect performance? The processing of this activity will inform the work that students do together on timed tasks during their school day. It will lead to defining behaviors that will support more effective functioning, as part of developing a of a Full Value Commitment.

Cross Categories: Be Here, Be Honest

CHAPTER 10

LET GO & MOVE ON

Of all the Full Values, Let Go & Move On tends to cause adults to wince when introduced. While students, particularly in the earlier grades, are often able to dust themselves off and re-friend their peers, this appears to be more difficult as we age. Older students and adults tend to hold onto unpleasant interactions and experiences and find it difficult to forgive and forget, or at the very least come to terms with the conflict and find ways to continue to engage with the person who offended them. Conflicts in the classroom, playground, lunchroom, and on the bus are a predictable part of life. This is also the case at home, in the community, and in the workplace. Developing adaptive skills to reconcile and resolve differences, agree to disagree, and possibly forgive are essential for healthy, resilient functioning. It is knowing when and when not to own responsibility for interactions. The following activities allow students to develop the behavioral norms associated with this Full Value and practice these skills across settings.

Outcomes of Let Go & Move On

- Revenge Versus Reconciliation
- Accepting Complexity
- Resiliency
- Accepting Difference
- Accepting Unenforceable Rules

ACTIVITIES

Activity Difficulty Scale

1 (Easy) ------- 2 (A bit harder) -------- 3 (Pretty complicated) --------- 4 (Difficult)

The Activity: Alligator River Time: 60 minutes

Difficulty: 2

How you do it:

Students will be read a story that asks them to rank the behavioral choices of characters interacting around a problem that needs to be solved. They will then rank the characters based on likability. Ranking can be done individually or in small groups. Where possible, a list should be kept of what behaviors contributed to each ranking.

The Story: Once there was a girl named Abigail who cared about a boy named Gregory. Gregory had an unfortunate accident when he fell and broke his glasses. Abigail, being a true friend, volunteered to take his glasses to be repaired. But the repair shop was across the river, and during a flash flood, the bridge was washed away. Poor Gregory could see nothing without his glasses, so Abigail was desperate to get across the river to the repair shop so she could get his glasses fixed.

While she was standing forlornly on the bank of the river, holding the broken glasses in her hand, a boy named Sinbad came by in his rowboat. She asked Sinbad if he would take her across the river. Sinbad agreed to take her across on the condition that while she was having the glasses repaired, she would go to a nearby store and steal a candy bar that he had wanted to have but didn't have any money to buy. Abigail refused to do this and went to a friend named Ivan, who also had a boat.

When Abigail told Ivan her problem, he said he was too busy to help her out and didn't want to be involved. Abigail, feeling she had no other choice, went back to Sinbad and told him she would agree to his plan.

When Abigail returned with the repaired glasses to Gregory, she told him what she had to do. Gregory was furious at what she had done and told her he never wanted to see her again.

Abigail, sad and upset, went to Slug with her tale of woe. Slug, feeling so sorry for Abigail, promised her he would get even with Gregory. Slug and Abigail went to the school playground where Gregory was playing ball with some of his friends. Abigail watched happily and was laughing while Slug took the glasses from Gregory and broke them again.

Once the ranking sheets are completed (requiring consensus in the small group), the teacher can stop there or consider having the smaller groups reach a whole class ranking consensus. Whether it is in small groups or during the entire class discussion, take careful note of how students arrive at an agreement.

<u>Alligator River Ranking Sheet</u>
(Form available in Chapter 16, Printable Materials)

1 = Person you like the most
5 = Person you like the least

1. _____

2. _____

3. _____

4. _____

5. _____

Reflection: In a group setting this activity generates a good deal of emotional involvement where students may attempt to attack and criticize each other's rankings. This creates an opportunity for students to become aware of their values and appreciate that when someone won't budge from their position(s), it becomes difficult to Let Go & Move On. Reflection questions should be framed to help students focus on self-control and how they will move forward to reach compromise.

Cross Categories: Be Honest, Care for Self & Others

The Activity: Balance Broom   Time: 30 minutes

Materials: Whisk broom with long wooden handle   Difficulty: 3 (Good spotting is essential)

How you do it:

To Let Go & Move On sometimes means acceptance of the loss of control of a situation. This can be made more bearable if there is a trusted support system around you. The Balance Broom offers this opportunity. Choose a soft grassy area or, if indoors, use gym mats. Reviewing spotting from a technical and commitment perspective is essential before starting this activity. Frontloading the activity by asking students to identify an experience where they felt a loss of control, due to the behavior of self or others, would be helpful during reflection time.

After going over spotting responsibilities, have students form into a tight circle. Ask for a student volunteer. Explain to the volunteer that they will hold the broom straight up above their head and spin rapidly 360 degrees while staring at the thatch, or if you are a balance broom purist, direct the volunteer to place the handle on top of their forehead and spin around the broom. Either technique will produce the necessary vertigo. Ask the circled-up students to count, never to exceed fifteen spins. After the turning is complete, the student should place (or throw) the broom on the ground and attempt to step over it. The dizziness that spinning around the broom creates makes this an almost impossible task. The student volunteer will usually stumble over the broom and end up in the arms of a group member who will break their fall.

Reflection: This can focus on how it felt to lose control (as a metaphor for dealing with a situation where people behave in ways that can be unkind) and how it felt to be supported by the circle of students. Students who serve as catchers will have the experience of protecting their peers from a fall. This is also worthy of reflection.

Some safety notes: This is a challenging activity to spot due to the unpredictable movements of the spinner, whose balance center is experiencing a major meltdown. The group members must have the emotional commitment, physical capability, and sufficient training to provide for a safe catch. The spotting goal is not to keep the student upright but to break the fall. For some people spinning is a really bad idea; those prone to vertigo or who have other problems related to balance. Check in with the group (and the school nurse) on this and have those who cannot tolerate spinning act in a spotting or observational capacity. Those with a history of seizure activity should only participate as spotters.

Cross Categories: Be Safe, Care for Self & Others

The Activity: Bridge-It Time: 2 hours (two class periods)

Materials: An ample quantity of paper cups, tongue depressors, Popsicle Sticks, masking tape, glue, Legos, rubber bands, wine corks, straws (or any other construction material that you have lying around), two tape measures, paper and pencils, large card table, teacher made language sheets (See Chapter 16 for printable sample), a vertical shield to prevent seeing each group's construction work before a mutual decision that the work is completed, and the bridge is revealed.

Difficulty: 3-4

How you do it:
> This activity aims for two groups of students to construct a bridge out of provided materials that look exactly the same, including size, shape, color, and position. The major wrinkle is that each group constructs half of the bridge behind a barrier without seeing what is happening on the other side. Ideally when the two halves of the bridge are revealed they will meet in precisely the same place.
>
> Depending on the size of the class, one or two bridges will be built. Construction groups for one bridge should be no larger than 16 students.
>
> - All materials provided must be used and be visible in the final design and construction. Only provided materials can be used.

- During planning and building time segments, respective teams are not to communicate with each other.

- Contact (communication) between the teams may only occur during negotiation sessions. A new negotiator is appointed for each session.

- During negotiation sessions only designated team negotiators may communicate with each other. Other team members may attend the negotiation sessions, but they are not allowed to share in any way with each other or between teams.

- Negotiators must use their native language (assigned by the teacher, see group language sheet) during sessions. However, any language may be used during individual planning and building sessions.

- Negotiators may not pass or show one another any written information during negotiation sessions.

- Promptness in attending negotiation sessions is essential as the clock starts at the time designated by the teacher.

Rules:

- Give each team a set of the same building materials.

- Decide what the penalties will be for any rule infractions. Usually, a time reduction for a particular building or negotiation session works well.

- Language or gestures you create for the language sheets (see the sample below) present a great opportunity for creativity and good comedy, if not confusion in the communication process. However, if not sure of what is acceptable to your group, it is better to err on the conservative side.

- If tangible success is important for the group, and it is clear that the bridge sections are not alike, consider offering an extended but final negotiation session. Usually, the negotiators who have met in the last talking session continue in this role. This extended offer is a chance for the groups to review their confidence in the project thus far, and helps them determine what needs doing to complete the project.

- Because this initiative presents significant difficulty and has so many opportunities for rule changes and variations, the teacher should set clear rules and expectations based upon observations of group and individual behaviors and what is important to the group.

- During the individual planning and building sessions, try to visit the respective teams to observe the interactions. This will help to guide the conversation during reflection time.

- Using different languages/gestures for negotiators during negotiations creates humorous interactions but makes the communication process more difficult. Generally, using a new language for five to six different materials adds sufficient difficulty.

- Physical setting up of spaces requires that you have designated areas where teams can go for their respective planning and building sessions. Teams should not be able to see each other or their projects. You should also have a designated negotiation area (tables, chairs, and maybe flowers included) where negotiators and their peers can come. This area should be out of visual range of the planning and building sites.

Group Language – Team A	
Words (not spoken)	Words, Sounds, Gestures Used
Corks	Pull right ear three times
Bottom	Top
Glue	Shake hands with negotiating partner
High	Laugh
Legos	Clap twice
Masking tape	Stick your tongue out at negotiating partner
No	Nod and say "yes"
Paper cups	Quack like a duck
Rubber bands	Hold up five fingers
Straws	Big smile at negotiating partner
Tongue Depressors/Popsicle Sticks	Pull left ear three times
Under	Side
Yes	Say "maybe"
Group Language – Team B	
Corks	Hold up ten fingers
Glue	Blink slowly three times
How Many	Banana
Legos	Stand and sit twice
Masking tape	Tap forehead three times slowly
No	Say "I don't know"
Paper cups	Stomp feet
Parallel	Criss-Cross Arms
Rubber bands	Flap arms like a bird

Straws	Pull right ear three times
Tongue Depressors/Popsicle Sticks	Sing the first line of Twinkle Star
Wide	Tape
Yes	Nod and say "no"

Bridge-It Sample Time Frames (in minutes): (Written on a large Post-it or easel)

- Initial small team planning & building session   10
- Negotiation session #1:   8
- Planning & building session #2:   8
- Negotiation session #2:   7
- Planning & building session #3:   7
- Negotiation session #3:   6
- Planning & building session #4:   5
- Negotiation session #4:   5
- Planning & building session #5:   4
- Negotiation session #5:   4
- Final planning & building session: 10
- Show and tell session: (Bridges Revealed!)   10

Reflection: The nature of this activity lends itself to within group and between-group friction as students sort out the language issues and how that will affect their part of the bridge construction. Compromise and consensus must be reached relatively quickly, given the time deadlines for negotiation and building sessions.

Some questions might include:

- What process did you use to reach consensus on language and construction issues?

- How did it feel to let go of a specific position?

- Was it challenging to balance out personal needs/positions and group needs?

- How did the time constraints affect your decision-making, particularly in the area of coming to consensus?

- How did the different languages contribute to misunderstandings between groups?

- Which role did you enjoy the most, negotiator, builder, etc.?

- How did you manage your irritation when grappling with differing opinions?

- Did you check out of the process and, if so, why?

- What behavioral norms and distractors can you take away from this activity to contribute to the class Full Value Commitment?

Cross Categories: Be Here, Set Goals

The Activity: Change Up   Time: 40 minutes

Materials: Thirty colored index cards and a marker, stopwatch   Difficulty: 2

How you do it:

The task is to have students line up in numerical order as quickly as possible. Create thirty cards numbered one through thirty. Make sure that the numbers are not visible through the card backs. This preparation piece is very important.

- Do not show the students what is on the cards.

- Shuffle the cards.

- Give one card to each student. If you have fewer than thirty students, do not distribute the extra cards. Tell students not to look at their cards or to allow anyone else to peek.

- Tell the group that they must line up in order relative to what is on the cards.

- Yell "start" and start timing their performance.

- Give them three tries, and record the time of each attempt. Between each trial, they need to exchange cards with other group members at least three times. Each exchange must be with the card numbers face down. A mini reflection time can be offered to allow students to discuss how to improve their performance after each round.

- Change up! Ask group members to exchange cards once again. But this time, tell them that they must line up alphabetically by how each number is spelled (e.g., 1 = <u>o</u>ne, 2 = <u>t</u>wo).

A variation for more capable/older students is to have them complete the activity in total silence.

Reflection: The Change Up that takes place is embedded in the letting go of a previous and perfected ability to work together. Suddenly, even though the materials are the same, the task is different. The response of students to this change, and to change in general, is an important topic for post activity reflection.

Cross Categories: Be Here, Be Honest

The Activity: Cross the Line   Time: 1 – 10 minutes

Materials: 20-foot rope, stopwatch   Difficulty: 2-3

How you do it:

Lay a rope down on the ground/floor that is sufficiently long so that the number of students in each group can stand opposite one another. Divide the students into two groups, with each half of the group standing opposite the other. Group A students stand on their side of the rope (their homeland) facing people in Group B, and Group B students stand on their side of the rope (their homeland) facing Group A. Ask that each student face the person standing opposite them on the other side of the rope. An uneven number of students by one is fine.

At this point, make sure to have everyone's attention before you go further with the directions. Depending upon your leadership/facilitator style in focusing attention, you may add a whistle, bell, or gong, or simply employ your very best are we ready yet glare.

Before stating the goal take some time to remind students about behavioral norms and distractors connected to Be Safe in your Full Value Commitment and extract a solemn promise from all that they will exercise care with one another in this activity.

Explain to students that you will only be stating the goal of the activity once, and no questions from the group will be answered, whether it's for seeking further clarification or for any other reason. No time to check for understanding will be offered. You should, however, make sure they understand the directions. Remind students that once you have stated the goal the clock starts ticking for them to solve the problem.

Here is a suggested script:

- Rule # 1 is Attend to Safety. Everyone needs to promise without any fingers, legs, or eyes crossed that they absolutely will not hurt anyone else while trying to reach the goal. No fighting of any kind is allowed, etc. How well you dramatize the Be Safe norm tends to go a long way in moving students more deeply into their already established cultural mindset that this must be about competition.

- Explain that the rope boundary that separates the two homelands should be thought of as fixed and cannot be moved in any way.

- Explain that they are standing in their own country, separated from the other country by the boundary rope on the ground. In your explanation you should play up how their respective countries represent the best of everything. Life is good here, and their land is sacred ground. It has been thus for generations that their well-established culture is loved and cherished. Therefore, it must endure for future generations to enjoy and prosper. The main idea here is to convey that the land on their side of the rope needs to be preserved and protected.

- Then state the goal as follows: "The goal for the group on the left side of the rope is to get as many people who are standing opposite them onto their side of the rope. The goal for the group on the right side of the rope is to get as many people who are standing opposite them onto their side of the rope. OK, that's the goal… Ready, Set, Go!" Then start the stopwatch.

Generally, you can let students try to solve the problem for anywhere up to five to eight minutes, sometimes longer. It is important to allow enough time for students to act and react to the various behaviors employed to reach the goal, and to observe these behaviors. More often than not, you will witness a host of futile, non-productive actions that represent lose-win and lose-lose behaviors sprinkled with some more positive interactions. It is fascinating to note that while the goal of the activity is mutual and hence collaborative/cooperative behaviors work best, most participants infer that it is competitive and that to win requires that someone has to lose.

<u>Reflection</u>: If it does not naturally occur from posing the questions below, it is essential to connect how letting go and moving on from a preconceived competitive mindset can completely alter the dynamics of the activity. This discussion can lead to trying again with the reframed focus on how to accomplish the activity. Successful completion can simply be each group voluntarily switching places. The whole thing can be over in 10 seconds. Some questions to consider:

- What was your problem-solving process?

- Based upon what you heard as the goal & rules for the activity, what were your preconceived notions?

- What were the behaviors that got played out between you and the student(s) standing opposite you? How about between the two groups?

- Did anyone have a different view about a possible easier win/win solution to the problem? If yes, what did you try to do to have others accept your opinion? How did others react to your suggestion?

- Why do you think you quickly demonstrated more competitive, if not aggressive behaviors, to solve the problem?

Note: There may be a slim possibility that a student has participated in this activity before. Give that student the task of timing the event or recording observations.

Cross Categories: Be Here, Set Goals, Care for Self & Others

The Activity: Elbow Tag   Time: 35 minutes

Materials: Cones or a rope to designate boundaries   Difficulty: 1

How you do it:

This Activity is all about letting go and moving on, literally. Have students find a partner. Pairs then stand with linked arms in a large play area. Pairs do not move. Create a large circle with the rope or cones. Boundaries are established with the size determined by the age and capabilities of the group. A student will need to volunteer to be "it." They will tag one member of a pair, hooking their arm (see illustration). The far side of the pair must immediately let go and hook up with another pair. That far side of the pair then let's go and so on. Three people cannot stay linked together.

When the "it" person tags an unlinked student, that person becomes "it." The new "it" person must spin around once to give the previously "it" person a chance to find a pair to link to. The chasing activity takes place <u>outside the circle</u>, which keeps students from plunging across the circle or trying to get through the locked elbows of the participants. It is important to keep the action within three to five feet of the outside circumference of the circle, so that the chasing does not go all over the field or room. If one student proves to be faster and more elusive than the other, and if the pursuit is beginning to go on too long (the chased is not hooking up, but simply staying away from the chaser), then the teacher or selected student leader can yell "switch," whereby the roles reverse. The student being chased becomes the chaser.

Reflection:

- Was it difficult for you to leave the safety of your partner? Why?

- When you were tagged and became "it," what thoughts and feelings did you have?

- How is this game connected to your letting go and moving on experience?

Cross Categories: Be Safe, Be Honest

The Activity: Lost at Sea Time: 60 minutes

Materials: Paper, pencils Difficulty: 2-3

How you do it:

Asking any group of students to make choices provides ample opportunity for disagreements. That is the point of this activity. A quick Internet search will yield many different scenarios. We provide one for your use, but depending on the age group and sophistication of your students, it will be very easy to find another.

Everyone is together on a spacious boat sailing across the Atlantic Ocean. Somewhere between the coasts of North America and Spain, the wind suddenly stops blowing. As it is a lovely day at sea, everyone lies around sunbathing, confident that the wind will kick up again. After a day of tanning and drifting with no wind, the decision is made to fire up the diesel engine. There is enough fuel for one day of motoring. Unfortunately, the fuel runs out, and there is still no wind. The captain, who does not take outstanding care of his boat, neglected to fix his chronometer before leaving port. What items would be most important to have on hand for this emergency?

Divide students into small groups with paper and pencils for note taking. The task is to rank the following list of items in order of importance. They must completely agree on the order through consensus building and explain their reasoning to the whole class.

- Bottle of rum
- Can of gasoline
- Chocolate bars
- Emergency food
- Fishing rod
- Floating seat cushion

- Mosquito net
- Plastic sheet
- Radio
- Rope
- Sea chart
- Sextant
- Shark repellent
- Small mirror
- Water container

US Coast Guard priority list:

Mirror (for signaling), gasoline (can be lit on the water to attract help), water container (for collecting drinking water), emergency rations (basic food intake), plastic sheet (shelter and collect rainwater), chocolate bars (handy food supply), fishing rod (for catching fish and tent pole), rope (for tying down equipment), floating seat cushion (life preserver), shark repellant (protection when going in the water), bottle of rum (antiseptic), radio (most probably no one will hear you), sea chart (need working navigation equipment), mosquito netting (on the Atlantic Ocean?), sextant (need tables and working chronometer).

Reflection: Students typically have strong opinions during these kinds of scenarios. During reflection time, ask students to talk about the process they used to reach consensus and what kind of letting go was required of strongly held opinions.

Cross Categories: Set Goals

Activity name: The Luminaria Circle Time: 60 minutes
(best done after dark or in a darkened room)

Materials: Sand, small LED candles, brown lunch   Difficulty: 2-4
bag, markers, glue, sparkles, etc.

How you do it:

> Luminaria… The word conjures up images of fireflies, moon on water, the glowing orb of the magician. Luminarias are lanterns often set out in lines to light the path from one place to another. As the light is candle driven, the Luminarias dance in the wind, casting growing and receding flickers into the darkness. They are easy to make, requiring a brown lunch bag, a small votive candle, and a bit of sand to provide stability against the wind. How they are used is limited only by the teacher's imagination.

Using markers, watercolor paints, and decorative materials such as tinsel and stars, group members create symbolic representations of their letting go and moving on experience. Once created, the Luminarias are assembled by simply opening the bag, pouring in a sufficient amount of sand for stability, and placing the candle in the bottom center. Then the Luminarias are lighted!

Note: This activity may require a period for constructing Luminarias and a period for lighting and sharing.

Reflection: This activity is ripe for symbolism. As the light emanates from each Luminaria, ask students to describe the situation they let go of and the feelings associated with their experience. Also, prompt for key learning that occurred, which will help to resolve future concerns. This may require acceptance of the degree of personal control one does or does not have over the outcome.

Another way to frame this activity is the letting go and moving on from the group. Students invariably experience transition and separation issues at the end of the school year. Some may be leaving for other communities, and there is the possibility that scheduling and unique interests will result in separation within school during the following year. Luminarias can be used to depict these concerns as well as hopes for the future. The focus of reflection can then be on summing up the present and expressing thoughts and feelings about the future. Each group member sits just behind their candle, forming a circle of glowing memories, contemplation, and bright faces of hope. Each takes a turn sharing their representations, as the candles continue to burn brightly, illuminating the way forward from the group on the path to a fulfilling future.

Cross Categories: Be Honest, Set Goals: Luminarias can also represent individual, group, and spiral goals.

The Activity: Negotiations Square   Time: 30 minutes

Difficulty: 2-3

How you do it:

Explain to students that they will be dividing into four small groups. Each group will need to develop a gesture and sound to share when they come back together. Make sure the groups are well separated so they cannot overhear each other when developing their sound and gesture. Explain that the activity is successfully completed when all four groups make the same gesture and sound in unison. In the extremely unlikely event that all four groups produce the same sound and gesture during the first round, the activity starts again. During round one, each group takes a turn sharing their sound and gesture. Each sound and gesture should be practiced until learned by all groups. The groups go off and decide which gesture they will reveal, of the four they have learned. When they come back together on the count of three, all sounds and gestures are displayed simultaneously. If they match, the game is over. If not, all groups go off to choose again what sound and gesture they will use. Students may discuss, debate, and argue about their choice in their small group, but not speak to other groups. The next round occurs with a simultaneous presentation. This continues until all of the sounds and gestures are the same.

<u>Reflection:</u> Some questions to consider:

- Can you describe what your group considered/did in making the decisions you made?

- What did you and the groups need to do to reach the goal as efficiently as possible?

- To be successful some groups had to let go of their motion and sound. Can you describe what that process was like?

- What are the obstacles that get in our way and don't allow us to reach compromises to achieve win-win situations?

- What are the obstacles that get in your way and prevent you from reaching compromises?

- What might be a key learning we/you can take away from this activity and apply to our Full Value Commitment?

- What might be some things we can do as a class to reach compromises and win-win results?

Cross Categories: Be Here, Set Goals, Care for Self & Others

The Activity: Paradigm Shift Time: 20 minutes

Difficulty: 2

How you do it:

With the group standing in a circle, have members point their index fingers to the sky or to the ceiling. Then, have them draw a hypothetical circle above their head. The circle must be scribed in a clockwise manner, as they look up at it. The circle must also be horizontal, as if holding a plate over their head on the end of their finger. Then, slowly, they bring their finger (still drawing the circle in a horizontal clockwise manner) to a position where they are looking down at it. When their hand gets to waist height, ask them which direction their hand is going. Some students will get the perspective shift right away, while others will struggle with it. "How did that happen, that our fingers are all of a sudden going counterclockwise?"

Reflection: Recognizing a difference in perspective is central to letting go. It requires openness, a lack of defensiveness, flexibility, and, in some instances, empathy and compassion. This activity literally requires coming around to recognizing a different perspective. Reflection on what it takes to do that could be a focus of discussions with students.

Cross Categories: Be Here

The Activity: Personal Coat of Arms Time: 60 minutes

Materials: Poster paper, markers, crayons, pencils, cut out pictures, etc. Difficulty: 2

How you do it:

Provide students with an example of a personal coat of arms to help them understand the shape. Within the shield outline, have students draw a vertical and horizontal line to create four equally sized quadrants. This can be modeled or drawn for students.

On a whiteboard, post questions connected to Let Go & Move On. Examples might be:

- Think of an argument/disagreement you had with a friend or family member where you could not Let Go & Move On. What was it?

- Think of an argument/disagreement you had with a friend or family member where you could Let Go & Move On. What did you do?

- What is something you think you can do to Let Go & Move On in the future?

- What is something you think others can do to Let Go & Move On? Something that would make you happy.

Each quadrant can be used to respond to a question. Depending on the age of the group, Students can write, draw a representation of their response, or use cut out pictures.

Reflection: After completion, the coat of arms can be hung about the room for a gallery walk. Ask for volunteers to explain their coat of arms to the rest of the class. Three or four can be reviewed each day to spread out the experience. The whole class can contribute to finding words from each coat of arms that can be used within the Full Value Commitment.

Cross Categories: Set Goals

The Activity: Rearrange the Furniture Time: 60 minutes +

Materials: Sheets of newsprint, markers, pencils Difficulty: 2

How you do it:

> This extends the idea of co-creation into the physical space of the classroom. It is logical that students should have a voice in determining how their daily workspace is organized. Keeping in mind the guideline of control to empowerment, divide the class into small groups and, within certain design parameters, tell students that they will be submitting proposals for a classroom redesign that will be presented to the class and voted on by all students. Here are some of our suggested ground rules (you most certainly may want to add others). The following workspaces will be needed:
>
> - Individual, small group, and large group workspaces.
>
> - A clear visual line to whiteboards, SMART Board, etc.
>
> - Open paths to exits and windows.
>
> - Certain things in proximity (i.e., the teacher's desk and file cabinet).
>
> - A new space that has not existed before.

Give students an entire period to work on their design. Make sure they understand that small groups need to reach a unanimous consensus. Ask them to keep a log of their disagreements and how they were able to resolve them. After your review and edits, use another period for each group to present their plan. To make this a win-win experience, explain that the vote is to determine the order of rearranging, and that throughout the year each small group plan will be used.

Reflection: The letting go and moving on is the work students do to reach a compromise when constructing their small group plan, and what internal and external processes were used to do that. This can be the focus of the discussion.

Cross Categories: Be Here, Be Honest

The Activity: Red/Yellow/Green Time: 10 minutes

Difficulty: 2

How you do it:

> The activity starts with each student choosing a partner. When you call out,

"red" partners hold hands and form a bridge with their arms above their heads. When you call out, "yellow," students continue to hold hands and add jumping up and down together. When you call out, "green," the pairs separate and students must quickly find a new partner. If a new partner is not found within five seconds, unpaired students are out of the game.

Explain that the goal of the activity is for the entire group to ensure that as many students as possible should still be in the game at the end of ten minutes. This will incentivize finding a partner as quickly as possible, no matter what feelings you might have about being partnered with that person. Play successive rounds to improve performance.

Begin the activity at a leisurely pace for the first few rounds until students master the calls. Then speed up the tempo so that, in finding a partner, there is very little time to make a preferential choice.

<u>Reflection</u>: Partner choices will invariably cause some students to feel left out and marginalized initially. As the pace of the game quickens, and finding a partner is the only way to continue participation, unlikely pairings will occur out of necessity. There will be feelings associated with not being chosen, being paired with someone you don't have much of a relationship with, or being paired with someone you don't really like. Some questions to pose to students might include:

- What did it feel like to not be immediately selected by a partner?

- What did you do with those feelings to stay in the game?

- Did you choose not to partner with someone? Why?

- Did it help to have a group goal? Did that make choosing a specific partner less important? Why?

- How does this activity connect to Let Go & Move On? What can we take from this activity to add to our Full Value Commitment?

- What were some thoughts and feelings that got in the way of making a quick choice to improve the group's success?

Cross Categories: Be Here, Be Honest, Set Goals, Care for Self & Others

The Activity: Run – Shout, Knock Yourself Out

Time: 10 minutes

Difficulty: 1

How you do it:

This comes as close to a Primal Scream adventure experience as you can get. Line the class up at the end of a long, open field, preferably free of woodchuck holes. On your command have them run as far as they can while screaming as loud as possible <u>on one breath</u>. Once out of breath, the person stops. Aside from the cleansing quality of this activity, a weird Doppler effect occurs as the screamers recede into the distance. That's it!

Reflection: Students will have a different amount of lung capacity and stamina, which will determine how far they can go before running out of air. This will result in a range of behaviors from frustration to cheating (that quick sip of a second breath of air) to amusement. The focus of the conversation can be on how students felt about their performance (distance times yell) in comparison to their peers. What choices did students make around how they participated in this activity? How important was it to do well at any cost, and why?

Cross Categories: Be Here

The Activity: Stepping Stones

Time: 60 minutes

Materials: Fourteen rigid foam blocks or 12-inch x 12-inch carpet tiles that your local carpet store will surely donate, tape or rope for boundary markers

Difficulty: 2-3

How you do it:

This is a crossing activity, meaning that the purpose is to go over something to get to the other side. It is a great place to introduce a metaphor. For example, "Our class needs to get past all of the complaining that is going on. By doing this activity, by crossing safely over to the other side of the Poison Thought Pit, we will use some strategies and get ourselves free of complaints so that we can get our work done." A nice co-creation idea for this activity is to ask students to label each block with a behavioral norm from their Full Value Commitment that will assist in a successful crossing.

A crossing area is identified. Start and finish lines are laid out with tape or rope on the floor or the carpet. 6-inch x 10-inch Styrofoam blocks are made available, which are about a ½ inch thick. The distance between the start and finish needs to be roughly four feet per foam block (i.e., ten blocks for crossing forty feet of space between the start and finish lines). The blocks are resources for crossing; students must use the blocks for stepping across the Poison Thought Pit. They cannot step on or touch the floor. All the blocks are stacked on the beginning side of the pit. All students crossing the pit must maintain physical contact with the blocks at all times. If physical contact is lost with a block, it gets taken away. Blocks can be passed to other participants, but they cannot be thrown. If a student touches the floor, they must go back to the beginning.

Reflection: There are lots of letting go and moving on outcomes in this activity. If students do not carefully attend to maintaining contact with blocks and each other, the stepping stones are taken away. Some questions for students to consider:

- When a stepping stone was taken away because you lost attention, what thoughts and feelings went through your head? Did you feel amused, guilty, unconcerned, responsible, angry, or anxious? Why?

- How did you feel other members of the group reacted to the loss of the stepping stones?

- Did the reactions to losing the stones help or hinder the progress of the group? Why?

- How did letting go and moving on help the group's journey?

- How did this activity connect to conflicts that you have had with classmates that will help you resolve those conflicts and maintain a relationship?

Cross Categories: Be Here, Be Safe, Set Goals, Care for Self & Others

The Activity: Turning Over a New Leaf   Time: 60 minutes

Materials: 4-foot x 8-foot tarpaulin (size of the tarp may be varied   Difficulty: 2
to adjust to different size groups or level of difficulty)

How you do it:

The goal is to completely flip over a tarpaulin without students stepping off and touching the floor. Before beginning, offer the group time to co-create a metaphor for the experience and to plan. A suggested prompt is to ask students to describe a conflict that occurred with a peer or sibling left unresolved. Reduced to a few words like "not taking turns, cutting in line," or "copying on a test," the issue(s) are written on masking tape and stuck to the bottom of the tarp before setting off on the journey. Begin with all students standing on the top of the tarp together. As students progress through the activity, have them think about how the work of turning over the tarp (and a new leaf) connects to resolving differences and letting go of the negative feelings associated with the issue(s). The level of difficulty can be varied by:

- Timing the task

- Setting difficult performance standards (e.g., one person touches the ground and the tarp is set back up in its original position)

- Varying the size of the tarp

Reflection: The obvious metaphor is that the expression "turning over a new leaf" is directly related to repairing the damage that a difficult interaction can cause between people. It means starting again and looking at things a bit differently. The framing of this activity (which should connect directly to reflection) could involve defining what the disagreement is, brainstorming what might help to address the conflict (in terms of a change in thinking, feeling, behavior), and practicing those strategies. This will lead to a conversation about how deliberately identifying strategies to resolve conflicts can lead to a successful resolution. It will also provide behaviors and perhaps new distractors to consider for the classroom Full Value Commitment.

Cross Categories: Be Here, Set Goals (Also see application to academic content areas in Chapter 12)

Activity: Zoom and Re-Zoom   Time: 1 hour+

Materials: Zoom/Re-Zoom images may be   Difficulty: 2
purchased from Flaghouse.com

How you do it:

This activity is based on the picture books *Zoom* and *Re-Zoom* by Istvan Banyai (1995).[65] The goal is to put the images into the correct sequential order.

Set Up

- Randomly put aside eight images (these will be placed face down on the ground in the middle of the group after all other images have been distributed).

- Randomly distribute the remaining images to the participants. Depending on group size, some students may get more than one image. Inform students that they may look at only their image(s) but may not look at other students' images.

- Instruct students to study their image(s). They may talk about their image(s) as much as they'd like, but cannot display them until the entire group agrees that the images are in the correct sequential order.

- Place the eight drawings on the floor or table with the images face down. Each image may be looked at twice with the following rules.

- First look: The group may request to turn over two images at a time for ten seconds for each pair.

- Second look: The above process may be repeated, but the pairs do not have to be the same as the first look.

Students may talk or act out their image(s). However, they may not show it to anyone. Once the students feel they know where their image goes, they may place it on the floor or table. Once an image is placed down, it may not be looked at until the end of the activity.

Ending: Once the designated time is over or the group agrees that they have the right sequence, the images may be turned over in order. If any mistakes happen, allow the group to correct the sequence.

Reflection: Zoom and Re-Zoom help students to find their voice when working together on any activity. For the problem to be solved students must contribute to sharing their piece of the puzzle, leading toward the ultimate solution. Conversely, honoring the contributions of classmates is the only way to figure Zoom or Re-Zoom out. The focus of reflection involves what action students took to be heard, and what skills students used to create opportunities for their classmates' contributions to be shared. For older students (grades 6-12), the following quote from Shakespeare can be presented for discussion: "This above all: to thine own self be true, and it must follow, as the night the day, thou canst not then be false to any man."[66]

How might this quote relate to this activity and the effort the group just made? What does it mean to be true to yourself? What interferes with people being true to themselves? How does being true to oneself help the group? How does this activity reflect the Full Value of Care for Self & Others?

As noted under Cross Categories, this is also a wonderful goal-setting activity. The problem is clearly defined. Students need to commit their resources to solving it, and cannot reach the solution without asking for help from their peers. Reflection time can also be focused on drawing out from students how Zoom or Re-Zoom mirrors the steps for goals they have set for themselves and with peers.

Cross Categories: Be Here, Be Honest, Set Goals

CHAPTER 11

CARE FOR SELF & OTHERS

The world would be a much better place if we related to each other with empathy and compassion. Attention to emotional and physical self-care would also help. Altruism is a noble thing, but without looking out for one's own needs, the well can run dry. It is important not to experience caring for self as a selfish act. Recharging your batteries serves as a foundation to have the strength to offer support to others. Care for self is indistinguishable from care for others in many ways.

Ongoing horrific events in our nation's schools reinforce the need to attend to this Full Value carefully. Students are often reticent to inform on a peer who has made a threatening comment for fear of retribution from other students, or to report a student who has expressed an intention to hurt themselves. It is not unusual to receive a report about suicidal intent from a student about a peer until the last possible moment during the school day. This is due to a misplaced internal struggle between loyalty and betrayal. When a student truly cares about self (and others), there is little ambivalence about doing the right thing.

The profile of students who have committed homicidal acts in schools is consistent with observed behaviors that demonstrate alienation and isolation. This can be evident in the early academic grades. If all of us in schools came from a place of empathy and inclusion, this marginalization could be avoided. Students labeled as "quirky," "different," or "weird" would be fully integrated into classroom life. They would have a voice, be recognized, and have their individuality applauded. And, they would be more able to ask for help. Care for Self & Others is at the core of maintaining safe and civil schools.

This Full Value is not for students alone. Imagine building caring and compassionate relationships with colleagues using the outcomes of Care for Self & Others. There would be less isolation, less competition, and more sharing and support, to not just survive but thrive in this exhilarating but also stressful and exhausting career.

Outcomes of Care for Self & Others

- Compassion/Self-Compassion
- Empathy
- Interdependence
- Recognizing Personal Needs
- Recognizing Self-Worth
- Self-Empathy
- Self-Sacrifice
- Personal and Social Responsibility

ACTIVITIES

Activity Difficulty Scale

1 (Easy) ------- 2 (A bit harder) -------- 3 (Pretty complicated) --------- 4 (Difficult)

The Activity: Accepting Yourself Time: 2 hours

Materials: Provided template (see Chapter 16, Printable Materials) Difficulty: 2-4

How you do it:

It is sadly true that we are better at giving positive feedback than receiving it. More difficult still is to speak publicly about our positive attributes. Students (and adults) struggle when talking about their strengths and achievements. It is often frowned upon as bragging or egotistical. Further, it is often difficult for us to accept praise from others.

We believe it is important to recognize and celebrate student and staff achievements and strengths. This activity offers students permission to do just that, hence the name Accepting Yourself. The connection to Care for Self & Others is pretty straightforward.

With older groups, make sure there is a box of tissues handy.

Here is a script you can follow when introducing the activity to your group:

In this exercise, you will be invited to discuss your strengths openly with other group members. There is no place for modesty. You are not being asked to brag, only to be realistic and open about the strengths that you possess. Take five to ten minutes to think it over and make notes. Then, follow this procedure for the exercise:

- Think of all the things that you have done well during the school year (or marking period), all the things for which you feel a sense of accomplishment.

- In the group as a whole, each person should share the full list of their strengths. Then ask the group, "What additional strengths did you see in me?" Add these to your list.

- Think about your successes and your strengths. Think about how your strengths may be utilized to improve your relationships, school, work, etc. Then set some goals around these issues.

Once the lists have been developed, students circle up. Each student gets to share their strengths with the group. Once finished, members of the group get to add to individual lists. Make clear to the group that every student shouldn't feel an obligation to offer positive feedback. However, more often than not, this happens, which can cause the activity to take a long time to complete.

This activity can also be saved for the end of the year as a closure experience for students. Depending on the age of the group, this can be a short experience or stretched out for several hours. It is worth taking the time.

Ask students to think about the school year and create a list of accomplishments or successes that they experienced and the strengths they brought to these successes. This could be connected to academic achievement, social experiences, or both. This list should be written down or, if working with younger students, can take the form of a collage or drawing. Students using a representation will need to be able to explain what their collage or drawing means.

Offer students a significant amount of time to create their lists. You might think about one full period for list building and another for sharing. It also might be interesting to ask parents to add to their student's list.

Reflection: Some questions to ask students after completing this activity:

- What feelings did you have when sharing your strengths and successes?

- What feelings did you have when people added to your list?

- Were there strengths that you were not aware of at the beginning of the year that you developed over time?

- How did your strengths contribute to your successes?

- Were you surprised at some of the strengths others saw in you? Why?

- Did you feel an obligation to add to each person's list? If so, why?

- Why do you feel it can be challenging for people to speak positively about themselves?

- Why do you feel it can be hard for people to receive positive feedback?

- Was this an emotional experience for you and, if so, why?

- How will this list of strengths and successes contribute to setting goals for the future?

Cross Categories: Be Safe, Be Honest, Let Go & Move On

The Activity: All Aboard   Time: 40 – 60 minutes

Materials: A 3-foot x 3-foot square piece of sturdy fabric, or if you wish to get fancy, build a wooden platform of the same size, four inches in height. This would be an excellent project for the carpentry program, if you have one. The size of the platform can be varied depending on the number of students in the group and the degree of challenge you wish to provide.

Difficulty: 2-3

How you do it:

The introduction is pretty straightforward. The object is to get the entire class within a designated space with no feet touching outside of the fabric, boundary area, or platform for a slow count of three (or longer if you want to up the challenge). There are several choices in framing this activity. It can be frontloaded with a discussion of the obvious necessity for people to get in close proximity to each other. This may be a Care for Self issue for some. The need to be mutually supportive can also be talked about, as well as the commitment involved in keeping group members on the platform.

Or, you can just give the group some planning time and leave the discussion for your post activity reflection. This will allow for more experiential discovery.

Aside from varying the size of the platform, you can also ask the group to decide how many touches outside of the boundary area require a restart. You need to be reading your group (GRABBSS). Some groups may be in a place where frustration may move them forward, whereas others may need a success. It is a continuum that you should always be aware of.

Reflection: When focusing on Care for Self & Others in the group's post activity reflection, several prompts can be used to promote discussion:

- When on the platform, what did you do to keep yourself from falling off? What did you need from the group?

- How did you support your classmates to stay on the platform? What was your level of commitment?

- Did you have any feelings, positive or negative, about being so close to your classmates?

- Did you need to ask for help? How did that feel to do so?

- How does Care for Self & Others connect to this activity?

- What behaviors in our Full Value Commitment did we use?

- What behaviors can we add to our Full Value Commitment as a result of this activity?

- Were there any distractors present, and do we need to revisit our Commitment as a result?

Cross Categories: Be Here, Be Safe, Set Goals

The Activity: Holy Alliance – (Four-Way Tug o' War)   Time: 45 minutes

Materials: Four-Way Tug o' War (see appendix for purchasing sources), earth or beach ball   Difficulty: 2

How you do it:

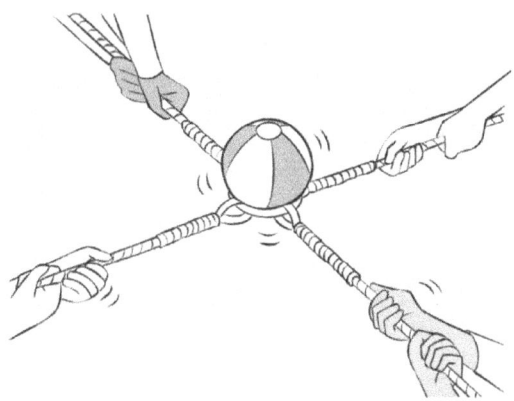

This activity uses one of the relatively high cost activity props that we would suggest you include in your program budget. If you are adept at weaving rope, which means you must know what a Fid is, then fabricating your own Holy Alliance can significantly reduce the cost. The apparatus consists of a heavy metal ring, approximately six inches in diameter, with four thick pieces of Multiline, approximately twenty feet in length, attached to it. This allows for a four-way tug of war with groups on each rope pulling the center ring over their side of the rope square. Temporary (unholy) alliances form when one group learns that if it helps another, it may ultimately guarantee its own victory. Teamwork, nah. Cooperation, nope. Guile and trickery, yep!

So, how about if from the very beginning all four groups were cooperating to complete a task? Now we have a very different but equally difficult scenario. Four groups of students holding four different ropes, delicately moving in unison, is no easy feat.

Set up your group at one end of a large field or in a gymnasium. Place an earth or beach ball in the center of the ring and ask the group to exert tension on their ropes until the ring lifts the ball off the ground. The initiative is to keep the ball balanced on the ring while moving the distance of the field or gymnasium and across a finish line. A more difficult goal for advanced alliances is to dump the ball into a box or crate after moving it some distance. Now that's a Holy Alliance!

Reflection: This activity requires an individual commitment to work in the service of the group. If a student is distracted, disinterested, self-absorbed, or needing to be the focus of attention, this will impact their success. A student may also feel the need to take charge, becoming overly directive without listening to input from others. When participating in any group activity, how do you make your needs known in a way that does not negatively affect the group? How might individual needs have impacted the success or failure of the activity? What strategies can be used to allow individuals the opportunity to articulate how they are feeling about their participation?

Cross Categories: Be Here, Set Goals

The Activity: Hospital Tag Time: 40 minutes

Materials: Boundary markers Difficulty: 3

How you do it:

Set up some soft boundaries, such as rubber cones or ropes on the ground. When you shout "go," all participants attempt to tag each other in out-of-the-way places. When tagged, participants need to place a hand or arm, or leg,

over the tagged area, as if it were a bandage. A bandage (hand, arm, leg, etc.) is placed on as many tagged spots as possible. If touched five times, the tagged person is rendered immobile, as they have run out of limbs to use as bandages. Tagging can be done with the hand, shoulder, knee, foot, or any body part that can touch another person. After this has gone on for some time, you can declare that everyone has gotten to the hospital and has been healed, at which point the game starts again, and again, and again right up to the point where it is clear that enough is enough is enough (this is a teacher judgment call).

Reflection: When one is hurt, either physically or emotionally, it can lead to some level of incapacitation, withdrawal, sadness, and isolation. How one copes with a temporary or permanent disability depends on the marshaling of personal resources and asking for help from those around us. Compassion and empathy play an important role. Connecting students to their human responsibility to others, support a classroom where Care for Self & Others is consistently evident. This activity can also focus on resiliency and adaptation, and the quiet courage that students with disabilities evidence daily. Some questions to consider:

- What are some things you can do to support a classmate or family member with a temporary or permanent disability?

- Why do you think that it can be hard to ask for help?

- How does this activity help us better understand how we often take for granted what we can do?

Cross Categories: Be Honest, Let Go & Move On

Note: Consideration needs to be given to the possibility that a member of your class may have a 504 or special education classification. A GRABBSS assessment needs to be done to determine the readiness of students to engage in this conversation without compromising the feelings or confidentiality of their classmates. This activity may provide those with disabilities the opportunity to speak to their life experience in a meaningful and powerful way, but only if they are ready to do so.

The Activity: Human Ladder Time: 45 minutes

Materials: 3-foot-long 1 ¼ inch diameter wooden dowels Difficulty: 3

How you do it:
Aside from being a handy item for getting stuff off high shelves, changing light bulbs, and house painting, the ladder has always been a symbol of upward mobility. The phrase "he is climbing the ladder of success" is a part of our upwardly mobile vocabulary. Up is good; down is clearly not so good. However, ladders, when used in group learning experiences, are not always

vertically oriented, which can be a very good thing!

The human ladder requires a significant commitment from spotters and participants alike for the trip to be a successful one. The group breaks out into pairs who are each given a dowel approximately three feet in length and at least 1¼ inches in diameter. Pairs line up with their dowels braced between them (held firmly with two hands) to form a large horizontal ladder. If only a limited number of students are available, pairs can move their rung to the front of the ladder once it has been climbed over. Rungs can either all be at the same height or varied in altitude, distance from each other, and angle.

As for setup variations, we wonder if the dowels could be held to create a gradual spiral, allowing for the climber to do a 360 as part of the traverse? We haven't tried that yet, but perhaps someone will and let us know!

Reflection: Completing a safe traverse relies on the commitment of the ladder climber and the dedication of the students holding each ladder rung. The climber must be focused on moving from rung to rung without behaving recklessly. Those holding the rungs must stay focused on providing vital support by holding their dowel end in position. Some questions to consider:

As a climber:

- How did it feel to trust your classmates to hold the ladder? If you had any concerns, what were they?

- Did you have doubts about your ability to traverse the ladder? If not, why? If so, how did you manage those uncertainties?

- How does this activity connect to Care for Self & Others?

As a holder:

- What responsibilities did you feel?

- Did your attention wander, and if so, why? How did you bring your focus back?

- How does this activity connect to Care for Self & Others?

Cross Categories: Be Here, Be Safe, Set Goals

The Activity: Letters of Appreciation   Time: 45 minutes

Materials: Paper, writing and drawing materials, envelopes   Difficulty: 1

How you do it:

Letters are one of the oldest methods of communication. Before e-mail and text messaging provided the ability to edit writing instantly, letters required taking the time to organize what you had to say and how you were going to say it. The importance of style and presentation contributed to being careful before putting pen to paper, unless the writer was OK with a messy finished product. It is akin to the days of print film, when careful composition had to be considered before snapping a picture due to the expense.

An excellent place to start is to write a letter of appreciation to yourself. A letter to yourself can go like this, "Dear Jim, when you listened closely to your classmate, you let yourself learn about his concerns. Your listening also showed your classmate that you cared about what he was saying. This helped you begin a friendship with him." Or, "Dear Richard, when your friend dropped all of his books in the hallway, you said a kind word to him and helped him pick them up. That was a thoughtful thing to do."

A letter of appreciation can also be written to a classmate. With the word, *appreciation* being stressed, students will hopefully adhere to that spirit when communicating. However, reviewing the letters before delivery is suggested. Let students know you will be looking them over.

For younger students, providing a format for a self or other letter can be helpful:

- When I helped my friend pick up the books that he dropped in the hallway, I...

- When I got my project back with a good grade, I...

- The things I like about you are...

- I appreciate working with you on our group project because...

Variation: Put all students' names in a hat and have a drawing. Ask students to think back a week and write a brief positive letter about the person whose name they have drawn.

Reflection: Was it helpful to begin by writing a self-affirmation letter, or was reporting your own positives more difficult? If so, why? How often have we felt like offering positive and caring feedback to others, but not found the words or opportunity to do so? This activity provides a structure to facilitate this communication. Check in with students as to how it felt to offer positives to a classmate. How is caring for others connected to caring for self? Check in with students as to how it felt to hear affirmations from peers. Were they surprised, moved, happy?

Cross Categories: Be Safe, Let Go & Move On

The Activity: Panic Evac Time: 45-60 minutes

Difficulty: 3-4

Materials: Two ropes (100 feet & 150 feet in length), two smaller ropes (see drawing), #10 tin can, carpet squares, six – 1-inch x 6-inch x 8-foot boards, balloons, plastic cups, trolleys*

How you do it:

There is truth to the observation that families in crisis and larger communities often tend to pull together. Aside from the more publicized baby boom resulting from the great New York City blackout of the sixties, also noteworthy was a reduction in crime, folks directing traffic, helping people in and out of darkened apartments, and a general reaching out to offer mutual support for each other. While it would be somewhat difficult (and illegal) to turn off all the power in the school to provoke a caring community outcome, this activity might be the next best thing. Make sure you have a large town like crowd, say twenty-five or more participants. The setup is a bit complicated, so bear with us.

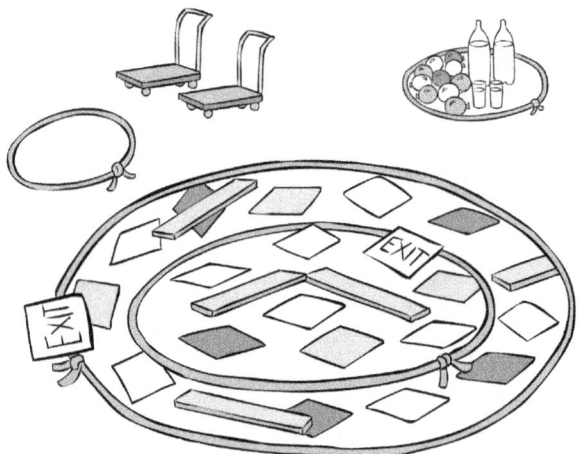

Grab two long ropes, one approximately 150 feet and the other around 100. Knot each one together to form two circles, one inside the other. Spread a bunch of carpet squares donated by a local store or snapped up at a flea market around the inside of both circles. Two special squares should be placed as exits adjacent to the rope edge of each circle. They may be red in color or have the word "EXIT" drawn on them. Now using maybe five or six, 1-inch x 6-inch x 8-foot boards, lay them down amid the squares, creating transit barriers that block participants from directly proceeding from one carpet square to another. In essence, you have created a ground maze.

Next to the EXIT sign, outside of the larger rope, lay a small diameter rope for participants to stand in as a safe island, once they have successfully made it out of the two rope circles. Next to this safe island is a set of trolleys, placed within easy reach.

Approximately thirty feet from the safe island, inside another small rope circle, are placed two one-liter uncapped plastic bottles filled with water, two plastic glasses, and ten water balloons (glasses and balloons are also filled with water).

Bring your group to the masterpiece you've created and instruct them not to discuss what they see until the activity has begun. Ask them to position themselves on the carpet squares, with some group members with eyes closed. Now, a sample metaphor:

> You are a group of neighbors, all living in an apartment building together. One of the apartments has caught on fire. Power has gone out in the neighborhood, and while someone has attempted to call the fire department, they still haven't arrived. The person in the burning apartment is old, frail, and has poor vision. You have all looked after him over the years, benefiting from his wisdom and humor. You have decided to attempt a rescue!
>
> You must all first find your way out of the pitch-black apartment complex, then carry water back in to put the fire out. The carpet squares are safety zones, and the wood boards are impassable walls. You must get a group out to the trolleys, retrieve the water supply, and use it to douse the apartment fire by filling a # 10 tin can (which you have previously placed at the center of the inner rope circle) until it flows over. The bottles and glasses may be passed from one student to another. The balloons must be tossed from one circle to another, and then broken over the can. If you touch the ground (outside of a carpet square or the ground underneath the trolleys), you have suffered an injury and must stop actively participating. However, you may still offer advice to your co-rescuers. If you can successfully fill the bucket to overflowing within eight minutes (or whatever time fits for your group), the old man has been saved!

Before making visual contact with the activity, introduce it. The introduction of this activity is critical to establishing a metaphor within the context of Care for Self & Others. Ask the group to imagine the thoughts and feelings they might have in this scenario. Encourage honest disclosure by sharing your ambivalence implicit in potentially risking your own physical safety for the life of another. Each carpet square can be labeled with behaviors, thoughts, and feelings that students decide are essential in attempting a successful rescue, such as focus, selflessness, planning, cooperation, communication, etc. Ask students to keep a mental note of some of the thoughts that run through their heads. They can even call them out on the fly with you acting as group scribe.

By the way, if you want to add a touch of realism to the basic scenario, get a sound effects app for your phone that has loud fire engines/police car noises and play it during the activity. Nice touch, eh?

Reflection: The nature of this activity (that of a rescue) leads naturally into reflection, with students focusing on the tension between helping and the emotional or physical risk this may involve. While it is unlikely that your students will be rescuing people from a burning building, there will be times when they are faced with the choice of doing nothing or doing something, and the choice to do something may cause some personal sacrifice or risk. How might this choice connect to intervening in a bullying situation, reporting to a teacher the friend who has expressed depressed thoughts, or shared discomfort, and not participating in a hurtful act? Expressing compassion for another student? Sticking up for oneself in a disagreement with a peer or teacher? What behaviors contribute to finding an effective balance between caring for self and for others? How can caring for others contribute to caring for self?

Cross Categories: Be Here, Be Safe, Be Honest, Set Goals,

*Trolleys are easily made. Materials: 2 – 4-inch x 4-inch by eight or ten-foot posts and 3/4 inch nylon rope (the posts can be shorter if the groups typically using it are smaller). A portable option is to make each trolley three or four feet in length and hook them together using a sturdy eye hook on one end. Drill through each post at 2-foot intervals along its length, starting about 6 inches from the front of each post. Holes should be at least 5/8 inches in diameter. Drill a larger hole into one side of the 5/8-inch hole to a depth of about 1 inch. This will serve as an inset for the knot that you tie at one end. Thread a four-foot rope through each hole and tie a knot at the top and bottom. The bottom knot will stop the rope from slipping through the hole, and the top knot will help students get a grip on the rope. They can also be purchased from Flaghouse.

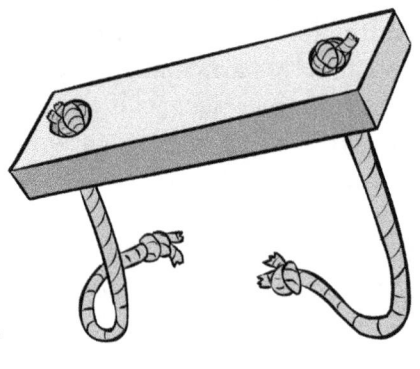

The Activity: Stonehenge   Time: 45 minutes (or longer)

Materials: Small stones and other objects   Difficulty: 2
of various sizes and shapes

How you do it:

    The name Stonehenge comes from a place in England where large stones were positioned so they could connect with the movement of the moon and stars. The practice of balancing stones into a multi-stone sculpture prompted the naming of this activity.

    Stonehenge is perhaps the world's most famous prehistoric monument. It was built in several stages: the first monument was an early Henge monument, built about 5,000 years ago, and then one was erected in the late Neolithic period about 2500 BC. In the early Bronze Age, many burial mounds were built nearby. Today, along with Avebury, it forms the heart of a World Heritage Site, with a unique concentration of prehistoric monuments (English Heritage).[64]

    The teacher first builds a balanced rock sculpture with a particular purpose in mind. That purpose can require disclosure, such as "How am I feeling about how the class is working together?" Or the purpose can be more general, such as "What I want to see my students achieve." The important thing is that the purpose is metaphorical insofar as it is represented by the construction of the sculpture.

    The class observes the teacher's work. As the building goes on, the thoughts that go through their mind are noted so that, once completed, they can verbalize them to the class. Of course, not all thoughts can be revealed, for the building and the experience of reaching and risking for balance is evocative, and appropriate boundaries need to be observed. However, that very evocation is the power of Stonehenge: it draws out thoughts-ideas-feelings.

    There needs to be a balance aspect to Stonehenge, at least from the teacher's construction experience. For the balanced stones have a mystery to their construction, a risk, a sense of vulnerability, while at the same time tapping into the gravitational power of the universe. There are many ways to build a sculpture, but the idea of the metaphor is the essential thing. What is it that I am doing, and what does it mean?

The teacher is modeling the process. Once the teacher has finished their work, they speak to the experience. It is important to take the time to do this, slowly, with meaning, humor, gravity, and honesty.

Now it is the students' turn. Setting them free in an outside area, or with a pile of rocks, sticks, and so forth inside, they create their own individual Stonehenge. Once completed, a gallery tour is conducted of each student's creation. They tell their story during the tour, and everyone has a chance to comment if they'd like.

If Stonehenge is used early in the school year, students can build a second sculpture in late spring and compare the two. Before and after pictures can be taken. Each sculpture is unique, and if the student can take it along as a photo, it becomes a reminder that promotes reflection and remembrance. The sculptures are not intended to be permanent. However, some classes construct a sculpture garden. In this way, the sculptures can be added to, changed, and reconstructed. It is a caring activity because of the balance work that has to take place in order to build a sculpture. Also, by sharing one's work with others, everyone is uplifted.

On Balancing Stones

The odd shapes and textures
will cling to each other
if given the chance,
    holding on to the slightest
interface.

Boldly, I step up to the world
and take charge
humbled by the weight of the task
yet drawn to climb
into that space.

I work and work to find that one moment of
release.
And finally, there it is,
 a miracle of touching,
a mysterious line running top to bottom.

The step away is cunning
as if by taking my eyes off,
or stumbling slightly
or changing the pattern of my breathing,
the stones will scatter.
I am quiet as I observe the spaces they make,
hands in the shape of the grain and the struggle,
breath still halting while

> backing further away,
> I defer to the wisdom of my companion.
> August 1997-Jim Schoel

Reflection: Implicit in this Full Value is balance. It is important that students find a balance between selfishness and selflessness. Both are at either end of the continuum and can be destructive. As this activity has the focus of balance, it can be used as a reflection springboard for students around this topic.

Some questions to consider:

- What might the different objects you picked for your sculpture represent?
- Why did you choose them?
- What was your construction secret for maintaining balance?
- How might technique relate to your life experience?
- Why is balance important?

Cross Categories: Be Honest, Be Here

The Activity: The Balance of Full Value   Time: 30+

Materials: 13, 20 penny nails, 6-inch x 6-inch by 2-inch wood block   Difficulty: 3

How you do it:
> First, some construction. You will need to drill a hole in the center of the flat part of the block that will hold a nail firmly upright. That's it! Place one of your nails into the block. The explanation of the task is simple. Students must <u>suspend</u> the remaining 12 nails from the top of the nail placed in the block. "Suspend" means that none of the nails can touch the wooden block or be held up or supported. Sounds impossible, well it isn't! The solution can be found on the Internet under the name "Porcupine Progression."

Reflection: The successful solution requires that all nails are in balance. Once correctly positioned, the platform that the block rests on can be smacked, and the assembly will not collapse. This activity is rich with metaphorical connections. What do the individual nails represent? How do they work together to keep the structure in balance? What happens when one nail is removed? How is their balance connected to the needs of self and the needs of others?

Cross Categories: This activity may be connected to any of the Full Value Behavioral Norms as a way of illustrating the balance that exists within and between them.

To ensure that the entire class is involved, a giant apparatus can be built using four-foot lengths of 1¼ inch PVC pipe and pipe tees to serve instead of nail heads. The base is also constructed of pipe, formed into a square with two additional fittings to hold a center sleeve that the upright pipe slides into. The smaller version can be purchased from Flaghouse under the name "Porcupine Progression."

The Activity: Trust Line Time: 30 minutes

Difficulty: 3

How you do it:

This is an extension of the Three Person Trust Fall (Chapter 7). Have the group form two equal lines facing each other. At the head of each line are the first two spotters. A volunteer is needed to fall backward and forward between them. The second person in each line is considered to be on deck and also in a spotting position.

After going through the spotting calls (Chapter 7), the faller sets off either forward or backward. If the initial fall is backward, then the forward spotter is replaced by the second person in line who announces, "I'm here" and the name of the person he is protecting, i.e., "I'm here, John." The original spotter moves to the rear of his line. While the forward catch is being made, the rear spotter is replaced by the second in line, who announces their presence and commitment using the same language. This rolling-spotting progression continues until the faller indicates he is nauseous or just finished by announcing "I'm done." A new faller moves in between the two lines, the spotting cadence is spoken, and the activity continues.

Reflection: Trust activities such as this one find a comfortable home in Care for Self & Others. This is a very good example of the cross-categorical use of many of the activities presented in this book. All trust activities can be used in the category of Care for Self &

Others. They serve as a powerful experiential metaphor. Effective spotting of the activity demands caring for others. Poor spotting has obvious emotional and physical consequences. Spotting entails much more responsibility than that of participation. It can be physically hard work, require heightened vigilance, rapid response, and the willingness to protect someone who is falling at one's own expense. This reflection is a wonderful place to make connections for students between the activity and caring.

Cross Categories: Be Safe

The Activity: Web Wave Time: 10 minutes

Materials: 1-inch diameter Multiline rope (length to be determined by group size) Difficulty: 2-3

How you do it:

The Web Wave is a truly elegant activity. It is simple, yet powerful. It requires nothing more than a length of sturdy rope and a group that needs to really feel what it is like to literally support each other. Find a piece of comfortable rope that students won't mind wrapping their hands around for a while. A piece of 1-inch diameter Multi-line is the crème de la crème. Secure the ends of the rope together using a triple Fisherman's Knot (See Chapter 9 for tying instructions). Once the knots have been put under a significant load, which they will be in this activity, don't plan on untying them without the use of a hacksaw.

Once your hardware is ready, it is time to assemble the group. Have them spread out along the rope to form an even circle. Since there is a natural tendency to start pulling on the rope once held (no doubt a remnant of too many tug o' war games of youth), remind your students that holding does not mean pulling.

Now, once everyone is set, ask students to spread their legs into a comfortable standing position, with each foot set in one spot. With hands spread approximately shoulder width on the rope, have each student slowly lean back until the rope is singing (taught, that is). There may very well be some slipping and sliding as group members adjust their stance and lean to maintain balance. This will be followed by ongoing minute adjustments as the group and rope gently sway and pull as all work together to stay safe and balanced.

There are lots of variations to this activity. While leaning back, ask the group to slowly go down into a sitting position, and then lift themselves back up again. While in the sitting position, get the rope pulsing rapidly in a circular rotation, three times clockwise, and then reversing to counterclockwise. Now ask each student to rotate their upper body in the same manner. You're really webbing and waving now! In order to truly experience the feeling of the group working together through the rope, have everyone close their eyes while in the leaning back position. It is truly remarkable to feel the rope shifting, pulling, and relaxing as the group supports itself in this endless, undulating circle.

Reflection: This is a sensory activity. If the group is truly committed, continuous minor and major adjustments will be felt through the rope, particularly if they have their eyes closed. Each student must choose to make a personal commitment to keep the larger group in balance, or the Web Wave will collapse. Some suggested questions:

- What did you need to do to make sure that you kept your balance?

- What were you thinking and feeling as you made these adjustments?

- How does making sure that the circle stays balanced connect to caring for self and caring for others?

Cross Categories: Be here, Be Safe, Set Goals

The Activity: Yurt Circle Time: 20 minutes

Difficulty: 3

How you do it:

The Yurt is a portable hut still utilized on the steppes of Central Asia, generally by the Mongolian nomadic people. It is typically built of animal hides. It is circular in shape with a domed roof. And, it has a tension band that holds it together, made out of rawhide. The Yurt has been adapted to Western climates and technology, made from fabric or wood. When all of its pieces are intact and the tension band is in place, it is strong, easily holding back the elemental forces of nature. However, should the tension band weaken and let go, then the whole structure is subject to collapse. And so, this might be said for groups. The one disaffected child, the one alcoholic parent, or the one member of the class that can't or won't work with others, can unbalance an entire system, sending it crashing to the ground.

The Yurt Circle activity allows for the group to practice physically constructing a Yurt-like structure through the use of their bodies and their willingness to make the emotional commitment to maintaining healthy interdependence.

Have students form a circle, and then hold hands. Back the circle out until arms are stretched out to provide tension. Ask the group to spread their legs comfortably apart. Starting from anywhere in the circle, assign the number 1 or 2 to alternating group members. Clearly, this will either require an even number of participants or one person with four arms, two of which are exceedingly long. Another odd number option is to rotate two student volunteers in and out. Anyway, if you need a person, here is your chance to step in and experience the Yurt Circle with students. Now tell them the history of the Yurt so that they get to thinking about how a structure like that might have implications for the group, how it's currently operating, and possibilities for the future.

On the count of five (three is so tedious), have all of the 1s slowly lean back, keeping their bodies stiff and arms extended, while all of the 2s lean forward at the same time, also keeping their bodies still and arms extended. If this is done slowly and with care, you will have created a self-supporting circle, just like the Yurt. You may find the need to have the group adjust the circle, depending on body weight and position. Once a stable Yurt Circle has been formed and held, try having the 2s slowly lean in, and the 1s lean out, then alternate back and forth between the in and out positions.

Reflection: Some questions to consider posing to students after this activity include:

- What responsibility did you have in this activity to keep other students safe?

- What did you need to do to ensure that your safety was maintained?

- How does this activity connect to the expression, "One for all and all for one?"

- How does this activity connect to the Full Value of Care for Self & Others?

- What distractors did you notice that got in the way of establishing and maintaining a safe balance with the group?

- When can caring for self becomes more important than caring for others? Talk about a circumstance in your life where that might have happened.

Cross Categories: Be Safe, Set Goals

The Activity: Zen Count Time: 15 minutes

Difficulty: 2

How you do it:

This activity connects to the intuitive part of us, which is able to will an event to happen. Or a successful result could simply be dumb luck. Have the group try to count to a certain number. That's easy. Now, have the group count to that number without anyone saying the same number at the same time. That is, if I say "three," it needs to be clear and distinct, coming from my voice only. If someone else says "three" at the same time that I do, then we need to start over. The goal is to get to the intended number without any duplication.

There are rules. First, the group must stand in a circle, not a line. Second, the group cannot organize in such a way that the count is a simple go around the circle. Third, there can be no direction from one leader, who points to people before saying the number. Spontaneity is the motto of Zen Count. When we insist on it, then the game has the potential of becoming one of chance and of mystique. The feeling of getting to ten, or fifteen, or twenty is, well, incredible.

Reflection: Successful completion of this activity requires focused anticipation. If you jump too early, then the activity starts again. If you wait too long, there is the distinct possibility that two people will tend to speak at once, again causing the activity to restart. When we genuinely care for others, we anticipate their needs. This requires empathy and active listening. Making this connection for students will help them to generate behavioral norms that contribute to the successful caring for others. Caring for self also requires active listening, self-compassion, and empathy. It is paying attention to when you need to rest and recharge to continue to effectively support the life journey of others. Again, important behavioral norms can come from this conversation.

Cross Categories: Be Here, Set Goals. Let Go & Move On

CHAPTER 12

FULL VALUE & ACADEMIC CONTENT AREAS

Integration into Content

Viewing social emotional learning as a burden reflects a lack of understanding as to how a self-regulating class of students can increase the quantity and quality of instructional time. Students who formulate and employ common goals and who create and implement agreed-upon behavioral norms are more invested in each other and continually use abstract reasoning skills as part of their problem-solving process. As discussed in Chapter 2, the practicing of abstract reasoning in the social arena naturally crosswalks over to the academic process.

There is no debating that creating and maintaining a positive culture and climate within the classroom takes some work and some time. But the outcomes, aside from significantly reducing classroom management concerns, can engender profound and positive changes for students and teachers alike.

While learning Full Value requires teaching some skills to students, its application can be directly woven into all classroom activities. We have already referenced this in the co-creation process of behavioral norms using a Full Value Commitment and the Calling Group process that sets the behavioral norms into motion.

Here we link Full Value with academic content areas, using an activity base to help students make emotional, cognitive, and behavioral connections to lessons in history, social studies, science, English, mathematics, and the visual and performing arts.

Other chapters of this book provide activities specific to teaching the individual behavioral norms. Typically, some, if not all, of the norms are either being honored or challenged during an activity. It is also important to stress that any interactions between students are an activity, and much more natural than the games and initiatives that can be used to teach the components of Full Value. Viewing a classroom lesson as an activity that will provoke behavior opens the door for using all interactions between students and between students and teachers as opportunities to teach, model, and reinforce agreed-upon behavioral norms.

While this chapter will not provide an exhaustive list of lessons to shape behavioral norms, it will provide a foundation for some creative thinking on your part. Once you begin to connect the dots concerning how these activities can be used for the dual purpose of teaching academics while also enhancing classroom culture, the process will start to feel like second nature. The creativity in this process provides opportunities for lesson adaptations.

What would this look like? A daring first year teacher[67] excited at the prospect of embedding Full Value into her English lesson, was observed implementing the following adaptation of a specific experiential activity. The activity she chose was Mine Field (Chapter 7).

This is how she framed her lesson:

Objectives:

- Identify the difference between perceived and actual risks.
- Analyze the perceived and actual risks experienced by the main character, Kino, from John Steinbeck's novella, *The Pearl*.

Teacher will set up activity and follow procedures as outlined within the experiential curriculum. Adaptation: designate an object to represent *The Pearl*. Have students lead one another to retrieve it.

Provide students with an exit ticket to make connections to text.

Example:

1. How does this risk activity connect to *The Pearl*?
    a. What is the pitfall/minefield Kino will be journeying through?
    b. What does Kino perceive to be the risks he faces?
    c. In what way is Kino "blindfolded" as he begins this journey?
    d. What predictions can you make about the outcome of Kino's risk-taking?

This lesson was used in a high school resource center class with eight 10th-grade students. Students evidenced some academic challenges, which kept them from participation in a general education English class. However, they were still required to master the general education curriculum with appropriate modifications and accommodations. While no overt behavioral problems were noted, students presented with varying degrees of disaffection as they continued to struggle with academic content from one grade level to the next.

The following was witnessed in observing this lesson:

- All students were completely engaged.

- The classroom teacher noted that one student, in particular, was animated and smiling for the first time all year (this was late November).

- Co-created behavioral norms were in play:

    o Be Here: As students took turns guiding each other through the Mine Field searching for *The Pearl*, clear communication and attention were essential to success.

    o Be Safe: As the students within the Mine Field were blindfolded, their guiding peers appropriately assumed the responsibility for keeping them safe.

- o Set Goals: This activity lent itself to a group goal-setting process with the class defining the task, resources needed to accomplish it, and their measure of success.

- o Care for Self & Others: In an activity where one person is blindfolded, there is an obvious responsibility on the part of the person's partner to ensure their physical safety.

- o Let Go & Move On: There were times when inadvertent misdirection was provided, or a student moved too far or too quickly in the Mine Field. These provided natural opportunities for students to discuss their experiences when group was called.

- During the Ticket Out process, students were able to make clear connections from activity to text.

The affect and behaviors provoked by the activity, built capacities in the areas of internal locus of control. There were many opportunities to make choices that would compromise the emotional safety of a peer. There were also choices that were made by students to disrupt the activity by engaging in off-task behavior. The activity became the vehicle for practicing socialization and for giving and receiving feedback connected to witnessed behaviors.

The reflection model (Calling Group) provides the second essential benefit for students by empowering them to voice their concerns when they feel that behavioral norms have been violated. What they have to say will make a difference.

In the example below, a fifth-grade language arts teacher[68] used Full Value as part of the writing process and text analysis rather than as part of the reading process. In this scenario, the class lesson itself was the activity, which speaks to our point that what happens day to day can be sufficient for creating and maintaining a Full Value instructional environment:

- Students chose a Full Value Behavioral Norm they would like to use as a trait for their main character when writing. Through actions and dialogue, the writer showed their readers this character trait instead of telling the reader.

- The teacher created six baskets labeled with a behavioral norm (e.g., Be Here, Be Safe, etc.). After reading, students placed their book in the basket that they believed most represented their book. Then they were asked to explain either verbally or in writing why they chose a specific basket, using evidence from the text to support their choice.

In the following example, Full Value is infused into a district's reading curriculum (See graphic below).[69] The need to make these connections is often required in a formal lesson-planning document. The Kinnelon Borough Public Schools lesson plans require specific language that articulates how Full Value links to content. The particular curricular piece is drawn from New Jersey's Language Arts/Literacy – Primary, grade 1 reading curriculum. In reviewing the Process Skills under Learning Objectives, the eye is drawn to the 21st Century Life and Career Standards:

- 9.1.4.A.5 Apply critical thinking and problem-solving skills in classroom and family settings. (**triangle**)

Unit/Topic Title	Reading Workshop: Readers Build Good Habits		Approximate Pacing	September, October	
UNIT/TOPIC ENDURING OBJECTIVES/UNDERSTANDINGS					
Students will understand that: • There are expectations for independent reading workshop time. • Readers read every day. • All readers have needs in order to read well. • Readers read for meaning.					
PRIORITY NJ CORE CURRICULUM CONTENT STANDARDS/ COMMON CORE STATE STANDARDS					
NJCCCS/CCSS	• Reading : Literature • Language				
CPI #/CCSS #	CUMULATIVE PROCESS INDICATOR (CPI)/CCS STANDARD				
RL.1.10	With prompting and support, read prose and poetry of appropriate complexity for grade 1.				
L.1.6.	Use words and phrases acquired through conversations, reading and being read to, and responding to texts, including using frequently occurring conjunctions to signal simple relationships (e.g., *because*).				
21ST CENTURY LIFE AND CAREER (STANDARD 9) AND/OR TECHNOLOGY STANDARD (STANDARD 8)					
CPI #	CUMULATIVE PROCESS INDICATOR (CPI)				
9.1.4.A.5	Apply critical thinking and problem-solving skills in classroom and family settings. ▲				
9.1.4.C.1	Practice collaborative skills in groups, and explain how these skills assist in completing tasks in different settings (at home, in school, and during play). ▲				
STUDENT LEARNING OBJECTIVES WITH CONCEPT ATTAINMENT *Are concepts being introduced, reviewed, or mastered in this Unit/topic?(For LA, use direct, guided or independent)*					
Key Knowledge		D, G, I	Process/Skills/Procedures/Application of Key Knowledge		D, G, I
Students will know: • Students will know themselves as readers and develop reading identities. • Students will know the routines and expectations for the reading workshop structure. • Students will know how to take care of books. • Students will know that partners are needed to assist with reading development. • Students will know that readers think about the text they are reading. To help themselves think about their text, they will think about what may happen next. ■		G I G G G	*Students will be able to:* • Students will be able to think of the types of books they enjoy and are interested in; and memories attached to reading. • Students will be able to follow the set routine established during the reading workshop. • Students will be able to practice taking care of their books. • Students will be able to work with partnerships in order to grow as readers. ● • Students will be able to make predictions in order to help themselves think about text.		I I I I G

- 9.1.4.C.1 Practice collaborative skills in groups, and explain how these skills assist in completing tasks in different settings (at home, in school, and during play). (**triangle**)

At the core of the co-creation process of a Full Value Commitment within the classroom is critical thinking and problem-solving. Students are empowered to determine the behaviors that will maximize their learning, and then use the Calling Group process to sort through the complexities of maintaining that environment. The standards, then, are continually being reinforced using the Full Value classroom process.

In looking at the Student Learning Objectives under Process/Skills/Procedures, it is noted that:

- Students will be able to work with partnerships to grow as readers. (**oval**)

All six of the Full Values are in play, and the co-created classroom Commitment can be used to reinforce appropriate behaviors in this partnership, while deepening its effectiveness. Again, this illustrates and reinforces the idea that any interactions between students are an activity that can be processed and used to enhance the classroom's social/emotional learning climate.

We have not even touched upon the curriculum's integration of Full Value. Let's look at the indicator under Key Knowledge:

- Students will know that readers think about the text they are reading. To help themselves think about their text, they will think about what may happen next. (**square**)

Prediction in literature can readily be connected to the goal-setting process. When setting a personal or academic goal, major questions to be asked are, "How will I know when I have gotten there? What will be my criteria? What might happen along the way to alter the outcome?" In directly relating goal setting to literature, the reader asks the question, "Where have the characters come from and where are they going?" In all literature, characters change with exposure to life experience. Most set short and long-term goals, either explicitly stated or played out via plot, conflict, theme, and characterization. Utilizing SMART Goals in examining a character's growth in literature serves the dual purpose of understanding the character while teaching students a goal-setting methodology.

How might an experiential activity be used to teach the goal-setting process with links to literature in the classroom? Let's look at Number the Stars (Lowry, 1989)[70], a fictional accounting of a Jewish Family's escape from Denmark during World War II. The Rosen family must flee and is assisted by friends. The story is rich with opportunities for making connections to Full Value Behavioral Norms. The activity Turning over a New Leaf (Chapter 10) provides a perfect opportunity for students to explore this journey together experientially. To briefly review the activity, students are given a large tarpaulin and asked to stand together on it as a group. The goal is then to completely turn over the tarp without students stepping off of it. This requires movement of the tarpaulin in one direction or another, which can be framed as a journeying activity.

Depending on the needs/capabilities of the group, layers of difficulty can be added to the experience:

- The activity is completed in total silence (this might reflect the reality of sharing no verbal information for fear of discovery).

- Some students can be blindfolded and looked after by a partner (this might represent a younger child in the story who would need to be guided).

- All students must remain in physical contact with each other. If contact is lost, the tarp is returned to its starting point, and the activity begins anew.

- Set a time limit for completion to raise the anxiety associated with being discovered.

Changing the physical demands of the activity can serve the curriculum while also testing the behavioral norms that students have agreed to when using their Full Value Commitment.

In brainstorming activity-to-text connections, several ideas come to mind:

- Use SMART goals to organize the process from start to finish.

- Label the top of the tarp with the country of origin.

- Label the bottom side of the tarp with the country they are journeying to. This will be revealed when it is successfully flipped over.

- Ask students to think about personal resources they might use for this journey and what they might need from their classmates.

- Ask students to think about the feelings they might be experiencing around the potential of being caught.

- Ask students to think about the feelings they would have before, during, and after this experience.

Reflection: During the reflection on the activity, students, if necessary, can be guided to make experience-to-text connections. As they 'live' the experience, making connections to the characters' experience becomes more easily integrated. The reflection can also address adherence to or departure from agreed upon behavioral norms. For example, if it was observed that a student lost contact with a classmate who was blindfolded (if that was one of the rules) and no one owned the violation, how does that respect the commitment to Be Honest? This discussion is not framed as a gotcha but rather as an acceptable and expected way to explore the genuine difficulties of adhering to behavioral norms. The students who witnessed the violation might not have wanted to put their classmate on the spot, or perhaps they felt they would be blamed for revealing a breach that would compromise the group's success. When looking at why people make these types of choices, the possibilities are varied, and there are often understandable reasons. These complexities can find a productive voice in reflection, the concepts of right and wrong, loyalties, desire to achieve goals, and potential for shame and humiliation.

Now, let's take a look at an application to science using the activity called Pipeline (Chapter 9). To review, this activity uses varying lengths of PVC pipe ramps to move rolling objects (e.g., marbles, golf balls) from a start to a finish line (hmm, perhaps a journeying activity that focuses on scientific discovery!). Each member of the group gets a PVC pipe. A basic ground rule is to keep the object constantly in motion, although additional rules can be added to raise the difficulty level. Some of the physical principles embedded in this activity are the effects of mass, friction, gravity, and incline on the movement of objects. If you are teaching middle or high school physics, perhaps some idea bells are going off in your head. This lesson might start with predictions related to the incline of the plane (pipeline) and the size and mass of the object(s) being transported. Strategies will need to be devised to control the motion of the objects, given what is being predicted about how these objects will move.

And then there is the community building, the goal-setting, the problem solving, all framed within operating behavioral norms that piggyback on the content being conveyed, in what can be a very high thrill-aerobic experience.

History and social studies particularly lend themselves to embedding Full Value within activities. For example, a high school teacher decided to frame the co-creation of the classroom behavioral norms as an exercise in a constitutional democracy. The classroom Full Value Commitment was their constitution. Representatives were selected within the classroom who met with their constituents to draft Full Value Articles. The representatives then met to hammer out compromises to the document, reporting back to their constituents on a regular basis. Finally, a vote was taken with a 2/3 majority required for approval. This experience offered students an activity-based window into what the process entailed to reach agreement through negotiation, on a document guiding and defining the rights and responsibilities of individuals and groups. Students were better able to make connections between their classroom Constitution and the US Constitution because it had now become more relevant. Because the repetition of Commitments across classrooms can become cumbersome, particularly at the high school level, there is a consideration to use the same representative system to create a grade-wide Full Value Commitment.

In making a connection to historical events, the Helium Hoop (Chapter 9) offers an engaging metaphor concerning conflicts between competing forces and how these disagreements can or cannot be resolved. As a refresher, in the Helium Hoop, students circle around a Hula Hoop placed at shoulder level on an extended index finger from each participant's hand. The object is simple: to lower the hoop to the ground without losing finger-to-hoop contact with it. This is actually far from simple and rapidly becomes conflicted as the hoop rises instead of sinking, fingers lose contact, and blame starts to fly.

It is often the case that the group is no closer to a solution after fifteen minutes of effort. In most instances, the group would be allowed to break and discuss what was not going well and why. But if you wish to use this to demonstrate how irresolvable conflicts can arise, there would be no time allowed for reflection. At some point, when tempers begin to flare, a reflection time should be provided connecting hoop behaviors to how conflicts come to a head between people and governments and lead to 'war.'

An unsuccessful Helium Hoop provides an experiential understanding of how emotions can defeat reason. This could easily be used as an activity embedded in the study of any of the great wars. To be clear, this activity does not address the political and economic forces at work that can lead to the breakdown of civilized behavior. But it does illustrate how working at cross-purposes or with a zealous personal agenda (hence the fingers pushing up to keep contact with the hoop) can cause irrational conflicts to arise. Not every activity requires finishing to be effective. The process during the activity is often of far greater importance than finishing the activity in terms of fostering learning.

Integration of Full Value through the visual and creative arts is perhaps the easiest to accomplish. This is because the content areas of graphic arts, dance, or music are already activity-based.

A striking example of this was an elementary art teacher's decision to have all of her students paint a Full Value mural to adorn the lobby of their school (above). The medium

used aligned with the demands of the curriculum, and each student chose the content of their painted block. The picture eloquently expresses the outcome of this curricular and Full Value integration. The Full Value Mural was designed and painted by students in the entranceway to the Kiel School. This is a preschool through grade two building.

Tools for Lesson Planning[71]

To assist in making connections between academic content areas and experiential learning, we have provided an example of an organizational template completed for a primary Autism class. A plan for these non-verbal, significantly challenged students was selected to illustrate the broad range of applications of Full Value. Each Full Value is listed, followed by anticipated outcomes related to the activity. For a blank copy, please see Chapter 16, Printable Materials.

Primary Autism

Lesson Planning Sheet   Student Name: _____

☒ Language Arts ☐ Reading ☐ Math ☐ Science ☐ Social Studies   ☐ Other:

Teacher: Building: Grade: K-1   Program: Primary Autism

Activity Name: Fill the Basket   Lesson Length: 45 minutes

Academic Goal(s): Identify things that are important to us and create a visual Representation of them

Enduring Objective: Sharing what is of value (important) to us with others

Social Emotional Goal(s): Full Value (Circle specific component(s) to be addressed)

☒ Be Here Active Listening, Becoming Comfortable in One's Own Skin, Building Relationships, Self-Reflection
☒ Be Safe Trust/Mistrust, Feeling Secure, Responding Rather Than Reacting, Self-Regulation, Welcoming Authentic Interaction
☐ Set Goals Exploring the Truth, Integrating Feedback, Practicing an Ethical Code of Behavior, Values
☒ Be Honest Achievement/Failure, Accepting Help, Brainstorm and Plan, Cooperation Versus Competition, Growth Oriented, Defining Clear Objectives, Intelligent Risk-Taking Independence, Intention into Action
☒ Let Go & Move On Revenge Versus Reconciliation, Accepting Complexity Resiliency, Accepting Difference, Accepting Unenforceable Rules
☐ Care for Self & Others Compassion/Self-Compassion, Empathy, Interdependence, Recognizing Personal Needs, Recognizing Self-Worth, Self-Empathy, Self-Sacrifice, Personal and Social Responsibility

Materials: Tennis balls, tape, colored markers, rope to be used for a boundary
Procedure:

Grounding (How to do it): Students may pick from the generated list. Assist them in writing their choices on strips of tape. Attach the tape to objects. Standing outside of a previously positioned rope circle, students will toss their objects into a box at the center of the circle. If they miss, they can go into the circle, retrieve their object, and try again. Position the diameter of the rope to ensure success. Students then take someone else's item from the box and sit outside the rope circle.

Framing (What does it mean?): Explain, using examples, how people and things in our lives are important to us. Allow time for students to react to this idea. Make a list of student responses on the board. (Non-verbal students may use icons and pictures throughout this activity).

Reflection (List strategies): Students, who are now holding someone else's value object, will point at the person they think it belongs to. If they are correct, they will pass the ball to that person. If they are not correct, the person who it belongs to will identify themselves, and the object will be given to that student. The student will then gather all of their objects and use the words/pictures on them to construct individual values posters. These posters will contain either the words or pictures describing the student's list of important people and things in their lives. Students will share the information on their posters with classmates.

Evaluation:

- Academic outcomes

Students will successfully pronounce and write words describing who and what they value (pictures may be used, but saying the words should be attempted by all students).

- Social/Emotional outcomes

Students will successfully identify a minimum of one important person and one important thing in their lives. Students will attempt to share the information on their posters with the group.

Next step:

- Activity extension:

Homework: Poster will be brought home to share with parents. Parents will add to the poster at least one person and an object that is of importance to them. Posters will come back to school, and students will share with the class the parent contributions to the poster.

Content Areas & Full Value Activity Connections

Look back at these activities and think about how they may be applied to academic content areas. We have grouped them to make the process easier. However, tapping into your creativity, you will find that activities can be used across multiple academic areas. Each activity is listed with its chapter location.

Easily adapted to all content areas

Peek A Who, 6
Mine Field, 7
Human Camera, 8
Have You Ever, 8
Truth Drawings, 8
Group Juggling, 9
Moonball, 9
Traffic Jam, 9
Zoom & Re-Zoom, 11
Web Wave, 11
Stepping Stones, 10
Turning Over a New Leaf, 10

Language Arts

Mind Mapping, 3
The Being, 3
Back Stabbers, 8
Luminaria Circle, 10

Mathematics

Toxic Waste, 3
Toss a Name Game, 6
Zen Count, 6
Star Wars, 7
Blindfold Square, 8
Compass Walk, 8
Calculator/Key Punch, 9
Bridge-It, 11
Change Up, 10

History

Full Value Speed Rabbit, 3
The Village, 3
Coming and Going of the Rain, 6
All Aboard, 11
Stonehenge, 11
Negotiations Square, 10

Performing Arts

Human Sculpture, 3
Near-Far, 6

Science

Blob Tag, 6
Fire in the Hole, 6
Flungee, 6
Impulse, 6
Trust Falls, 7
Evolution, 8
Duct Tape, 9
Great Egg Drop, 9
Leaning Tower of Feetza, 9
Pipeline, 9

Social Studies

Everybody's It, 6
Island of Healing Circle, 6
People to People, 6
Balloon Trolley, 9
Electric Fence, 9
Human Knot, 9
Panic Evac, 11
Yurt Circle, 11
Cross the Line, 10

Visual Arts

Claytionary, 6
Personal Coat of Arms, 10

Project Adventure Physical Education Cycles & Full Value

Project Adventure has been a disseminator of experiential learning for over 40 years. As such, many school districts currently integrate a low and high ropes course experience into their physical education programs. Working with physical education staff, the classroom teacher can create Full Value peak experiences with their students, using an existing ropes course facility in the school. Because of their training in using ropes courses, many physical education teachers are familiar with social emotional learning practices and how Project Adventure integrates them into the student experience. Full Value can operate to support all elements of Project Adventure programming. The physical education teacher can develop a Full Value Commitment with their students and support the work of the classroom teacher through collaborative planning.

Summing Up

The recipe for success in linking activity to content is a pretty simple formula. First, find activities that you like! This is critical, as it is easier to convince students of the value of an activity that you are already sold on. Learn the activity well. Think about the dynamics that are naturally present in the experience. Think about what the activity represents (e.g., journeying, circling, individualizing, grouping). These are adventure archetypes (Schoel & Maizell, 2002)[72] that are present within specific activities. They can help with the fit between the activity and the curriculum. Include your students in connecting the activity to the curriculum content. This is a naturalistic way to enter into the content and empowers students to take responsibility for their learning. Do not be afraid of a bumpy ride. Discuss this with students and link it to their behavioral norms. The commitment to maintain emotional safety and to Care for Self & Others casts them as your helpers in finding success within the activity. And if there are problems, the behavioral norms are there to provide ground rules for discussion and promote learning. Most importantly, embrace the fun and excitement of the experience.

CHAPTER 13

MINDFULNESS & FULL VALUE

To begin, it is important to note that the practice of mindfulness is woven into all of the Full Value Behavioral Norms, not just Be Here. The chart below summarizes the connections:

Full Value Behavioral Norm	Connection to Mindfulness
Be Here	Attention, Mindfulness
Be Safe	Physical and Emotional Well Being
Be Honest	Integrity, Trust and Values
Set Goals	Intention into Action Effort
Let Go & Move On	Acceptance and Forgiveness
Care For Self & Others	Empathy and Compassion

These connections will be addressed in this chapter.

Note: You will see that this chapter contains several uses of the Helium Hoop Activity. It can also be found in the chapters on goal setting and academic content areas. This reinforces that activities can be used for multiple purposes, all depending on how they are framed.

Overview

The task is simple; just lower the hoop to the ground as a group in 10 minutes or less. To recap, the rules are that it must rest on only two fingers of each participant and that no one may physically disconnect their fingers while it is being lowered. These are part of the instructions that are delivered when we introduce the Helium Hoop (Chapter 9). This seemingly modest task tends to get out of control rather quickly. There are many reasons for this. It may be that students do not want to experience or take responsibility for failure, which means losing contact with the hoop. The desire to maintain contact at all costs forces the hoop upward. Some students do not feel a commitment to participate. Others may find satisfaction in actively working against success. In some instances, a paralysis sets in, perhaps due to the fear of making a mistake. Then the hoop does not move at all.

Rarely does a group get this on their first attempt. After letting the group struggle for a few minutes, we provide a brief relaxation technique called *Positive Emotional Refocusing Technique* (Luskin, 2001, pg. 119).[73] The group almost always initially improves, but then reverts to its previous state of chaos or rigidity. The framing and build up to this activity include discussion around the behaviors and norms of effective groups and the psychological safety needed to allow these norms to thrive. It also includes introducing the six behavioral norms of the Full Value Commitment (written on the hoop). It is only when students become more connected and practiced in the Full Value norms that they are more likely to be successful in lowering the hoop. This experience becomes a living metaphor for the group's functioning and well-being.

What initially allows the group to begin their path to success is each student's ability to stay focused, receptive, and to remain calm and even tempered. Students need to be responding to each other in a deliberate manner rather than reacting haphazardly. This requires awareness of their own and others' connection to the hoop and adjusting accordingly from moment to moment. The individual choice by each student to be mindful exponentially increases the group's success at this initiative.

Mindfulness is a perfect companion to Full Value and social-emotional learning in that it offers techniques that enhance our inner ability to practice the Full Value norms. In this section, we offer you an introduction to mindfulness through the lens of the Full Value Behavioral Norms. We hope that the reader's interest will be piqued enough and convinced of the importance of this practice to seek out further education and training. At the end of this section there will be a variety of resources provided to support the development of competencies in this area.

The words mindfulness and meditation have become part of our modern vernacular through a multitude of mediums. A recent Google search of the terms yielded 1,250,000 hits. Books have been written on mindfulness in business, the military, law, sports, and education. One can access various trainings in person or online, utilize apps, and even read Mindful Magazine. Mindfulness and meditation have achieved such an increased awareness in the popular culture that they have been featured on the cover of Time magazine three times. There have been a variety of quick fixes that some have referred to as "McMindfulness." Retailers have caught on by creating things like Mindful Mayonnaise and other products that make light of the importance of this practice. However, even though this awareness has become part of the zeitgeist, these terms and techniques are greatly misunderstood.

Let's first look at these concepts and start with what they are not. They are not recently discovered new age concepts that require adherence to a particular belief system, joining a religion or cult, participating in navel gazing, brainwashing, spacing out, or even reaching something called "enlightenment or nirvana." They are, however, a means to living a more deliberate, meaningful, and engaged life.

When you do that Google search on mindfulness and meditation, you will also get some descriptions that can be very confusing on the precise meanings and distinctions between the terms. There are a variety of relaxation and breathing techniques, guided meditations, visualizations, and somatic and mindfulness practices that may all be referred to as mindfulness or meditation. These debates and discussions have existed for a long time, and they will not be resolved here. However, we do want to make you aware of the overall difference between relaxation techniques and meditation.

Relaxation techniques refer to activities like deep breathing and progressive muscle relaxation. The main goal of these practices is to calm or regulate the nervous system. The main goal of meditation is to become more familiar with the workings of the mind. To make this all simpler, just think of the concept of exercise. There are plenty of exercises, and they are all practiced to assist us in achieving overall physical health. However, exercise also has some secondary impacts on our mental health, sleep, intellectual capability, and a variety of other benefits. Many people at first take up exercise to work on singularly focused areas like losing weight, becoming more toned, or dealing with a specific physical ailment. Likewise, many people start practicing meditation to deal with overwhelming feelings associated with anxiety, depression, and anger that we tend to clump under the word "stress." When people start to practice meditation earnestly, they also begin to discover that it can greatly impact overall well-being and relationships. Instead of just focusing on the body or nervous system, meditation is a way of working on our inner lives. Like running is one type of exercise, mindfulness for our purposes should be considered one type of meditation. In some meditation traditions, it is the foundation of contemplative practices.

Mindfulness's main objective is to help us develop our attention. In some settings, people will refer to mindfulness as attention or focus training. The military has chosen the term *situational awareness* to describe mindfulness practices. Mindfulness's entry to the present moment is through developing our awareness of thoughts, emotions, and senses. Another view of this is to look at the actual meanings from the ancient language of Pali, where these terms are believed to have originated. In this language, meditation means *to become familiar with*, and mindfulness means *to remember* (Lozzio, 2015).[74] If the object of awareness in a mindfulness meditation is the breath, then the person becomes *familiar* with their breathing by sensing it in the present moment. When the attention goes off the breath, one *remembers* to bring it back. Awareness can be practiced through any of the five senses by focusing our attention on an object like food (taste) or a bird singing (hearing) and continuously bringing one's attention back when distracted by a thought, feeling, or sensation. The senses can only be experienced in the present moment, and they allow a perfect platform for the practice. Mindful practices can be formal, like seated meditation and mindful walking sessions, or informal, like focusing your attention on a daily activity. These could include brushing your teeth, washing the dishes—anything you can experience through your senses. As physical exercise or training can prepare us for a specific event (like a bike tour), mindfulness practices can prepare us for real life.

Let's explore mindfulness through the lens of the Full Value Behavioral Norms and its role in developing the CASEL five social and emotional competencies and a safe and effective school community. A popular definition of mindfulness comes from Jon Kabat-Zinn, the founder of the University of Massachusetts Mindfulness Based Stress Reduction program, who has been instrumental in making mindfulness more generally accepted:

> Mindfulness is the awareness that emerges through paying attention on purpose, in the present moment, and non-judgmentally to the unfolding of experience moment by moment as if your life depended on it (pg. 17).[75]

Be Here: In the Present Moment

What is the present moment for you? If you are not here, where are you? While doing the Full Value Helium Hoop, are the participants thinking about a time when they were a child playing with a hoop, are they worried that people are judging them in the group, or are they fully present with the task, feeling the hoop on their fingers and adjusting effectively to others' movements? How many times have you had the experience of reading a passage and having no idea what you read because your thoughts or senses have taken you away? Our attention has a tendency to wander.

There is so much vying for our attention and removing us from the present moment. These distractions are both external and internal. Mindfulness helps us become aware of these distractions and to refocus our attention. But our attention cannot be redirected without developing this initial awareness. For many of us, our attention is like an atrophied muscle and needs a good workout. Try this experiment for the next ten seconds.

Try not to have a thought. How did you do? The average person has between 50,000 and 85,000 thoughts a day. Skeptical? Sit for a few minutes and count your thoughts. Double the count, because each number is also a thought, and then multiply this by the number of hours you are awake. Watch how easily your thoughts add up. The other interesting thing about our thoughts is that approximately 96 percent of them are exactly the same thoughts that we had yesterday.[76] We are not as unique or creative as we imagined. What we begin to discover is that our thoughts are just mental events that we have limited to no control over. We are never taught this. A basic understanding of the brain and the mind helps tremendously in accepting how hard being mindful can be.

The primary focus of education is on this concept called *thinking*, but practitioners rarely explore what it is. We are not talking about brain processes but rather a practical, user-friendly understanding.

So, what is a thought? How do you even know that you have had one? Do you hear a voice in your head, or maybe see an image? Perhaps the two are combined, at times. Imagine if that voice was a real, live person who followed you around all day. It might just drive you crazy with its incessant chatter. Then imagine a person holding up an image in front of you all day. Now that you are noticing this voice and image, have you ever realized how negative these sometimes could be? This is what neuroscience refers to as *negativity bias*. It originally evolved for our protection to make us alert to any possible danger. It is the immediate emergency reaction of thinking or imagining a bear rather than a chipmunk when hearing a twig snap in the woods. This default was very effective in protecting us when we were cave dwellers, but today it is an overactive and usually critical voice that creates fear, avoidance, and pessimism. Now imagine that the voice in your head was attached to a loudspeaker or your images were projected above you when walking around. How embarrassing!

Our thoughts and images can be fairly weird, wild, and almost completely random. They can also be creative, brilliant, kind, and humorous. Unfortunately, due to the negativity bias, we focus on and give much more weight to the negative ones. There is an old saying that goes, "For every one negative event in our lives, we need five positive ones to balance it out." It's like when we get evaluated, and our supervisor tells us so many great things about our work, but we only focus on one negative piece of feedback. Understanding how easily thoughts can take us away from being here helps us understand how mindfulness can counter these tendencies and allow us to be more present. It is like lifting a weight, where the upward and downward movements of a curl build the muscles. Through the practice of concentrating on a sense, we are developing our muscle of attention and being cognizant that our attention has shifted. This allows us to build our muscle of awareness. Mindfulness helps us become more familiar with this inner voice, bodily sensations, and emotions, thus allowing us to become capable of responding rather than reacting. There is a neuroscience saying that goes, "Where your attention goes, neural firing flows, and neural connections grow." Current science demonstrates that mindfulness practice produces physical changes in the brain, positively impacts bodily processes, and improves our well-being and relationships. All this just by Being Here.

Be Safe: Non-Judgmentally

While doing the Helium Hoop activity, will students start judging other people? Are they having strong feelings around the lack of success and blaming others? Do they attack or blame themselves that it can't be done? For the most part, physical safety is pretty straightforward in this activity. The group can easily identify that moving rapidly across the room with the hoop could cause someone to trip and fall. It is also easily remedied by asking students to stand still while attempting the task. However, we are now talking about inner processes that are not easily identified or dealt with so simply. A student may become frustrated and start blaming another participant for not being able to assist properly. They may believe this person is deliberately lifting the hoop rather than lowering it. The student may make silent judgments about their peers; judgments like this person is "stupid, lazy, does not care," or is "not a team player." These are thoughts that automatically arise from that inner critical voice. A reactive student may have these thoughts and instantly lash out at classmates. If the student can become more aware of their bodily sensations, thoughts, feelings, and the potential for an adverse reaction, then the potential to successfully self-regulate becomes more likely. They begin to develop a filter, moving away from blame and seeking understanding.

It is almost impossible to find out who is pushing the hoop up because of the reactivity of all the group members. A student may even realize that they could also be the one who is raising the hoop and that attacking does not help. Again, understanding a little about our brain processes and our need to categorize and judge for our protection and safety allows us to become more aware and skillful in our responses. Studies have shown that mindfulness practices have increased people's empathy and compassion: both areas that enable students to intentionally practice being safe with themselves and others.[77]

Be Honest: Awareness That Emerges

As the group continues attempting the Helium Hoop, people may notice that more and more feelings and judgments occur. Are these now true? Before we start talking about feelings, a brief note. The words *feelings* and *emotions*, and even the word *moods*, are frequently interchanged in the English language. One can find numerous debates in journals and articles about the specific differences. We have chosen to base the following on the works of psychologist Paul Ekman and the neuroscientist Antonio Damasio (2009).[78]

What is a feeling? How do you know you have a feeling? Right, you just feel it. Well, not exactly. We experience sensations in our body that some internal or external stimulus has provoked, and these sensations provide us with information. This information almost simultaneously combines with our emotions and possibly our moods, and presto, we have feelings. This information almost simultaneously combines with our emotions, and possibly our moods, and presto, we have feelings. This state then gives us the option as to how we should cope with the situation. We may experience our eyes dilating, profuse sweating, heart racing, legs shaking, and a surge of overall energy as one group of sensations. But is this due to a friend jumping out and scaring us, being cut off by a rude driver, or going on a first date? According to Paul Ekman's research, we have six basic emotions: anger, disgust, fear, happiness, sadness, and surprise.[79] These emotions are activated in a part of our brain that is illogical, reactive, and serves to protect us. The bodily sensations associated with these emotions are instinctual and almost always autonomic, but our feelings are not. Much of what we know about our feelings is learned, and we can work with them. There are over 4,000 words that represent feelings in the English language, and they come from our experiences. Moods are emotional states that are not as intense but can also impact our feelings. They are generally either positive or negative and do not have an immediate impact.

> My wife does a spectacular job decorating our house during the holidays. We celebrate it all during the winter season. Her family is Jewish and mine is Catholic. So we have snowmen with yarmulkes, towels with Santa and a dancing rabbi, a Christmas tree topped with the star of David, and a plethora of decorations representing each tradition. All these decorations require large bins that are stored in the attic after the holidays. It takes two people to lift these containers up the attic stairs. Last year, I figured I would take advantage of my sons being home from college and asked them to take the bins up to the attic. Their response was, "No problem dad." Now it is important to know that was my older son's last day before he returned south to Charleston and I wouldn't see him for a few months. I left for work with both boys sitting bookend on the couch playing FIFA on the X-Box comforted in my belief that the job would be completed. I returned later that evening and saw my boys in the exact some positions now watching TV and not a single bin moved! How would you feel? Me too. I felt my hands clench, stomach tighten, and an increase of energy in my body. Anger! How dare they not help their dad! But all this mindfulness stuff really does work sometimes. I caught myself before I exploded and searched for a source of wisdom. That would be my wife. I asked her if she knew why the bins were not put away. She shared that my younger son was out at the gym lifting and just returned a few hours ago. And my older son? Well, he is an EMT and when home goes out on emergency calls. My wife then shared that he had just sat down five minutes before I came home after his third consecutive call. The last call had a fatality. Now how do you feel about the bins? Me too. They meant nothing compared to what my son had just witnessed. I could have really messed up our last night together by attacking him. By being aware of all of this, I was able to better understand the situation and respond appropriately. I know I can't do this all the time but I have found that the more I practice, the more I realize that I don't always know the truth of the situation. - John

Mindfulness practices, like the body scan, offer the opportunity to become aware of our emotions through bodily sensations. The more you practice, the more familiar you are with reactions and can intervene effortlessly. Knowing that anger may be felt through your tightened fists, the burning sensations in your belly, and a rapid heart rate allows you to catch and work with the feeling. As another neuroscience adage says, "If you can name it, you can tame it." Again, research has shown that just by naming an emotion, "I am feeling angry," a shift happens that takes it away from just a bodily response, engaging the prefrontal cortex and releasing chemicals that relax the body. Being honest requires awareness of the sensations and includes our emerging emotions, feelings, and thoughts. This is very hard work for most of us and causes us to ask the question, "Do I really know what is going on?" Without taking into consideration all the information mentioned above, we most likely have no idea. It is like when we get cut off by a reckless driver. We may have a strong reaction that may lead to a choice finger gesture and words aimed at the other driver. But if we find out that the driver cut us off because they were racing to the hospital with a badly bleeding child, we would most likely let go of our anger and respond with empathy and understanding.

Set Goals: Attention on Purpose

The Full Value Helium Hoop goal is pretty straightforward: Lower it to the ground in 10 minutes or less. This is a specific, measurable, and easily trackable goal for the group. Whether they can achieve it within the allotted time is a whole other question. What interferes is the myriad of ways that the group members lose attention and thus physical contact with the hoop. Instead of just focusing on the overall goal, the members must continuously attend to the immediate goal of just staying connected to the hoop. Paying attention to the moment and continually adjusting to each other gets the group to the larger goal. It is a scaffolding of many emerging goals that build into the larger goal. This is like setting the goal of losing weight and creating a comprehensive plan to accomplish this desired outcome. But when that doughnut is in front of you, the immediate goal is not to eat the doughnut. Many people pursue mindfulness with lofty goals of being more patient, becoming kinder, finding inner peace, and enjoying life. These are noteworthy ambitions. However, when you attempt to focus your attention on your breath and get distracted by a thought, the more immediate task is to bring your attention back to just this breath. You can't be thinking about the bigger goals because they then become the distraction.

How many times have you been stridently told or told others to "pay attention?" We bark out this demand without ever taking the time to define, teach, or practice it. We need to start with the understanding that our minds have a natural tendency to wander. Researcher and Harvard Professor Dan Gilbert has shown that the average person spends 47% of their time mind wandering (2010).[80] A study in Canada reports the average human attention span has fallen from twelve seconds in 2000, or around the time the mobile phone revolution began, to eight seconds in 2016. The age of smartphones has left humans with such a short attention span that even a goldfish can hold its attention for longer than we can (McSpannen, 2015).[81] Like the tendency of our muscles to atrophy if not used, our attention needs to be worked out. We need to develop exercises and repeated practices that strengthen this ability. Neuroscience has shown that "neurons that fire together wire together." If we are practicing inattention, these neural pathways become more developed as our natural default. Unfortunately, we have an inordinate amount of practice in not paying attention and being distracted. Developing intentional practices that are repeated to work on concentration and awareness allows new neural pathways to develop. These new pathways enable us to remain more focused and capable of bringing our attention back.

The idea of keeping your eye on the prize is not helpful when you are just trying just to keep your fingers connected to the hoop. If you do, you miss what is happening right now, and you disconnect, don't move, or push the hoop away from your fellow students. This purposeful goal of attention becomes an emerging process that needs continual assessment and adjustment. It is like sailing to a destination. You must map out an overall course to reach your destination. However, it is the constant adjustments of the sails and rudder that get you there. It is also being open to the possibility of developing a new course when needed. How often have you had to adjust your approach to a student when teaching them a new concept, when your original strategy was not working? Mindfulness is one such practice to develop the ability to be purposeful with our attention and keep us with the emerging goals of the moment.

We need to develop practices that strengthen our attending ability. We devote an inordinate amount of practice to not paying attention. Developing intentional, repeated practice to work on concentration and awareness allows new neural pathways to form. These new pathways permit us to remain more focused and capable of bringing our attention back. Mindfulness is one such effective practice to develop this skill.

Let Go & Move On: Unfolding of Experience

What really makes the Hula Hoop descend is the student's ability to let go and not control the hoop. The more receptive a participant becomes, the easier the hoop moves. It is the desire to control the hoop that keeps pushing it upward. If we accepted the properties of the hoop (lightweight) and adjusted our attempts to just let go, it would lower quickly. It is a true revelation in our lives when we discover what we can and cannot control. It is the misunderstanding that we have control over our thoughts and emotions that leads to many problems.

What we do have control over is our response to our thoughts and emotions. Attempting to control things that are not controllable gives us a false illusion of stability. Fred Luskin (2001) refers to these as *unenforceable rules*.[82] It is running an outdoor field trip with your students and expecting it not to rain, then getting angry when it does rain and freaking out all day, ruining the trip for yourself and students by not adapting to this situation. Another saying from the mindfulness world states, "If you have a problem in life and you can do something about it, do it. So why worry? If you have a problem in life and can't do anything about it, why worry?" In the example of the rainstorm, it would be to either postpone the trip or have students wear raincoats.

The act of letting go allows us to develop what many refer to as wisdom. In the Alcoholics Anonymous 12 Step program, this wisdom has been known for years, and the Serenity Prayer clearly points this out. In mindful meditation on the breath, this letting go muscle is developed when we become aware that our attention has been hijacked and then kindly and gently returning our attention to the breath. ABC Newsman and self-proclaimed mindfulness evangelist Dan Harris has been heard to say, "Learning to let go and start over is all there is to mindfulness."

Care for Self & Others: As if Your Life Depended on It

By attending to your efforts in attempting the hoop, you are better able to assist others. By creating your own stillness, you are better capable of responding to others' efforts. An analogy that works well is the instructions given by flight attendants regarding oxygen masks. "Place the oxygen mask on yourself first before your child or loved one." We cannot be helpful to anyone when we are unconscious. This image is true in our lives but is often dismissed and overlooked. The lack of Care for Self is especially true in the education and helping professions. It is, for example, the dedicated teacher who shows up sick and wears herself down, becoming more ill. This does not mean that we become more self-involved and just focus on ourselves all the time. Self-sacrifice is part of caring for others. It does mean developing the wisdom to know when to take care of ourselves to be more available for others. It also means that we become more committed to our own physical and emotional health and growth.

Our lives do depend on our attention. Just walk through midtown Manhattan on a busy day without being cognizant of your surroundings and the many obstacles that could harm you. Buses, cabs, trains, cars, bikes, and pedestrians could easily hit you with some dire consequences. The potential danger of not paying attention to our physical safety is clear. This lack of attending to and taking care of our inner lives may seem to have no immediate consequences. However, this deprivation will have a negative cumulative effect. It may result in us automatically going through life, not paying attention to our own emotional needs. This impedes our ability to live our lives to the fullest and be as present as possible for family, friends, work, and communities.

There is an essential differentiation between self-attention and mind wandering. When your mind drifts, this does not equate to paying attention to oneself. It is more of a distraction and can often represent fixation on tangential or anxiety-provoking thoughts. If the studies by Dan Gilbert are accurate, we miss almost half our lives due to mind wandering. Mindfulness offers the tools to remedy this and to be more engaged with each other. Mindfulness practices like *Loving Kindness* have been shown to impact parts of the brain that are responsible for mind wandering and to lessen it.

There is an ancient term in Buddhism called *Bodhisattva*. One who becomes a Bodhisattva dedicates their life to bettering all humans. However, before one can reach this title or take the Bodhisattva vows, one must commit to rigorous training to better themselves. Educators have dedicated their lives to improving our youth and thus humanity. As a society, we need to value the personal development of teachers and realize that the healthier they are, the more they can offer their students. As the French philosopher Simone Weil stated, "Attention is the rarest and purest form of generosity." Caring for Self is strengthened through the practice of mindfulness, allowing educators to bring their full attention to caring for students.

Full Value & Mindfulness in Action

Here is a practical example to help deepen your understanding. Imagine walking down the street and seeing a good friend on the other side of the street. You wave and call out her name, but she doesn't respond. What sensations do you feel in your body? What is the emotion you experience? What is your first thought? What is your first feeling? When this scenario is presented at trainings, we typically get the following responses in order of popularity:

1) An anger-based response that usually consists of referring to the non-responder as some lower body part or product of that area.

2) A hurt response that is usually overly self-conscious or guilty. They are mostly worried that they did something wrong to the person and that the non-responder is angry with them.

3) A response of equanimity or neutrality that is inquisitive in nature and wonders if the non-responder actually saw or heard them. This is the rarest of all the responses.

Further information reveals that your friend had earbuds in, was listening to deafening music, and was in her own world. She never saw or heard you. But if you are aware and honest, you had immediate bodily sensations (emotion) and a predominant interpretation (thought), and thus a feeling was created. Add to this situation your mood, physical wellbeing, temperament, and other personal beliefs, and it can become the perfect storm of misunderstanding and emotional hijacking. Imagine that you were dumped by a loved one recently, or you won the lottery, or just had a nasty head cold. All of these will most likely influence your interpretation and reactions to the above scenario. Inherently, our emotions have little impact on us when they are not connected to a specific thought or feeling. It is the lack of awareness and understanding, and having these misinterpretations, that can impact our well-being. In emergencies, this process is highly effective in keeping us safe, but in our everyday lives, we are mainly dealing with perceived rather than actual threats. Through the lens of Full Value and mindfulness, an emotionally intelligent response to this situation would be number 3, above.

You would:

- Be Here by being aware of your current mood, emotions, and thoughts, and how they may be impacting your understanding of the interaction.

- Be Safe by not attacking the person or yourself with blame.

- Be Honest by realizing that you have no idea what is really going on with your friend.

- Set Goals by planning on meeting with your friend to talk about the interaction and discover the truth.

- Let Go & Move On by knowing that your initial reactions/interpretations may be wrong, and until you know more, you need to find ways to remain calm.

- Care of Self and Others by calming yourself down and finding ways to nurture yourself until you can talk with your friend. When you can do this, you may be more open to your friend in a kind and caring manner that will allow an authentic conversation. Responding to this situation mindfully permits the relationship to be more fully valued.

Bringing Mindfulness to Schools

Mindfulness in education is still in its infancy, and there is limited research on the best model for bringing these practices into an educational system. However, based on the current research and learning from established programs, such as Mindfulness Based Stress Reduction, Mindful Education, Mind Up, Search Inside Yourself, and others, there are three areas that these programs include: mentors, teachings, and community. The Full Value School model focuses on and incorporates all three.

Find a good curriculum and or develop your own that meets your students' needs. Become more conversant with the science that supports these practices and utilize this information to reduce misunderstandings. This is especially needed to make sure religion or biased belief systems are not brought into public education. Having access to scientifically based evidence of the efficacy of mindfulness is crucial. Make sure that the teachings are developmentally appropriate and sequenced for students. The pedagogy should also include the following literacies developed by Daniel Rechtschaffen (2014) of Mindful Education:

- Physical: Bodily sensations
- Mental: Thoughts
- Emotional: Emotions and feelings
- Social: Relationships
- Global: Interconnectedness[83]

This leads to an admonition about teaching meditation and mindfulness to staff and students without developing your own practice and being properly trained. Working with the mind for some may be a very anxiety provoking experience and more damaging than helpful. This is usually found with people who have experienced trauma. The act of closing one's eyes and looking inward at thoughts and feelings may be at the least uncomfortable, but for one with a traumatic experience in their past, it could be truly damaging. This is a rare occurrence, but we must be aware of the possible dangers and practice the behavioral norm of Be Safe. Staff should be informed of the role trauma can play in impacting student learning.

Develop a strong and safe environment for learning. Duhigg (2016)[84], in his research on teambuilding for Google's Aristotle Project, demonstrates the need for psychological safety to ensure group effectiveness. Studies have also shown that the more connected students are, the better access they have to the parts of the brain that potentiate learning. Understand that this takes time and practice (Barron & Darling-Hamond, 2008).[85]

3 New Rs of Education

Rechtschaffen has written that mindfulness offers the new 3 Rs of education: Reflection, Relationships, and Resilience. Developing a Full Value community promotes and strengthens all three areas and overall mental health.[86] The World Health Organization (2014) defines mental health as "a state of well-being in which every individual realizes his or her own potential, can cope with the normal stresses of life, can work productively and fruitfully, and is able to make a contribution to his or her community."[87] Well-being is our ability to understand and effectively self-regulate our thoughts, emotions, feelings, and moods, or what is now referred to as having emotional intelligence. Thoughts, emotions, feelings, and moods are the internal markers we use to process everything, developing the awareness and the skillful means to respond to our emotions and feelings effectively. This is at the heart of wellbeing. The tool that enables an awareness of our inner world. Our experiences of the external world can be referred to as the mind. Doesn't it make sense to also offer a method to train the mind? Mindfulness is this training. Doesn't it make sense to create an environment that fosters this training? A Full Value School allows for this to happen.

Activities that Support Teaching Mindfulness

Established meditation practice has traditionally been represented by the image of a bird and its two wings. The bird cannot take flight without the wings being strong and working in unison. If the body of the bird is the meditation practice, then the two wings represent the development of wisdom and compassion. Wisdom is the understanding of our own inner lives and their influence on our understanding of others and the world at large. Compassion is simply becoming kinder to ourselves and others. It is about acknowledging our connections to others and our interdependence. In today's terms, these two wings could be referred to as emotional and social intelligence.

The following activities and their sequencing have been created to introduce mindfulness and teaching related concepts connected to social emotional learning. It is strongly recommended that teachers educate themselves further in these specific areas to enhance the lessons. Resources are included with each activity to assist in this learning. The activities are also used to model the adaptability of experiential education when teaching various topics through metaphor. We encourage the reader to explore and create their own metaphorical connections to social and emotional learning topics.

Brain Basics

Teaching the basics of brain functioning assists students in developing a better understanding of how relaxation, mindfulness, and meditation practices work. These descriptions also include how the mind and body are connected and how this impacts our daily living and interactions. Teachers should become more familiar with the basics of neuroscience and the brain when teaching these practices.

The Triune Brain model (McLean, 1990)[88] is a representation of the brain and its basic functioning. While the explosion of recent brain scan imaging technology has shown the brain to be much more complex and interconnected than this original model, it still provides an excellent beginning overview for students. Resources throughout the activities and the index will offer opportunities to explore the more current research and findings.

The Triune Brain

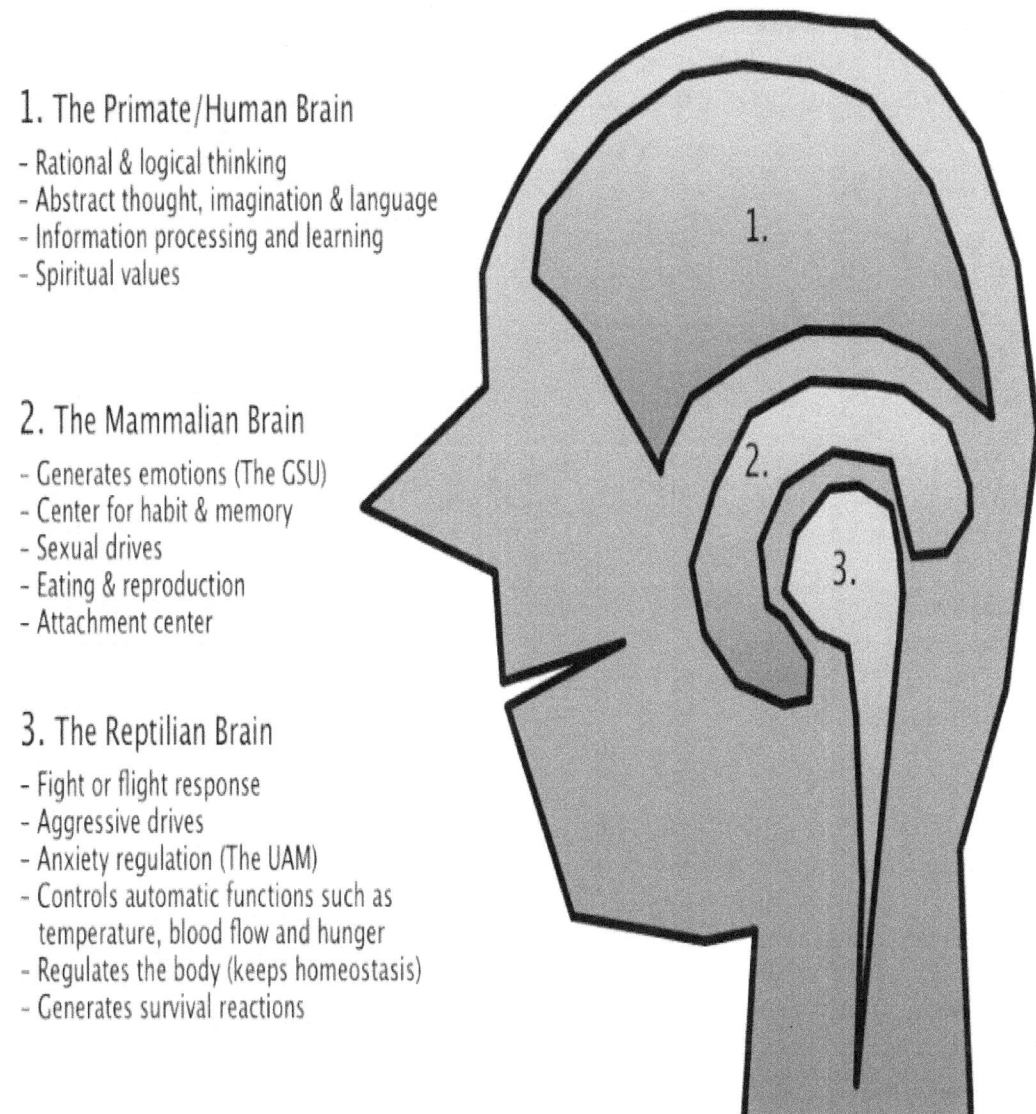

1. The Primate/Human Brain
- Rational & logical thinking
- Abstract thought, imagination & language
- Information processing and learning
- Spiritual values

2. The Mammalian Brain
- Generates emotions (The GSU)
- Center for habit & memory
- Sexual drives
- Eating & reproduction
- Attachment center

3. The Reptilian Brain
- Fight or flight response
- Aggressive drives
- Anxiety regulation (The UAM)
- Controls automatic functions such as temperature, blood flow and hunger
- Regulates the body (keeps homeostasis)
- Generates survival reactions

Mindfulness Activities

The Activity: Evolution of the Triune Brain   Time: 30 minutes

Difficulty: 2-3

Note: This activity is also found in Chapter 7, Be Safe; another example of multiple uses for the same activity. In this instance, it is being used to teach elements of the Triune Brain. The Triune Brain is a model that divides the brain into 3 areas.

When introducing the roles, ask the participants to describe how these animals interact with each other and their environments. Use this as an opportunity to teach the characteristics of each part of the Triune Brain through these behaviors.

For example, reptiles are usually solitary animals with little to no observable emotion other than fight or flight, whereas dogs are more social and emotional in their interactions. Feel free to replace the animals with your own preference of animal to represent each category.

Introduce the following roles:

Egg:
    Structure: Arms overhead with fingers interlaced and eyes downward
    Movement: Shuffling feet and slow
    Sound: Silent

Reptile: (T Rex)
    Structure: Arms at sides, hands out in front with claws showing
    Movement: Stamping feet in strong, deliberate movement
    Sound: Loud roar

Mammal: (Dog)
    Structure: Hands next to head with fingers spread out to make ears, wagging tail
    Movement: Quick and light
    Sound: Barking and howling

Primate: (Chimpanzee)
    Structure: Arms waving above head and legs bent
    Movement: Swaying movement mixed with bouncing around
    Sound: Hooting and howling

How you do it:

Only the same species can play against each other. Whenever someone loses, they always restart as an egg.

Play: All participants start as eggs and mill about.

- When an egg meets another egg, the two players participate in a single game of rock, paper, scissors, and the winner advances to a reptile.

- Reptile goes against another reptile. The winner advances to mammal and the loser returns to an egg.

- The mammal must find three other mammals for a total of four players and play against each other. No planning may occur, and the winner(s) advance to a primate(s). If one person plays a rock and the other three play scissors, then only the rock moves on. If three players throw rocks and only one throws a scissors, then all three move on, and the one throwing scissors goes back to an egg. If all the same symbols are thrown and it is a tie, then play continues until there is a distinct winner(s). If the four mammals tie three times in a row, they all must return to being eggs.

- When players reach the primate level, they must get into groups of three and compete with other groups of three primates. Each team of three primates must all agree on the same symbol when competing with another like team of primates in rock, paper, scissors. The winning team rises to human, and the losers become eggs.

- Humans just hang out with other humans and look down on the other animals.

Stop the game after about ten to fifteen minutes of play. Call out the roles and invite people to display their representation of egg, reptile, mammal, primate, and human, and to make the corresponding sounds.

Reflection:

What: What did you notice while playing this game?

So What: How did you feel throughout the game? What lessons can be learned from the game?

Now What: Teach the Triune Brain utilizing the hand model displayed through the video by Dan Siegel (2007).[89] Teach about *flipping your lid* and how the lower parts of the brain take over when experiencing strong, destructive emotions or stress. Help the students identify situations that flip their lids.

Connection to Mindfulness

Relaxation, meditation, and mindfulness practices have all been scientifically proven to change the brain, body, and especially the nervous system. Helping students understand how stress and emotions impact our brain and body offers the opportunity to teach them practices that can help with self-regulation and recovery from flipping your lid.

The Activity: Evolution of Compassion   Time: 30 minutes

Difficulty: 2-3

This is a great activity to play after the Evolution of the Triune Brain. It represents a clear introduction as to the importance of social emotional learning and the development of compassion. This is mainly played like traditional Evolution with some minor changes. There are four Structures (Germer, 2016)[90] in this variation that we will refer to as states.

How you do it:

State 1: Stress/Anger

Structure: Both arms bent in front like a fighter. Fists should be held tightly, and a scowl should be on the face. Limited, menacing eye contact with other participants

Movement: Breath should be rapid. Swaying movement mixed with bouncing around, like a boxer ready to fight

State 2: Relaxed

Structure: Open fists and palms turned outward toward other participants. Body should be relaxed. Limited eye contact with eyes half open

Movement: Breath should be slower with a 5 seconds in, 5-seconds out cadence. Slow meandering gait

State 3: Self-Compassion/Self-Care

Structure: One hand is placed over the heart, and the other over the stomach. Walking should be slower and more deliberate, with occasional breathing breaks of a four second inhale, a seven second hold, and an eight second exhale pattern.

State 4: Empathy and Compassion/Taking Care of Others

Structure: Put arms in front of self in a circle with hands touching around heart height. This should mimic the actions of giving a pretend hug to an invisible person.

All players start with the Stress state and play rock, paper, scissors, advancing to the next level like regular Evolution. However, once participants reach Compassion level, they may now go back and try to move other participants up. This is done by matching/mirroring the person's current state and then matching rock, paper, or scissor symbols rather than defeating the person. Once the symbols are matched, the person may move up to the next state. If other people who have reached the Compassion state, they too may assist in bringing people up to Compassion. Only one person in the group is required to match the person being helped for them to advance.

Reflection:

What: What did you notice while playing this game? What did you experience that was different from the first game of evolution?

So What: How did you feel throughout the game? What lessons can be learned from the activity regarding developing empathy and compassion?

Now What: Many components of this activity can become lessons in themselves and catalysts for teaching social emotional learning. Below are a few examples.

Self-Compassion:

The three components of self-compassion are:

- Self-Kindness: Being kind and understanding with oneself as one would be with a friend

- Common Humanity: Understanding that we're not alone in our mistakes, weaknesses, and failures, that making mistakes is intrinsically human, and that they are a normal part of everyone's life

- Mindfulness: Being mindful of one's emotions and feelings without over-identifying with them, i.e., validating our emotions without adding fuel to the fire (Neff, 2014)[91]

Empathy:

The term *empathy* is used to describe a wide range of experiences. Emotion researchers generally define empathy as the ability to sense other people's emotions, coupled with the ability to imagine what someone else might be thinking or feeling.

Contemporary researchers often differentiate between two types of empathy. Affective empathy[92] refers to the sensations and feelings we get in response to others' emotions; this can include mirroring what that person is feeling, or just experiencing stress when we detect another's fear or anxiety. Cognitive empathy, sometimes called *perspective taking*, refers to our ability to identify and understand other people's emotions.

Compassion:

Compassion means to suffer together. Among emotion researchers, it is defined as the feeling that arises when you are confronted with another's suffering and feel motivated to relieve it.

The Activity: The CASEL 5 Hoop   Time: 30 minutes

Materials: Poster paper, markers, Hula Hoops   Difficulty: 2-3

How you do it:

Review the CASEL 5 Competencies (see Introduction) by using mind maps (Chapter 3).

Write each of the competencies in the center of a large piece of poster paper. Split students into five smaller groups and hand out each of the competencies. Have each smaller group define and identify how this competency will be experienced in the group and its importance to well-being. Have each group Mind Map the competency. Have a representative from each group summarize their discussion and key points that their group agrees upon. After each competency is presented, hand each group a Hula Hoop with the five competencies written on it (one hoop for each six to eight students).

Task: The group must circle up shoulder to shoulder and start by placing the Hula Hoop on top of their two pointing fingers at shoulder height. The task is to lower the hoop to the floor without ever disconnecting from it. If a disconnection occurs, the group must restart the hoop at shoulder height. After about five minutes of attempting the activity, teach the group the following relaxation technique:

PERT Positive Emotional Refocusing Technique (Luskin, 2003)[93]

- Start with heart breath: breathing in through the nose for a five count and exhaling through the nose for a five count.

- Place one hand on the heart and one hand on the stomach, and continue breathing.

- Ask the group members to close their eyes or glance downward and to visualize a safe place. This place should be an environment where one is not judged, and they can feel relaxed and accepted. Participants can be by themselves or with a loved one. This loved one may also be a pet. Have each person experience the safe place with all their senses. What does it sound like, smell like, look like, and feel like when you are there? How do you feel emotionally in this place? Experience the body in this safe place and the accompanying thoughts and feelings.

After doing this exercise with the group for approximately five minutes, ask them to attempt the lowering of the hoop again. Instruct them to start in silence and to hold onto the feeling they had in their safe place for as long as possible. Talking may occur eventually if needed to complete the task.

Reflection:

What: What did you notice in your attempts to lower the hoop? What did you notice in your effort to lower the hoop after the PERT exercise?

So What: How do your attempts relate to the CASEL 5 Competencies? Which competencies were witnessed? Which competencies were missing?

Now What: Teach the concept of integration as used by Dr. Siegel in developing well-being. The concept of *integration* entails the linkage of different aspects of a system, whether they exist within a single person or a collection of individuals. Explore with students how this definition works well with the CASEL 5 and relates to the hoop experience.

Note: The following activity was also used to teach Set Goals in Chapter 9.

The Activity: Neural Pathways – Neurons that fire together wire together

Time: 30 minutes

Materials: 8 to 12 Fleece Balls

Difficulty: 2-3

Key Terms: (further information can be found at https://dictionary.apa.org/neuron)

Neurons: A nerve cell that receives and sends electrical signals over long distances within the body. A neuron receives electrical input signals from sensory cells (called sensory neurons) and from other neurons.

Neural Pathways: Any route followed by a nerve impulse through central or peripheral nerve fibers of the nervous system. A neural pathway may consist of a simple reflex arc or a complex but specific route, such as that followed by impulses transmitting a specific wavelength of sound from the cochlea to the auditory cortex.

Plasticity: The flexibility and adaptability of the nervous system. Plasticity of the nervous or hormonal systems makes it possible to learn and register new experiences. Early experiences can also modify and shape gene expression to induce long-lasting changes in neurons or endocrine organs.

How you do it:

>Round One: Have the group form a circle. Explain how each student will represent a neuron, and the fleece balls will represent the electrical impulse between each neuron. The first part of the activity involves establishing a pattern (neural pathway). Each student will receive and pass an object and thus create a distinct pattern. A volunteer starts by throwing to someone else in the circle. No one can toss to someone right beside them—it must go at least two people away. An easy way for the group to remember who has gotten the object and who has not is to have everyone start with their hands out in front of them. As players receive the object, they put their hands down. Everyone needs to remember who they received the object from and who they tossed the object to. Now that the pattern is established, begin Neural Pathways. Begin by throwing one object through the sequence and add other props periodically. The goal is to see how many objects the group can successfully juggle. Practice a few times until the established goal is reached or the pattern is clearly established.

>Round Two: Have the person who received the object third from the leader become the new leader. Have students create a new pattern. This is accomplished by challenging the group not pass to, or receive from, the same people in the first pattern. Give them several tries to again reach their goal number of juggled objects.

Reflection: Talk about how neural pathways get established through discovery, practice, and repetition (i.e., a child's first attempt to use a spoon to feed him or herself). Once the neural pathways are established, the child does not even need to think about the required movements. Change is the creation of neural pathways that are established through discovery, practice, and repetition. This applies to any physical, intellectual, social, or emotional change that we attempt. Habits are just well-established neural pathways.

What: What did you notice when trying to establish a pattern? When you changed it?

So What: How does this relate to habits and change?

Now What: What habits do you have that are hard to change? What new practices would you have to discover, practice, and repeat to make this change?

Connection to Mindfulness: Many of us have an abundance of practice at being distracted, angry, worried, or anxious. We do not have as much practice at being aware, focused, patient, and at ease. This activity reinforces the need to discover these practices and the work necessary for them to make lasting changes.

Note: The following activity was also used to teach Be Safe in Chapter 7 (Mine Field).

The Activity: Mind Field: Partner Meditation Time: 30 minutes

Materials: Mixed group of obstacles, large rope Difficulty: 2-3

The simple directions for mindfulness meditation are to pay attention to your breath by sensing it in your body. Whenever you get distracted, kindly and gently return your attention to the breath. Our attention is easily distracted by our thoughts, sensations, and feelings. Being mindful is not about denying or ignoring these distractions but instead learning to recognize, experience, and work through them. This activity works with our attention and the many obstacles that can impede our attempts to stay present.

How you do it:

Split the group into partners. Have each pair participate in the practice of Flow and Tell (See below) for two minutes.

Flow and Tell: Each person takes a turn in identifying one thought, feeling, or sensation that they are experiencing in that moment. They tell this to their partner using the following prompt. "In this moment I notice _____," then the next person goes following the same prompt with their observation. This goes back and forth until the teacher calls out, "Stop."

Have the partners calculate how many thoughts, feelings, or sensations were identified. Have each partnership discuss this experience. Were there any persistent distractions?

Task: To be led verbally by your partner through the Mind Field while eyes are closed.

Set Up: Place a thirty to sixty-foot piece of webbing or rope in a large rectangle and scatter objects in its interior. Make the difficulty level appropriate to the group (See Chapter 7, Mine Field, for more detailed setup instructions).

This activity becomes a partner mindfulness meditation in motion practice. The person going through the field wants to keep their attention on their guide and not get so distracted by the object that they bump into it. The guider's voice is the focal point, just like the breath. The obstacles are all the distractions that can take our awareness away. Ask the partners to agree on four distractions that impact their attention, as represented by the objects in the Mind Field, i.e., "The Beanie Baby rabbit is my racing thoughts, the ball is my wanting to always play, the rope represents feelings of being overwhelmed, the rubber chicken is my anxiety." The person walking through the Mind Field must pass over each of their identified four objects. This will represent working through the distraction rather than avoiding it.

All the other objects in the Mind Field may be avoided by walking around them, if possible.

Rules: Have the group split into partners and gather at one end of the Mind Field. One student keeps their eyes shut (or blindfolded) and starts going through the Mind Field. The second student may only guide the partner <u>verbally</u> through the maze. The guide can only stand <u>outside</u> the rope barrier and cannot touch their partner. Allow all eyes closed students to enter the field simultaneously. If a student with eyes closed touches an obstacle or another person, they must return to the beginning of the maze. Switch roles after completing a Mind Field traverse.

<u>Reflection:</u>

What: What did you notice going through the Mind Field? What did you see as the guide? What was harder to lead or follow? What made this so?

So What: Read the Guest House

The Guest House

This being human is a guest house.
Every morning a new arrival.
A joy, a depression, a meanness,
some momentary awareness comes
as an unexpected visitor.
Welcome and entertain them all!
Even if they are a crowd of sorrows,
who violently sweep your house
empty of its furniture,
still, treat each guest honorably.
He may be clearing you out
for some new delight.
The dark thought, the shame, the malice.
Meet them at the door laughing
and invite them in.
Be grateful for whatever comes
because each has been sent
as a guide from beyond.
— Jellaludin Rumi, translation by Coleman Barks (1995)[94]

How is the Mind Field experience like the Guest House?

Now What?: How can the Mind Field experience be applied to learning meditation?

CHAPTER 14

MODEL PROGRAMS & SUSTAINABILITY

A recurring theme that we hear from school staff is the transient life of social emotional learning programs. An in-house champion discovers a program that seems promising, provides training and materials, and implementation goes forward. But then something happens. The champion leaves, or money runs out for materials, or a new champion arrives and supports a different approach. An understandable cynicism develops among staff when presented with yet another new social emotional learning program. So how does one avoid the pitfall of this revolving door? This chapter provides a number of potential fixes for the problem: 1) presenting two demonstrably effective programs and 2) offering a sustainability model to provide ongoing support.

Under the Big Tent of Full Value

Full Value concepts, methods, and strategies can enhance but do not necessarily need to replace existing programs. The six Full Value Behavioral Norms encapsulate the underpinnings of the most widely used research-based programs. The Big Tent of Full Value allows teachers to continue using strategies, activities, and materials that they believe are effective from programs that currently exist in their classrooms and buildings. These elements can be piggybacked on the common language, goal setting, and group process that Full Value provides.

FULL VALUE	Restorative Practice	Honor Code	Project Wisdom	Open Circle
Be Here	Respect a Talking Piece	Responsibility	Responsibility	Identity & Inclusion
Be Safe	Peaceful Classroom Respect	Respect Trust	Respect Trustworthiness	
Be Honest		Academic Honesty Integrity	Citizenship	
Set Goals	Making Things Right			Youth Leadership & Development Growth & Innovation
Let Go & Move On	Conflict Resolution	Fairness	Fairness	Learning Through Relationships
Care for Self & Others		Supportive Connections with peers	Caring	Safe & Caring Environments Identity & Inclusion
Calling Group	Calling Group & Group Process		Group Process	
Co-Created Commitment	Contracting			

FULL VALUE	Second Step	RCCP	Responsive Classroom	Social Problem Solving & Decision Making
Be Here	Pay Attention Remember Directions (Pre-K)	Responsibility	Responsibility Academic behaviors	
Be Safe	Empathy Control behavior PreK	Judgment Respect	Self-Control	Self-Control
Be Honest	Problem Solving	Honesty Integrity		
Set Goals		Confidence, Perseverance	Establishing rules Perseverance Learning strategies	Social Awareness and Group Participation Skills Decision Making and Problem Solving Skills
Let Go & Move On	Manage Anger & Intense Emotions	Sportsmanship		
Care for Self & Others	Empathy	Courtesy	Assertiveness Empathy	
Calling Group				
Co-Created Commitment				

The Full Value School captures all of these components while also providing continuity across settings and grade levels. Further, our activity-based approach offers experiences that support understanding and practice, leading to a more deeply integrated assimilation of skills. However, there are instances where the disruption of existing programs that staff and students are familiar with and committed to does not serve a productive purpose. We identify the key elements of three of these programs and describe how Full Value is used to support them. Some examples:

How Full Value Supports the Responsive Classroom[95]

Academic Choice: Offering students a choice, even if it is a forced choice, promotes engagement. Full Value's Challenge of Choice (Chapter 3) provides a framework to empower students to choose the focus and intensity of their participation. The challenge is to choose something as opposed to nothing and to be stretched by the experience. This framework can be applied to individual assignments as well as to project based learning and large group instruction.

Establishing Clear Expectations: There will always be some expectations that teachers must initially set, mostly around student safety. Beyond that, when expectations are co-created by students and teachers, acceptance and adherence to them are much more likely. The Full Value Commitment is a dynamic document that establishes student defined positive behavioral expectations. Students check in with the Commitment often, which is displayed prominently in the classroom and modified throughout the school year.

Experiences That are Safe, Challenging, & Joyful: At the core of building a Full Value Community is activity-based learning. The hundreds of activities presented in this book to teach Full Value reflect this approach. Safety is protected by the Full Value Commitment and the Full Value of Be Safe (along with all other Values working together). The degree of challenge can be adjusted by the teacher or students (i.e., how many touches in the Mine Field should be allowed before we all have to go back?). The challenge of the activity pits students against a goal rather than each other. The unique aspect of the activities and their associated props (e.g., rubber chickens, Hula Hoops, trolleys) adds elements of surprise and fun. The activity-based learning process can easily be integrated into the Responsive Classroom design.

Morning Meeting: The Full Value Calling Group process (Chapter 5) helps students hone in on the content of Morning Meeting. We have found that defining the purpose of the meeting (e.g., Information, Feedback, Celebration) supports student attention. Younger students, in particular, tend to jump from one topic to the next depending on whatever thought is occurring to them at any given moment. With this increased focus comes more assured participation. The different meeting types broaden the purposes of the meeting time, which can be as simple as providing information or working through a situation between students experiencing problems in their small group. The Control to Empowerment Scale (Chapter 1) serves to help the teacher assess student readiness to take on a leadership role in Morning Meeting.

Proactive Approach to Discipline: While it is noted in the Responsive Classroom that students co-create classroom rules to live by, developing a Full Value Commitment (Chapter 3) extends and deepens the process. This is a physical representation of classroom rules and can take many forms, as agreed upon by students. The six Full Values (Chapter 1) provide common foundational language across settings. This reduces confusion for students moving from one location to the next, as the same language is used in all common areas and each classroom. Under the umbrella of Full Value, students are provided the opportunity to reach a consensus on how norms are operationalized and identify behaviors that can impede progress (distractors). These distractors are presented as opportunities rather than failures. The proactive approach (or prevention) occurs as students practice and absorb their own co-created positive behaviors via classroom interactions and structured experiential learning. Finally, student goal setting (Chapter 9) is nested within the Full Value Commitment. A positive behavioral repertoire and an awareness of distractors are essential to successful goal attainment. Asking for help from peers is another important aspect of this process.

Natural & Logical Consequences: The experiential basis of Full Value completely embraces Rudolf Dreikurs' formulation of natural and logical consequences (Dreikurs & Gray, 1970).[96] During any Full Value activity, students can potentially experience shame or embarrassment due to choice or happenstance. These consequences are baked into the activity and provide opportunities not for humiliation but growth. As noted, anticipating actions that may result in a natural or logical consequence is also represented in the classroom Full Value Commitment in the form of distractors. While distractors are behaviors identified by students to avoid, the Calling Group process provides an affirming and structured framework to learn from mistakes or a deliberate choice that a student has made to be disruptive. A number of group types often come into play when sorting out logical consequences, including Information, Feelings, Feedback, and Outcome.

Positive Teacher Language: Full Value provides an asset-based approach to social emotional learning. The program's name reflects this assumption; we fully value each other in all of our interactions, as reflected in our Full Value Commitment. Each Full Value provides a roadmap toward unconditional positive regard. They promote presence with each other, physical and emotional safety, honesty offered with compassion and empathy, goal setting with the support of our classmates and teacher, letting go and moving on from conflict, which teaches forgiveness, and caring for self and others. These foundational tenets become infused in all interactions between students and teachers.

How Full Value Supports the Resolving Conflict Creatively Program
-(Dejong, 1993)[97]

Active Listening: The Full Value of Be Here and its associated activities provide rich experiential opportunities to practice active listening. Full Value mindfulness activities provide techniques for being present within oneself and with peers.

Assertiveness: There are many tools for practicing kind and compassionate assertiveness within Full Value. These include Challenge of Choice, using the Calling Group process to have a voice, and taking on leadership roles during activities.

Celebrating Differences: The celebration of difference is reflected in many of the elements of Full Value. When engaged in any activity, having a choice is a celebration of differences; of individuality. Challenge of Choice allows for that to occur. This allows the opportunity for students to assert their differences in how they choose to participate. Most of what makes Full Value classrooms work is the amount of consensus building that goes into decision-making, whether it is co-creating a Commitment, setting a group goal around an activity process, or reaching an understanding via Calling Group. Building a consensus means recognizing, celebrating, and appreciating how differences, whether ethnic, gender, sexual, cultural, physical, or cognitive, contribute to a stronger whole.

Countering Bias: Confronting bias can be addressed through the implementation of all the Full Values. How Full Value is used through the co-creation process provides a focused structure for first defining behaviors that contribute to bias (distractors) and then developing positive behaviors to commit to and practice. At the root of bias is a lack of empathy and an egocentric view of the world, often stemming from learned preconceived notions. The co-creation of the Full Value Commitment and the genuine closeness that develops between students as an outcome of their participation helps to facilitate the breaking down of stereotypes and biases.

Handling Feelings: The Full Values of Be Safe, Care for Self & Others, Let Go & Move On, and their associated outcomes provide many opportunities for students to practice self-regulation. Their application occurs during Calling Group, participation in activities and associated reflection, and co-creating the classroom Full Value Commitment.

Negotiation: Frontloaded into each Full Value activity can be time for students to use problem-solving. This involves, among other things, defining the task, deciding who will do what, and establishing the degree of the challenge. When students participate in Calling Group, whether it is coming to a consensus around what happened via an Information Group or resolving differences through an Outcome Group, students are continually involved in negotiations.

Peace Lessons: The Full Values of Be Safe, Care for Self & Others, and Let Go & Move On all contribute to a focus on emotional safety, problem solving to resolve conflict and reach equitable outcomes, to hear and listen to differing opinions, and let go of the residue of conflict. Care for Self & Others, in particular, provides a foundational and compassionate roadmap for all interactions between students.

Peer Mediation: The Full Value peer leadership program provides student participants with a process for supporting each other via the creation of their own Full Value Commitment. It is essential that students participating in this program experience care for self, and establish trusting relationships that encourage self-disclosure and unconditional peer support. Training in Full Value allows students to effectively employ the behavioral norms during the mediation process. When in conflict, Be Here teaches students to be present with each other and to use active listening. Be Safe helps students make statements that do no emotional harm. Be Honest asks students to give and receive feedback. Care for Self & Others and Let Go & Move On set the stage for what RCCP calls a win-win resolution of disputes.

Sharing Power with Students: This is understandably a problematic Rubicon to cross for teachers who are used to a more directive approach to discipline. Control to Empowerment provides teachers with language and parameters for empowering students with increasing authority. Two other areas of power sharing are found in Calling Group and co-creation of the class Full Value Commitment. Again, the structure around each one of these elements provides opportunities for freedom within limits.

Teachable Moments & Experiential Learning Strategies: The activities described in this book are designed to elicit behaviors that become teachable moments. They generate real emotions, behaviors, and thinking. The activities naturally provoke dialogue, brainstorming, problem solving, disagreements, solutions, and cooperation. These outcomes become the focus of discussion and reflection. There is a world of difference between the acting associated with role playing and becoming truly immersed in an experience.

Units (Elementary): All of the programmatic elements can be integrated into the curriculum units of RCCP:

- Affirmation – Calling Group, Control to Empowerment, Full Value Activities, Goal Setting

- Appreciating Diversity – Calling Group, Challenge of Choice, Full Value Activities, Full Value Commitment

- Bias Awareness – Calling Group, Challenge of Choice, Full Value Activities, Full Value Commitment

- Communication – Calling Group, Full Value Activities, Full Value Commitment

- Cooperation – Calling Group, Challenge of Choice, Full Value Activities, Full Value Commitment, Goal Setting

- Countering Bias – Calling Group, Full Value Activities, Full Value Commitment, Goal Setting

- Peace & Conflict – Calling Group, Control to Empowerment, Full Value Activities, Full Value Commitment, Peer Leadership

- Peacemakers – Calling Group, Peer Leadership

- Resolving Conflict Creatively – Calling Group, Full Value Activities, Full Value Commitment

- Setting the Stage – Information Group, Full Value Commitment

- The Future – Calling Group, Control to Empowerment, Full Value Activities, Goal Setting

Units (Secondary):

- Concepts & Skills of Conflict Resolution – Calling Group, Control to Empowerment, Full Value Activities, Full Value Commitment, Goal Setting, Peer Leadership

- Concepts & Skills of Intergroup Relations & Bias Awareness – Calling Group, Full Value Activities, Full Value Commitment, Goal Setting

- Engaging the Students – Calling Group, Challenge of Choice, Control to Empowerment, Full Value Activities, Full Value Commitment, Goal Setting

- Warm Ups – Many of the activities in this book can be used as warm-ups or energizers. They are novel and fun!

How Full Value Supports Restorative Practice (Kiddie, 2018)[98]

Challenge of Choice: This element supports opportunities for students to find a way to participate within but not outside of their stretch zone. It reduces the pressure to have to contribute in only one prescribed way when participating in Circles.

Circles (the Centerpiece of Restorative Practice): Using the co-created Full Value Commitment, students bring a set of agreed upon behavioral norms to whatever the purposes of the Circle might be. As these norms have been taught, reinforced, and practiced in all aspects of school life, they operate naturalistically in the Circles setting. The identification and prior awareness of potential distractors as part of the Commitment bring attention to the destructive patterns that serve to derail resolution.

Control to Empowerment: This is an element of Full Value that provides teachers a lens to view student readiness to take on increasing responsibility for calling and facilitating Circles.

Full Value Mindfulness & Restorative Practice: Students and faculty engagement with each other to problem solve, resolve conflicts, heal, and determine consequences requires being present, being self-aware, and developing skills to self-regulate affective states. Mindfulness is embedded in all aspects of Full Value. The neurobiology of mindfulness and mindfulness techniques are taught and practiced via the games and initiatives unique to Full Value experiential learning.

Full Value Peer Leadership: This element of Full Value provides a roadmap to create a cadre of students who can model Restorative Practice in their classrooms and the larger school community. They are trained in all of the core Full Value elements using experiential methodology.

Global Support: Full Value provides foundational support to guide all Restorative interactions and a common language that travels along with students between classrooms, communal settings, grade levels, and schools.

Staff (engagement, relationship & community building, skill acquisition): Staff Co-Creation of their Full Value Commitments uses each Full Value to identify behaviors that will support self-compassion and self-empathy. Self-care goals, which can be represented within the Commitment, are defined by the individual and supported by colleagues.

Primary Prevention

Our Full Value wellness work is the primary focus of this book. It is appropriate for use as

Tier 1 and Tier 2 interventions.[99] These are typically not kids who present with significant behavioral concerns. For this population, we have referred the reader to two texts on Adventure Based Counseling, Islands of Healing (1998) and Exploring Islands of Healing (2002). Full Value primary prevention interventions inoculate against harassment, intimidation, and bullying by providing students with strategies and methods for self-regulation and confronting and positively resolving issues with peers.

Best Practices in the Schools

Kinnelon Borough Public Schools - Full Value Communities – The Foundation of Safe and Civil Schools

Program Description:

Well before legislation was passed in New Jersey to address Harassment, Intimidation, and Bullying, the Kinnelon Schools initiated a district wide social-emotional and character education program called Full Value. Over the last eight years, many Kinnelon staff experienced four days of immersive summer training in the theory and application of this model. Where the program is being implemented with fidelity, teachers are reporting a significant reduction in disciplinary issues within the classroom and a significant increase in student self-regulation. The building principals are uniformly supportive of implementing Full Value in their schools.

Issues such as bullying and harassment can be seen as symptoms of a school climate that does not systematically teach and reinforce pro-social behavior for all students, including students with 504 Plans and those classified as needing special education and related services. Students need to learn how to identify a set of behavioral norms or core values and apply them to every aspect of their school day, from the classroom to the lunchroom. Further, students need the implementation tools that offer safe and supportive opportunities for confronting behaviors that are devaluing and demeaning. To be truly effective, any intervention strategy must also be applied across all schools, K-12, to ensure a common language and process.

The Full Value model meets all the above criteria. It provides guided opportunities for students to co-create behavioral norms, develop a common language to discuss social and emotional concerns, and define a group processing structure to confront and resolve negative behaviors and applaud pro-social ones.

In each classroom, students work with their teachers to create their Full Value Commitment (Chapter 3). Practice comes from behavioral interactions of a typical classroom day, as well as via special activities designed to teach core values and to process the outcomes of the group experience. The core values that students select are universal in nature and tend to reflect such concepts as trust, listening, honesty, love, compassion, cooperation, friendship, etc. Outside of the Full Value Commitment are placed distractors that get in the way of implementing pro-social behaviors. The bedrock for the creation of the Full Value Commitment resides in the following six Full Value Behavioral Norms (Chapter 1):

- Be Here
- Be Safe
- Be Honest
- Set Goals
- Let Go & Move On
- Caring for Self and Others

Students are taught the skill of Calling Group (Chapter 5) to provide a structured communication forum for discussing issues with their peers. Teachers also use the Calling Group process for classroom management. The groups listed below are called to address a variety of needs:

- Information
- Celebration
- Feelings
- Growth
- Feedback
- Outcome

Initially, teachers control the Calling Group process, but as students become more empowered and secure, they take increased responsibility for calling them. Offered opportunities to assume increased responsibility, students feel empowered and valued. Teachers learn a corresponding group assessment technique to help determine how and when to most effectively and gradually release control to students.

Specific Program Goals:

- Provide all students with common foundational behavioral norms.

- Foster empathy and support for and between all students.

- Weave social emotional learning into the fabric of day-to-day school functioning.

- Create a common language that can be used across classrooms, grade levels, and schools.

- Engage students in co-creating behavioral commitments predicated on these norms in each classroom.

- Teach a goal-setting process where students set personal and content connected goals using the SMART Goals or 4 Square methods, supported by their Full Value Commitment. Students must state goals unequivocally, commit personal resources, define how they will know the goals have been accomplished, and ask for help from peers and teachers to support goal attainment.

- Learn and utilize a Calling Group process for working through issues with their peers or celebrating their achievements.

Professional Development:

Primary prevention activities take time and significant effort to implement and sustain, but pay enormous dividends over time. The program adoption has been phased in over several years. Every summer, a new cohort of twenty-four teachers and staff are provided in depth training. These participants become enthusiastic Full Value representatives, collaborating in its evolution, and promoting interest among other staff. The Kinnelon district is committed to training all staff in this model, including administration, certified staff, cafeteria aides, bus drivers, and maintenance staff.

Unique to the training is that faculty become immersed in what their students will experience. They have opportunities to reflect on the transfer to their classroom settings, then provide feedback to one another as they co-create model lessons. An important outcome is that staff advance their personal growth and deeper collegial relationships. A highly developed social emotional learning program effectively inspires staff and allows for increasingly effective collegial relationships. It is this depth and change in adult culture that helps to support a parallel process in classrooms.

Implementation Responsibilities:

The program is coordinated through the Kinnelon Department of Special Services and began in 2011. It has been funded primarily using district resources and supplemented with some funds associated with the New Jersey Harassment, Intimidation, and Bullying laws. Four day workshops are provided for staff. Refreshers are then offered via the district after-school institute and during in-service days as a means to share practices and increase program integration.

Additionally, a sustainability team of in-district staff has been created to provide ongoing collegial support. The team is comprised of two faculty members from each of the four district schools; educators who have successfully implemented the program with students and who have expressed a desire to serve in this capacity. During staff orientation, before school starts, all new staff are introduced to the program by teacher facilitators who have attended the full training. Though some staff have a much deeper familiarity with the pedagogy and methods than others, everyone is provided a basic introduction through this formal orientation session or informal meetings.

Population Serviced:

All special and general education students throughout the district participate in Full Value. This program is particularly valuable to students with learning disabilities as it provides them with concrete and explicable tools to engage with the hidden social curriculum.

Curriculum Connections (Chapter 12):

To respond to the legitimate concern that this is another program that pulls time away from instruction, teachers have been trained to integrate the six Full Values into elements of the social studies, mathematics, and integrated language arts curriculum. At the basis of this process is using their Full Value Behavioral Norms to work as a high performing team when engaged in all manner of academic content.

Outcomes:

As part of the school climate survey for preschool through grade two, students were asked, "Do you think the Full Values help you solve problems? If yes, tell how." 99 percent of the students who responded to this question answered, "Yes."

Here is a representative set of comments from the open-ended question:

> Yes, because when we get into fights we Let Go & Move On and use I statements and we solve and it helps us to get over it and move on and have good feelings about it.
>
> I say yes so let's say Let Go & Move On and you let go of the bad stuff and carry on with good stuff. That helps us so we can be happy and not fight so we can pay attention.
>
> When I look at the Full Values it helps me to solve my problems for example, I get into fight with somebody I look at the Full Values chart and say, "Let Go & Move On!"
>
> Full Values do help us solve problems of somebody hurts somebody's feelings and then you have to use the Full Values Be Safe and Let Go & Move On and those help me solve my problems for solving bad problems.
>
> The Full Values help me soo... much because they are something that can stay in my whole life and they help me solve problems all of the time.
>
> I think Full Value solve problems because if you do Full Values you'll stop problems before they start because you keep your hands to yourself there won't be fights.
>
> Yes, because when someone is mean to me I do my Full Values like Let Go & Move On and it actually works.
>
> Yes because when someone is being mean it makes me want to use my hands I remember to Care for Self & Others.
>
> Yes because if I'm in a fight I tell him/her to follow the Full Value road signs and if someone is screaming I will tell them to commit to goals and stay quiet.

I think Full Values help our class because when we use Full Values like Be Safe no one gets hurt and if they use Be Here we will always know what to do in class and that's why I think Full Values help our class.

Other qualitative and quantitative feedback from teachers and students would indicate that far less time is spent on discipline. Students have become more adept at self-regulating within their classrooms. Having a common language helps students to feel a sense of predictability and comfort when moving from classroom to classroom, grade to grade, and school to school. The evaluation process has included, 1) online teacher surveys to ascertain use and commitment to the program, 2) videotaping, 3) analysis of the Calling Group process 4), inclusion of Full Value activities as a component of the district teacher evaluation rubric under classroom climate, 4) tracking of changes in attendance and disciplinary referral rates, and 5) qualitative feedback from stakeholders.

An examination of harassment, intimidation, and bullying data yields the following since the implementation of the Kinnelon Full Value Schools program.

Parent/Community Involvement:

An overview of the Full Value program is featured prominently on the district's website.

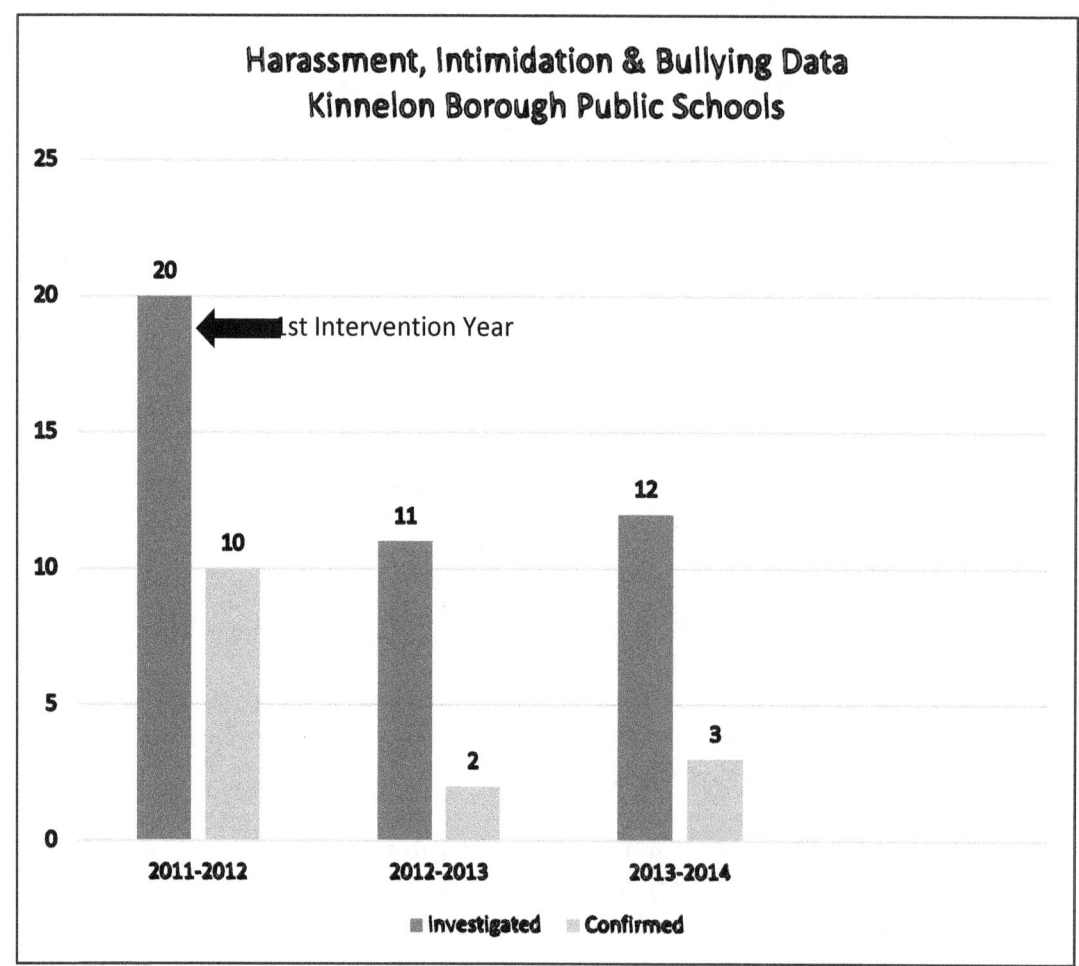

Parents receive an informational flyer about the program and a refrigerator magnet listing the six Full Value Behavioral Norms for their homes. Students routinely report that their families use the behavioral norms within their homes.

Peer Leadership: Student Led Support of Full Value – Bernards High School, Bernardsville, NJ

Peer leadership programs are a powerful expression of the Full Value of Care for Self & Others. They provide an opportunity for juniors and seniors (the elders) of the school to pass along their experiential wisdom by offering a support system and road map for the novitiates entering into the daunting world of high school. In the spirit of Care for Self & Others, mentors or peer leaders gain tremendous fulfillment and learning by providing guidance to the younger generation.

Peer leadership programs have taken on an increasingly important role in high school settings. Educators must continually seek out more effective methods of integrating young people into an environment fraught with increasingly dangerous temptations, particularly in the area of drug and alcohol abuse. It is known across multiple disciplines, including psychology, sociology, nursing, public health, social work, and medicine, that enhancing positive factors in the lives of youth, such as connectedness to family, school, and community, can reduce the likelihood they will engage in health-jeopardizing behaviors.

The Bernards High School peer leadership program creates this connectedness through their semester long 9th grade orientation program. Peer leadership has been a tradition at Bernards High School for over 20 years and has proven effective in creating a welcoming and safe environment for all incoming first year class. Evaluations completed by 9th graders at the end of the program consistently reflect the value they derive from it.

Ninth grade students were asked the question, "What was helpful about the peer leadership orientation program?"

They offered the following:

> That there are people here to help and that other people share my feelings.
>
> Being able to talk with upper class students about the worries of starting high school.
>
> That there are people here for you and you can depend on the majority of your peers, and most importantly, Bernards High School.
>
> Knowing that there is a group of peers that will be supporting us to do well in school and to live a healthy, drug free life.

Student evaluations parallel the above quotes in reflecting positive feelings and attitudes toward the peer leaders and the entire school community. When asked what could improve their experience, the majority of respondents wished for a full year program. In a time of what is perceived as pervasive school violence precipitated by a lack of tolerance, this type of transition program for junior high school students becomes an essential component of a K-12 intervention plan to positively affect school culture and climate.

The student created a mission statement for peer leadership reads:

> Peer leadership is committed to providing leadership for the Bernards High School community via student directed activities and programs that foster a healthy learning and social environment.

This mission is accomplished through the following goals:

- To establish a comfortable, positive atmosphere where first year students feel involved and accepted.

- To provide guidance and assistance to incoming first year and transfer students.

- To provide positive role models who disseminate information, encouraging healthy lifestyles and positive decision making for all students.

- To provide a link between students and staff.

- To assist with programs that support the peer leadership mission.

The peer leadership program has been using the Full Value Commitment as its main theoretical framework for over twenty years. Peer leadership consists of carefully selected students who lead a semester long 9th grade orientation. There is a student peer leadership advisory board, approximately forty peer leaders, and two adult advisors. The advisory board is responsible for the selection and training process of the entire program. The remaining peer leaders facilitate 9th grade orientation that occurs once a week in physical education classes. The advisors provide overall direction, training, and support to the program.

Peer leaders go through an extensive training process that prepares them to facilitate small groups of freshmen using experiential learning activities. This dynamic and effective approach provides a safe environment for the freshmen. Peer leaders begin their training in the spring with an overnight retreat. During the first semester, the peers meet once a week for two hours. The entire peer group is split into four separate work groups meeting weekly to learn adventure activities, the use of a challenge course, stress reduction techniques, mindfulness, Full Value (social emotional learning), and leadership skills. Peers are required to teach/facilitate at least a weekly meeting for their work group. The training process not only teaches the peer leaders about Full Value but also about group dynamics and leadership. The program integrates current research on emotional intelligence, mindfulness, stress reduction, and leadership and group process.

The advisory board begins its training in the winter and assists in the spring training. They are also required to attend a youth leadership program during the summer. This advanced training focuses on the theories surrounding leadership, group dynamics, social emotional learning, mindfulness, adventure, and the use of a challenge ropes course. The training prepares the board for its role as leaders of the entire program.

Becoming a Peer Leader

Step 1: The Application, Commitment, Teacher Reference, Community Reference, and Peer Reference forms are submitted

Step 2: All potential peer leaders' names are put on two lists. One list is distributed to staff members, and the other list to current peer leaders. Both staff and peers are asked to rate only those candidates whom they know. Ratings are based on the candidates' ability to facilitate small groups and to support the goals and mission of peer leadership. Only the peer adult advisors see these original ratings.

Step 3: After the candidates are interviewed, the advisory board and adult advisors consider the following in determining the final group of peer leaders for the upcoming year:

- Application
- Staff ratings
- Peer ratings
- Teacher reference
- Peer reference
- Community reference
- Evaluation of candidates working through a group problem-solving task
- Interview
- Male/female ratio
- Grade level ratio
- Size of incoming first-year class

Step 4: The previous years and current board members make the final selection of the new group under the adult adviser's guidance

Orientation Overview

The program utilizes the Full Value Behavioral Norms to divide the semester long program into six sections. Each of these sections is about three weeks long and covers various topics related to creating Full Value Commitments. The following is an overview of these areas.

Full Value	School Related Topics
Be Here	Leaving middle school, high school layout, and general school rules and procedures
Be Safe	School and community resources, wellness and health related policies
Be Honest	Ethical and honorable behavior
Set Goals	Success in high school and beyond
Let Go & Move On	Diversity, cliques, and harassment
Care for Self & Others	Wellness and community service

Research has documented that peer-initiated and led activities are a key component in effective drug and alcohol prevention efforts (Bernat & Resnick, 2006; Griffin & Botvin, 2010).[100] Peer leadership continues to evolve to meet the changing needs of the incoming student class and fulfill its mission to create a healthy, supportive learning environment. Bernards has a group of talented students that the entire school community has identified as leaders. Even with this input and talent, peer leaders are adolescents who face the same issues that all teens face. We are asking students to be role models and leaders in areas where they also struggle on a daily basis. The trainings have evolved into a why to, rather than just a how to, focus on social and emotional learning and wellness. This approach encourages peer leaders to become more self-aware and develop their personal reasons for avoiding negative risky behaviors. This exploration focuses more on developing healthy habits rather than being told what not to do. A comprehensive program needs to include more of this rationale as well as hands-on leadership skills. A comprehensive program also needs to include community and family support. Parental involvement is critical to the issues that are being addressed. Peer leadership has always developed programs to create a better sense of community and connection. The inclusion of a peer leadership program in a Full Value School just makes sense on so many levels. It is authentically practicing co-creation by valuing students' input, leadership, and the key role they play in the community.

A Student's Voice

Over the years, many students at Bernards High School have written essays for English and college on Full Value. Here is an excerpt from a college essay written by a peer leader:

> With all the college stress placed on every senior, I began to feel trapped during the start of my senior year. My only escape from all the stress that my parents and I had placed on me, was the peer leadership program. This program let me forget everything for two hours and let me lead freely. As October rolled around, even more stress came with giving another shot at SATs and starting college applications. In the fall the Full Value Commitment was introduced to the 9th grade class. As I read them aloud, an imaginary bell rang in my head. It was as if I were reading these values for the first time. I saw a whole new insight in them and realized how truly they are helpful, not just to the program, but to my life in general. These

values let me breathe during stressful time periods and have become almost a mantra for me.

Be Here was always told to the 9th grade students so they wouldn't fool around on the ropes course. However, Be Here can be used anywhere in life. How many times have I truly taken a shower and thought about nothing else, except showering? I am always thinking about my day or work that I still have to do while showering. Or even these days I just wolf my food down; I haven't had time to eat with my family since the summer. Even when I eat, I am not present mentally or emotionally. When I am part of a conversation, I have also caught myself not being there mentally. With this realization, I am catching myself every day from getting distracted and truly trying to be there for everything I do. I am starting to succeed because now it's been a week and I have sat down and eaten dinner with my family and have been there the whole time.

Be Safe also had a positive impact on my life. I have always been the type to take on a project and do everything myself. This year it has been really hard, because I am in charge of many clubs and have to deal with a full load of AP and IB courses. My health suffered a great deal from this endeavor that I took on. With coming to realization, I have now started to sort out the work, so I don't hurt myself in any way. My health is on its way back to normal, and I have a better grasp on my activities.

Let Go & Move On has been the key mantra for me this year. I started to see how competitive all the "friends" I had acquired are getting about colleges. Even my best friend has started to get competitive with me, because we are both applying to the same college. I began to get frustrated with him and everyone else who I thought were my friends treating me maliciously with the college process. My only way to save our friendship was to let go of their actions and move on. I don't like some things they're doing and instead of pouting about it, I have learned to just move on. This has made me a calmer person and I have healthier relationships with everyone.

Finally, Be honest as clichéd as it is, this too has found meaning for me this year. I have had to be honest with my parents on so many occasions. I had to let them know that the colleges that they want me to go to aren't my choices, and I don't want to go there. I realized I had to be honest with myself first, because I am not going to disappoint them by going to a college they want me to go to and not being happy there. I need to be somewhere I will be happy and successful, and in the end that's what they want. Our relationship is a little better now that my parents know their dreams are not my dreams.

Now this alteration can be considered maturity or fate. I choose to believe in fate and that the peer leadership program was meant for me to discover myself in many ways. This can be looked at as maturity as well: however, fate sounds more cosmic. I wish I had this epiphany during my freshman year, so I would have not stressed over pointless things and gotten worked up. However, with time comes wisdom, and I am glad I received this knowledge before I spread my wings into the sky facing me.

Sustainability

Once the initial rush of enthusiasm passes, there are all sorts of reasons why programs can languish and die. This is particularly true of social-emotional learning programs, which, despite the reams of literature arguing otherwise, are seen as time consuming and better left to parents and community organizations to address. Often, there is a champion for a particular program. This could be an administrator or faculty member. When this person moves on to another district, it can also set into motion a program's demise. It is important, then, to start thinking about sustainability as part of the program implementation process.

In Kinnelon, for example, three strategies are in place to support sustainability:

- An internal advanced training group. Eight faculty were recruited, two from each building, who evidenced a passion for the work, a gift for explaining program elements to others, and skills in implementing the program. These staff members received an additional four days of training with a focus on teaching components of Full Value. A mix of classroom teachers and related service providers was chosen to increase the flexibility for co-teaching.

- The Full Value program was adopted as the identified primary prevention program for the school district. This provided a small sum of money for training each year, but more importantly, named the program as the district's program of choice.

- A staff member who was particularly articulate and passionate about the program was offered the opportunity to present an overview of Full Value to newly hired staff.

Bullet three is worthy of attention. A whole faculty may be trained in any given year. However, over time, people come and go. It is very important to provide a training path to new staff and, of equal importance, offering support to existing staff. Implementation across classrooms and grade levels must be consistent and clear.

Summing Up

We are excited and gratified by the diversity of applications of experientially based social emotional learning practices that are thriving across the country. Educators and counselors have used their imaginations, coupled with a fierce dedication to children, to create programs that are making a difference. At the root of their success is a clear understanding of their students' needs, strong leadership and social emotional learning skills, a commitment to intelligent risk taking, and the love of adventure and having fun. We hope that these sample programs have provided some inspiration. Knowledge of these programs, as well as the one that you may very well be running right now, provides us with a sense of just how vast and powerful the experientially based social-emotional learning community has become over a relatively brief period of time.

CHAPTER 15

ODDS & ENDS

We would like to share so much with you as you embark on this Full Value adventure with your students. Here are some loose ends for your information and enjoyment.

Creating Small Groups Can be Fun Using the Following Activities:

Activity Name: Categories　　　　　　　　　　　　　　　Time: 10 minutes

How you do it:

> If you need to form two groups (many of the activities require it), ask these questions and watch them form (with much laughter and surprise):
>
> - When you buy something at a store, do you count your change (coins) or just put it in your pocket?
> - When you put your pants on, which leg do you always put in first
> - When you fold your arms, which is always on top?
> - When you interlock your fingers, which thumb is always on top?
> - When you draw a circle in the air is it clockwise or counterclockwise?

Each time you ask a question, have the large group separate into one category or the other. Over the course of five questions, two equal groups will be created. If the groups are a few students off, just ask for a few volunteers to make them equal.

Activity Name: Draw a Dog　　　　　　　　　　　　　　　Time: 5 minutes

How you do it:

> Have students trace the face of a dog in front of them. If the dog's snout goes to the left, they are in group A. If the dog's snout goes to the right, they are in group B. If their tracing is head on, have them choose one of the other groups.

Activity Name: Picture Puzzle　　　　　　　　　　　　　　Time: 10 minutes

How you do it:

> Rip two pages out of a magazine. Cut each page into pieces (enough for half of a large group for each page). Put the cut pieces into a bag. Students draw the pieces out and assemble two separate puzzles. This becomes their group for the activity.

Activity Name: What's the Same? Time: 5 minutes

How you do it:

> This is a handy activity for forming pairs. Have your students circulate and find someone with the same color eyes. Other similarities can include hair, an article of clothing, identical knees, elbows, same birthday, closest shoe size down to a half size, etc. We are sure there are more you can think of.

Activity Resources

Within each of the Full Value chapters, we have provided an extensive sampling of activities to get you started on teaching each behavioral norm. Here we offer a list of resources that provide literally hundreds of additional activity options literally for you to draw upon to teach Full Value and to co-create your classroom Full Value Commitment. Many of these books are available through Flaghouse and can also be purchased through other online resources or ordered at brick and mortar bookstores.

Aubrey, P. (2008). Stepping Stones: A Therapeutic Adventure Activity Guide: Activities to enhance outcomes with Therapeutic Populations. Beverly, MA: Project Adventure.

Bower, N. M. (1998). Adventure Play: Adventure activities for preschool and early elementary age children. New York City, NY: Pearson Custom Publishing.

Chappelle, S. & Bigman, L. (1998). Diversity in Action. New York City, NY: Pearson Custom Publishing.

Collard, M. (2008). Count Me In: Large Group Activities That Work. Beverly, MA: Project Adventure.

Collard, M. (2018). No Props No Problem: 150+ Outrageously Fun Group Games & Activities Using No Equipment. Melbourne, Australia: playmeo

Folan, N. & Friends (2012). The Hundredth Monkey: Activities that Inspire Playful Learning. Beverly, MA: Project Adventure.

Panicucci, J. (2003). Adventure Curriculum for Physical Education. Beverly, MA: Project Adventure. (Note: This is available in three separate volumes for elementary, middle, and high school programs.)

playmeo.com

An innovative online platform that hosts the largest database of group games & activities in the world, featuring step-by-step instructions, video tutorials, leadership tips, variations & reflection strategies. Free app available on iOS & Android. https://www.playmeo.com

Rohnke, K. (1994). The Bottomless Bag Again, 2nd Edition. Dubuque, Iowa: Kendall Hunt.

Rohnke, K. (2004). Funn N' Games. Dubuque, Iowa: Kendall Hunt.

Rohnke, K. (2004). The Bottomless Bag Revival. Dubuque, Iowa: Kendall Hunt.

Rohnke, K. (2009). Silver Bullets, 2nd Edition. Dubuque, Iowa: Kendall Hunt.

Rohnke, K. & Butler, S. (1995). Quicksilver: Adventure Games, Initiative Problems, Trust Activities, and a Guide to Effective Leadership. Dubuque, Iowa: Kendall Hunt.

Rohnke, K. & Grout, J. (1998). Back Pocket Adventure. New York, NY: Simon & Schuster Custom Publishing.

Schoel, J. & Maizell, R. S. (2002). Exploring Islands of Healing: New Perspectives on Adventure Based Counseling. Beverly, MA: Project Adventure.

Schoel, J. & Stratton, M. (1990). Gold Nuggets: Readings for Experiential Education. Beverly, MA: Project Adventure.

Training Wheels: A premier experiential learning company offering training, materials, and supplies.

Mindfulness Resources

For those interested in a deeper dive into the practice of mindfulness, a wealth of resources is provided. It is very important to keep in mind that reading is not sufficient. Beyond using some of the basic techniques described in the text, training from a certified specialist in mindfulness is advised. Mindfulness techniques, when appropriately applied, will yield positive outcomes for students. However, the process of focusing and clarity can also provoke unanticipated negative emotional content. Understanding psychological depth and seeking appropriate training will help ensure that mindfulness is a positive experience for students.

Goleman, D. (2004). Destructive Emotions: A scientific dialogue with the Dalai Lama. Reprint ed. New York, NY: Bantam Books.

Hahn, T., & Weare, K. (2017). Happy teachers change the world. A guide for cultivating mindfulness in education. Berkeley, CA: Parallax Press.

Harris, D. (2014). 10% Happier: How I tamed the voice in my head, reduced stress without losing my edge, and found self-help that actually works, A true story. New York City, NY: Harper Collins Books.

Harris, D. (2017). Meditation for fidgety skeptics: a 10% happier how to book. New York, NY: Penguin Random House.

HH Dalai Lama, & Cutler MD, H. (1998). The Art of Happiness: A handbook for living. New York City, NY: Penguin Books.

Kabat-Zinn, J. (1990). Full catastrophe living, Using the wisdom of your body and mind to face stress, pain, and illness. New York City, NY: Delacorte.

Kabat-Zinn, J. (1994). Wherever you go, there you are. New York City, NY: Hyperion.

Kabat-Zinn, J., & Kabat-Zinn, M. (1997). Everyday blessings, The inner work of mindful parenting. New York, NY: Hachette Books.

Kabat-Zinn, J. (2005). Coming to our senses healing ourselves and the world. New York City, NY: Hyperion.

Kabat-Zinn, J. (2012). Mindfulness for Beginners. Louisville, KY: Sounds True.

Langer, E. J. (2014). Mindfulness, 25th anniversary edition. Louisville, KY: Boston, MA: De Capo Books.

Lantieri, L., & Goleman, D. (2008). Building Emotional Intelligence: Techniques to Cultivate Inner strength in children. Louisville, KY: Sounds True.

Lantieri, L. (2001). Schools with Spirit: Nurturing the inner lives of children and Teachers. Boston, MA: Beacon Press.

Rechtschaffen, D. (2016). The mindful education workbook. New York: W.W. Norton & Company.

Seigel, D. (2010). Mindsight: the new science of personal transformation. New York City: NY Bantam Books.

Seigel, D. (2015). The developing mind: how relationships and the brain interact to shape who we are, 2nd edition. New York City, NY: The Guildford Press.

Turtkle, S. (2011). Alone Together: Why we expect more from technology and less from each other. New York City, NY: Basic Books.

<u>Websites</u>

Association for Mindfulness in Schools: <u>http://www.mindfuleducation.org/research.html</u>

CASEL: Collaborative for Academic, Social and Emotional Learning. <u>http://casel.org/</u>

Dan Siegel: <u>http://www.drdansiegel.com/home/</u>

MBSR: Mindfulness Based Stress Reduction Program at UMASS
<u>http://www.umassmed.edu/cfm/stress/index.aspx</u>

The Mind Life Institute: <u>http://www.mindandlife.org/</u>

Mindful Magazine: http://mindful.org

Mindful Schools: http://www.mindfulschools.org/

Nalanda Institute: http://www.nalandainstitute.org/

Retreat Centers

Garrison Institute, Garrison, NY

Omega Institute, Rhinebeck, NY

Kripalu Center, Stockbridge, MA

Tibet House US, New York, NY

Mindfulness resources from Chapter 13:

The Triune Brain

Dan Siegel Hand Model Video: https://www.youtube.com/watch?v=f-m2YcdMdFw

Video and rap song by JusTme: Don't Flip Yo Lid
https://www.youtube.com/watch?v=he-fW9_3egw

Self-Compassion

Resource video: Kristin Neff, Ph.D. The three components of self-compassion:
https://greatergood.berkeley.edu/video/item/the_three_components_of_self_compassion

Empathy

Greater Good Magazine
https://greatergood.berkeley.edu/topic/empathy/definition#what_is

Resource Video: Brene Browne: Empathy:
https://www.youtube.com/watch?time_continue=42&v=1Evwgu369Jw

Compassion

Greater Good Magazine: https://greatergood.berkeley.edu/topic/compassion/definition
Resource video: The Center for Compassion and Altruism Research and Education Video: James Doty, MD, The Importance of Compassion. https://youtu.be/rUi40yTXrjY
Greater Good UC Berkeley, Greater Good
https://greatergood.berkeley.edu/video/series/science_meaningful_life_videos

Stanford University, Medicine: The Center for Compassion and Altruistic Research and Education http://ccare.stanford.edu/

Mind Life Institute: https://www.mindandlife.org/

Resource video: Dan Siegel: Integration as a source of power:
https://www.youtube.com/watch?v=0TK62FdzzTs

Full Value Communities

What we do:

Full Value Communities offers training opportunities for schools, agencies, and corporations to facilitate the creation and sustainability of affirming and respectful environments. Training is offered by experienced facilitators at your site and tailored to your specific needs.

We can be contacted at www.fullvaluecommunities.org or (947) 517-7924. We would love to discuss working with your school, agency, or business using the methodology presented in this book.

Who We Are:

Richard Maizell: Dr. Maizell has over thirty-five years of experience as an educator in the New Jersey Public Schools. He holds a Masters' Degrees in School Psychology and Special Education, and a Doctorate in School/Community Psychology. He has served as a teacher of English and special education, a school psychologist, and as Director of Special Services for the last eighteen years. His lifelong passion has been in the area of social emotional learning. Dr. Maizell founded Project Quest, a group-counseling program for court-involved youth in Sussex County, NJ. The program served students from nine county high schools, later expanding into middle and elementary schools as an after school primary prevention program. Dr. Maizell conceptualized and constructed a universal playground in the Sussex-Wantage Regional District, Wantage, NJ, which allowed for general education and differently abled students to play together on uniquely designed playground equipment. The social emotional learning program at Sussex-Wantage also involved a partnership with Dr. Maurice Elias and his social problem-solving and decision-making program. In his last district, the Kinnelon Borough Public Schools, Dr. Maizell implemented a district wide primary prevention program called Full Value Schools. As a result of this implementation, harassment, intimidation, and bullying referrals and confirmed incidents fell significantly over a three-year period. Students reported, via school climate surveys, feeling better equipped to self-regulate and confront inappropriate behaviors with their peers. Dr. Maizell's program has been presented at national and regional conferences. Most recently, he presented to educators at the Lausanne Learning Institute conference on social emotional learning, the Association of Experiential Education Northeast Regional Conference, and at the Schools of Character Conference. He is the co-author of the book, Exploring Islands of Healing (2002), and the principal author of The Full Value School: A social emotional learning community (2019). Dr. Maizell is the recipient of the following awards and honors: Innovations in Special Education Award, National Honor Society in Education, United States Jaycees Distinguished Service Award, The Distinguished Agency Recreation Services Award-New Jersey, and the Commission on Recreation for Individuals with Disabilities Award.

Jim Schoel: Jim Schoel has been an experiential educator for over forty years. He is a founding member of Project Adventure, Inc. and has served as their senior trainer and consultant for programs with at-risk youth. He has served as the director of the Gloucester Museum School, which provides interactive outdoor experiential opportunities for children in the greater Boston area. Mr. Schoel has extensive teaching experience in the Gloucester Public Schools and in the Hamilton-Wenham School District in Massachusetts. He is considered a national expert in experiential learning and activity-based counseling, and has routinely presented on these topics as the keynote speaker at national and international conferences. He is the recipient of the Practitioner of the Year award from the International Association of Experiential Education (2005). Mr. Schoel has published extensively in the field, including co-authoring Islands of Healing (1988), Exploring Islands of Healing (2002), and Gold Nuggets (1990). He is a co-author of the Full Value School. Mr. Schoel holds a Master's Degree in Education from Harvard University.

John Grund: Mr. Grund has over twenty-eight years of experience in the New Jersey public schools as a School Social Worker, a Student Assistance Counselor, and an Anti-Bullying Specialist. Mr. Grund's experience has been in both urban and suburban schools and in alternative as well as mainstream settings. He was at Bernards High School for 20 years, where he created and led a semester long Full Value based 9th grade orientations. At Bernards, he was a state champion tennis coach and was the 2015 Educational Professional of the Year. Mr. Grund has been a senior trainer for Project Adventure, Inc. for over twenty-five years and provides training for educators and therapists in Adventure-Based Counseling, Social Emotional Learning, and Adventure Programming. As an experiential practitioner, he has created and led community based experiential counseling and prevention programs for adolescents at the Somerset Hills YMCA and for the Municipal Alliance Committee in Verona, NJ. These programs have included Dr. Maizell's Quest model, youth leadership training, and wilderness expeditions. Mr. Grund holds a Master's Degree in Social Work from New York University. His postgraduate education has included training through the Institute for the Advancement of Group Studies, The Center for Mindfulness at UMASS, the Omega and Garrison Institutes, and Google's Search Inside Yourself program. He has received training in Mindfulness Based Stress Reduction, Mindfulness Based Cognitive Therapy, Stanford Forgiveness Therapy, and Stanford Cultivating Compassion. Mr. Grund is a graduate of the Nalanda Institute's Contemplative Psychotherapy and Compassion program. Mr. Grund is currently in private practice as a licensed clinical social worker and consultant to schools, community organizations, and corporations in developing mindfulness and SEL programs.

CHAPTER 16

PRINTABLE MATERIALS

Lesson Planning Template

Teacher: Building: Grade: Week of:

Activity Name:

Enduring Objective:

Common Core or C. C. C. S:

Other (Academic, OT, PT, Speech goals)

Enduring Objectives – Full Value

- [ ] Be Here Active Listening, Becoming Comfortable in One's Own Skin, Building Relationships, Self-Reflection
- [ ] Be Safe Trust/Mistrust, Feeling Secure, Responding Rather Than Reacting, Self-Regulation, Welcoming Authentic Interaction
- [ ] Set Goals Exploring the truth, Integrating Feedback, Practicing an Ethical Code of Behavior, Values
- [ ] Be Honest Achievement/Failure, Accepting Help, Brainstorm and Plan, Cooperation Versus Competition, Growth Oriented, Defining Clear Objectives, Intelligent Risk-Taking Independence, Intention into Action
- [ ] Let Go & Move On Revenge Versus Reconciliation, Accepting Complexity Resiliency, Accepting Difference, Accepting Unenforceable Rules
- [ ] Care for Self & Others Compassion/Self-Compassion, Empathy, Interdependence, Recognizing personal needs, Recognizing Self Worth, Self-Empathy, Self-Sacrifice, Personal and Social Responsibility

Materials:

Procedure:

Grounding (How you do it?):

Framing (What does it mean?):

Reflection (What, No What, Now What) (List strategies):

Academic Outcomes:

Social Emotional Outcomes:

Extension Activities (homework):   Notes:

Full Value Behavioral Norms & Desired Outcomes

Full Value	Outcomes
Be Here	- Active Listening - Becoming Comfortable in One's Own Skin - Building Relationships - Self-Reflection Specific to Mindfulness: - Attunement - Awareness of slipping into the past and future - Emotional Self-Awareness - Integration - Optimism - Organizational Awareness
Be Safe	- Trust/Mistrust - Feeling Secure - Responding Rather Than Reacting - Self-Regulation - Welcoming Authentic Interaction
Be Honest	- Exploring the truth - Integrating Feedback - Practicing an Ethical Code of Behavior - Values
Set Goals	- Achievement/Failure - Accepting Help - Brainstorm and Plan - Cooperation Versus Competition - Empowerment - Growth Oriented - Defining Clear Objectives - Intelligent Risk-Taking - Independence - Intention into Action
Let Go & Move On	- Revenge Versus Reconciliation - Accepting Complexity - Resiliency - Accepting Difference - Accepting Unenforceable Rules
Care for Self & Others	- Compassion/Self-Compassion - Empathy - Interdependence - Recognizing personal needs - Recognizing Self Worth - Self-Empathy - Self-Sacrifice - Personal and Social Responsibility

SMART GOALS

To set effective goals, it is important that one sets SMART goals

S - SPECIFIC You should set one goal at a time, stating exactly what you are responsible for. Research has shown that a person who says they want to do one thing or another, giving themselves an alternative, seldom gets beyond the "or." The individual does neither. This does not mean you can't be flexible with your goal. Flexibility in action implies the ability to be able to make a judgment that some action you are involved in is either inappropriate, unnecessary, or the result of a bad decision. Even though you may set out for one goal, you can stop at any time and drop it for a new one. But when you change, you again state your goal without an alternative.

M - MEASURABLE Your goal must be stated so that it is measurable in time and quantity. For example, suppose your goal was to finish writing a curriculum outline this week. You would specify your goal by saying, "I am going to finish the outline, complete with objectives, 1-week of lesson plans, and project ideas by Friday." That way, the goal can be measured; when Friday comes, you know whether or not you have achieved it.

A - ACHIEVABLE The goals you set must be accomplishable or reasonable with your given strengths and abilities. It is too easy to set impossible goals that are simply not realistic. While you want to stretch yourself, you do not want to set goals that are so difficult that they're unattainable and further frustrate you. For example, if you were a somewhat obese 45 year old, it would be foolish to set a goal of running the four-minute mile in the next six months—that simply would not be achievable.

R - RELEVANT About 80% of one's performance comes from 20% of one's activities. Therefore, a goal is relevant if it addresses an activity that makes a positive difference in overall performance. Clearly, your goal should never be destructive to yourself or others. Destructive goals should not be supported. If someone is seeking potentially harmful goals, a concerted effort to encourage that person to consider a different goal should be made.

T - TRACKABLE Ideally, you want to be able to monitor progress. To do that, you've got to be able to measure or count performance frequently, which means you need to put a record-keeping system in place to track performance. Monthly reports or time sheets are examples of systems that allow you to easily track performance.

S.M.A.R.T. Goal Planner

Specific	What **EXACTLY** do I want to happen?	
Measurable	I will know I have reached my goal when....	
Attainable	With hard work, is it possible to reach this goal by the deadline?	
Realistic and Relevant	My goal is important enough for me to put a plan into action. I will follow this specific plan to reach my goal:	
Time-Bound	I will reach my goal by:	

My SMART GOAL

I want to _____

_____

by _____

so I will _____

_____ to meet my goal.

4 Square Goal Setting Worksheet

What do I want to accomplish?	What will I need from my classmate(s)?

What personal resources/strengths will I need?	How will I know that I've achieved my goal(s)?

Bridge-It Language

Group Language – Team A	
Words (not spoken)	Words, Sounds, Gestures Used
Corks	Pull right ear three times
Bottom	Top
Glue	Shake hands with negotiating partner
High	Laugh
Legos	Clap twice
Masking tape	Stick your tongue out at negotiating partner
No	Nod and say, "yes"
Paper cups	Quack like a duck
Rubber bands	Hold up five fingers
Straws	Big smile at negotiating partner
Tongue Depressors/Popsicle Sticks	Pull left ear three times
Under	Side
Yes	Say, "maybe"
Group Language – Team B	
Corks	Hold up ten fingers
Glue	Blink slowly three times
How Many	Banana
Legos	Stand and sit twice
Masking tape	Tap forehead three times slowly
No	Say, "I don't know"
Paper cups	Stomp feet
Parallel	Criss-Cross Arms
Rubber bands	Flap arms like a bird
Straws	Pull right ear three times
Tongue Depressors/Popsicle Sticks	Sing the first line of Twinkle Star
Wide	Tape
Yes	Nod and say, "no"

Bridge-It Sample Time Frames (in minutes): (Written on a large Post-it or easel)

- Initial small team Planning & Building session   10
- Negotiation Session #1:   8
- Planning & Building Session #2:   8
- Negotiation Session #2:   8
- Planning & Building Session #3:   7
- Negotiation Session #3:   7
- Planning & Building Session #4:   6
- Negotiation Session #4:   5
- Planning & Building Session #5:   5
- Negotiation Session #5:   4
- Final Planning & Building Session: 10
- Show and Tell Session (Bridges Revealed)   10

Alligator River Rankings

1 = Person you like the most

5 = Person you like the least

1. _____

2. _____

3. _____

4. _____

5. _____

ACCEPTING YOURSELF

In this activity you will be asked to discuss your strengths openly with your classmates. This is no place for modesty. You are not being asked to brag, only to be realistic and open about the strengths that you possess. The process for this experience is as follows:

1. Think of all of the things that you have done well during this school year; all of the things for which you feel a sense of accomplishment. List all of your accomplishments and successes:

2. In the group as a whole, each person will share the full list of their strengths. Then ask the group, "What additional strengths did you see in me?" Add these to your list.

REFERENCES

INTRODUCTION

[1] Elias, M. J., Zins, J. E., Weissberg, R. P., Frey, K. S., Greenberg, M. T., Haynes, N. M., Norris, M., Kessler, R., Schwab-Stone, M. E., & Shriver, T. P. (1997). Social-Emotional Learning: Guidelines for Educators. Alexandria, Virginia: Association for Supervision and Curriculum Development. (pg. 2).

[2] Core SEL Competencies. (2019). Retrieved from https://casel.org/what-is-sel/

[3] CASEL Guide. Effective Social Emotional Learning Programs: Middle School and High School Edition. (2015). Retrieved from http://secondaryguide.casel.org/casel-secondary-guide.pdf

[4] Elementary and Secondary Education Act of 1965 [As Amended Through P.L. 114–95, Enacted December 10, 2015]. (2015). Retrieved from https://www2.ed.gov/documents/essa-act-of-1965.pdf

[5] What is SEL? (n.d.) Collaborative for Academic, Social, and Emotional Learning. Retrieved from https://casel.org/what-is-sel/

[6] Aspen Institute National Commission on Social, Emotional, and Academic Development (n.d.). From a Nation at Risk to a Nation of Hope. Retrieved from http://nationathope.org/report-from-the-nation/chapter-1-how-learning-happens/

[7] Durlak, K., Weissberg, P., Dymnicki A., Taylor, R., & Schellinger, B. The Impact of Enhancing Students' Social and Emotional Learning: A Meta-Analysis of School-Based Universal Interventions. Child Development. Jan./Feb. 2011, 82, (1), 405-432.

[8] Schoel, J., & Maizell, R. (2002). Exploring Islands of Healing: New Perspectives on Adventure Based Counseling. Beverly, MA: Project Adventure.

[9] Payton, J., Weissberg, R. P., Durlak, J. A., Dymnicki, A. B., Taylor, R. D., Schellinger, K. B., & Pachan, M. (December, 2008). Positive Impact of Social and Emotional Learning for Kindergarten to Eighth-Grade Students: Findings from Three Scientific Reviews. Collaborative for Academic, Social, and Emotional Learning (CASEL).

McCormick, M.P., Cappella, E., O'Connor, E. E., & McClowry, S. G. (September, 2015). Social-Emotional Learning and Academic Achievement: Using Causal Methods to Explore Classroom-Level Mechanisms. 1:3 https://journals.sagepub.com/doi/10.1177/2332858415603959.

Zins, J. E., Bloodworth, M. R., Weissberg, R. P., & Walberg, H. J. (2007). The Scientific Base Linking Social and Emotional Learning to School Success, Journal of Educational and Psychological Consultation, 17:2-3, 191-210, DOI: 10.1080/10474410701413145.

Schonfeld, D. J., Adams, R. E., Fredstrom, B. K., Weissberg, R. P., Gilman, R., Voyce, C., & Speese-Linehan, D. (2015). Cluster-randomized trial demonstrating impact on academic achievement of elementary social-emotional learning. School Psychology Quarterly, 30(3), 406-420. http://dx.doi.org/10.1037/spq0000099.

Corcoran, R. P., Cheung, A. C. K., Kim, E., & Xie, C. (November 2018). Effective universal school-based social and emotional learning programs for improving academic achievement: A systematic review and meta-analysis of 50 years of research. Educational Research Review, 25, 56-72.

[10]Felitti, V. J., Anda, R. F., Nordenberg, D., Williamson, D. F., Spitz, A. M., Edwards, V., Koss, M. P., & Marks, J. S. (1998). "Adverse Childhood Experiences." American Journal of Preventive Medicine. 14 (4): 245–258. doi:10.1016/S0749-3797(98)00017-8.

[11]Child and Adolescent Health Measurement Initiative (2013). "Overview of Adverse Child and Family Experiences among US Children." Data Resource Center, supported by Cooperative Agreement 1-U59-MC06980-01 from the U.S. Department of Health and Human Services, Health Resources and Services Administration (HRSA), Maternal and Child Health Bureau (MCHB). Available at www.childhealthdata.org. Revised 5/10/2013.

[12]Elias, M.J. (2001, September). Prepare Children for the Tests of Life, Not a Life of Tests. Education Week, Vol. 21, Issue 4, Page 40.

CHAPTER 1 – FULL VALUE

[13]Minor, J. (2002). Outward Bound: Crew Not Passengers. Seattle, WA: Mountaineers Books.

[14]Medrick, F. (1977). Confronting Passive Behavior Through Outdoor Experience: A TA Approach to Experiential Learning, Rocky Mountain Center for Experiential Learning, Denver, Colorado.

[15]Berne, E. (1964). Games people play: The psychology of human relationships. New York: Grove Press.

Berne, E. (1961). Transactional analysis in psychotherapy. New York: Grove Press.

[16]Schoel J., & Maizell R. (2002) Op. Cit.

[17]Kena, G., Aud, S., Johnson, F., Wang, X., Zhang, J., Rathbun, A., Wilkinson-Flicker, S., & Kristapovich, P. (2014). The Condition of Education 2014 (NCES 2014-083). U.S. Department of Education, National Center for Education Statistics. Washington, DC. Retrieved 10/31/18 from http://nces.ed.gov/pubsearch.

[18]Sumner Redstone Quotes. (n.d.). BrainyQuote.com. Retrieved April 17, 2019, from BrainyQuote.com website: https://www.brainyquote.com/quotes/sumner_redstone_227812

[19]Mental Health Facts: Children and Teens. (2016, September 21). National Alliance on Mental Health. Retrieved from https://www.nami.org/NAMI/media/NAMI-Media/Infographics/Children-MH-Facts-NAMI.pdf

[20]Parry, D. (1995). Warriors of the Heart: A Handbook of Conflict Resolution. Earthstewards Network.

[21]Statista. The Statistics Portal. https://www.statista.com/statistics/740222/number-of-lawyers-us/

[22]Simpson, C., & Gillis, L. (1998). Working with Those Who Hurt Others. ERIC Number: ED424075.

[23]van der Kolk, B. A. (2014). The Body Keeps the Score: Brain, Mind, and Body in the Healing of Trauma. New York: Viking.

CHAPTER 2 – THE IMPACT OF FULL VALUE ON AFFECT & ABSTRACT REASONING

[24]Lehrer, J. (2009). How we decide. New York: Houghton Mifflin.

[25]Immordino-Yang, M. H., & Damasio, A. (2007). We Feel, Therefore We Learn: The Relevance of Affective and Social Neuroscience to Education. International Mind, Brain, and Education Society and Blackwell Publishing, Inc.

[26]Corporation, The Psychological. WIAT III -- Wechsler Individual Achievement Test, Third Edition, 2009. The Psychological Corporation, 2009.

[27]Goleman, D. (n.d.). Retrieved from http://www.danielgoleman.info/topics/social emotional-learning/

[28]Schoel, J., Prouty, R., & Radcliffe, P. (1988). Islands of Healing: A Guide to Adventure Based Counseling. Dubuque, Iowa: Kendall-Hunt Publishing Company.

[29]Anderson, L. W., & Krathwohl, R. eds. (2001). A Taxonomy for Learning, Teaching, and Assessing: A Revision of Bloom's Taxonomy of Educational Objectives. New York: Addison Wesley Longman, Inc.

[30]Kincade, K. M. Patterns in children's ability to recall explicit, implicit and metaphorical information. Journal of Research in Reading. 1991, 14(2): 81-98.

[31]Elias, M. J., & Arnold, H. eds. (2006). The Educator's Guide to Emotional Intelligence and Academic Achievement: Social Emotional Learning in the Classroom. Thousand Oaks, CA: Corwin Press. Pg. 136.

[32]West, Martin R., et al. What Effective Schools Do. Education Next. Fall 2014, 14(4).

[33]Cattell, R. B. Theory of fluid and crystallized intelligence: A critical experiment. Journal of Educational Psychology, 1963, 54(1), 1-22.

CHAPTER 3 – CO-CREATING FULL VALUE COMMITMENTS & CHALLENGE OF CHOICE

[34]Random House Dictionary of the English language (Unabridged Edition). (1967). New York, NY: Random House.

[35]Buzan, T. (2015, January). Mind Mapping Genius. Retrieved from http://www.tonybuzan.com/about/mind-mapping

[36]Chase, Daniel Lyons, "Exploring challenge by choice in an adventure setting." (2009). Dissertations. 92. https://digscholarship.unco.edu/dissertations/92

[37]Schoel, J., & Maizell, R. (2002). Op. Cit. p. 14.

[38]Schoel, J., & Stratton, M., Eds. (1990). Gold Nuggets. Beverly, MA: Project Adventure Press.

CHAPTER 4 – ASSESSMENT AND REFLECTION STRATEGIES

[39]Tuckman, B.W., & Jensen, M.C. Stages of Small-Group Development Revisited. Group & Organization Studies, December 1977, 2(4), 419-427.

[40]Civic with Hart Research Associates (November 2018) for the Collaborative for Academic, Social and Emotional Learning (CASEL).

[41]Rolfe, G., Freshwater, D., & Jasper, M. (2001). Critical reflection in nursing and the helping professions: a user's guide. Basingstoke: Palgrave Macmillan.

[42]op. cit. Anderson, L. W., & Krathwohl, R., eds. (2001).

[43]Schoel. J., Prouty, D., & Radcliffe, P. (1988) Op. Cit.

CHAPTER 5 – CALLING GROUP

[44]Brown, B. (2017, September). Finding Our Way to True Belonging. Retrieved from https://ideas.ted.com/finding-our-way-to-true-belonging/

[45] Moyers, B. (1988, June). 'Masks of Eternity' Ep. 6: Joseph Campbell and the Power of Myth — Retrieved from https://billmoyers.com/content/ep-6-joseph-campbell-and-the-power-of-myth-masks-of-eternity-audio/

[46] Keltner, D. (2014, December). We Are Built to Be Kind. Retrieved from Good Science https://www.youtube.com/watch?v=SsWs6bf7tvI

[47] ibid.

[48] Doty, J. (2015, April). Power of Compassion & Importance of the work of CCARE. Retrieved from https://www.youtube.com/watch?time_continue=89&v=rUi40yTXrjY

[49] Op. Cit. Keltner, D. (2014, December).

[50] Waldinger, R. (2015, November). What makes a good life. Lessons from the longest study on happiness. Retrieved from https://www.ted.com/talks/robert_waldinger_what_makes_a_good_life_lessons_from_the_longest_study_on_happiness

[51] Ohio Means Jobs (n.d.). Top Ten Employability Skills. Retrieved from http://www.opportunityjobnetwork.com/job-resources/help/top-10-skills.html

[52] Covey, S. R. (2013). The 7 Habits of Highly Effective People: Powerful Lessons in Personal Change. New York: Simon & Schuster.

[53] ibid. pg. 219

[54] Dweck, Carol S. (2008). Mindset: the new psychology of success. New York: Ballantine Books.

[55] Project Aristotle, re: Work (n.d.). Understanding Team Effectiveness. Retrieved from https://rework.withgoogle.com/print/guides/5721312655835136/

[56] Schoel, J. & Schoel, N. (2012). I Am About Cards. Available from 13 Woodbury Street, Gloucester, MA 01930

[57] Wheatley, M. J. & Crinean, G. (2004). Solving, not Attacking, Complex Problems: A Five-State Approach Based on an Ancient Practice, para. 23. Retrieved from https://www.margaretwheatley.com/articles/solvingnotattacking.html

CHAPTER 7 – BE SAFE

[58] Indicators of School Crime and Safety: 2016. NCES 2017-064/NCJ 250650

CHAPTER 9 – SET GOALS

[59] Penman, M., & Vedantam, S. (2016, May 10). WOOP, There It Is! 4 Steps to Achieve

Your Goals. Retrieved from https://www.npr.org/2016/05/10/477379965/woop-there-it-is-four-steps-to-achieve-your-goals

[60]Rycroft, E. (n.d.). Proud to Be Primary. Retrieved from https://www.teacherspayteachers.com/Store/Proud-To-Be-Primary

[61]Connell, G. (2016, January 6). Setting (Almost) SMART Goals with My Students. Retrieved from https://www.scholastic.com/teachers/blog-posts/genia-connell/setting-almost-smart-goals-my-students/

[62]Boyatzis, R. E. (2000). Developing Emotional Intelligence. In Cherniss, C., Boyatzis, R. E., & Elias, M. (Eds.), Developments in Emotional Intelligence. San Francisco: Jossey-Bass.

[63]Adapted from Kenneth Blanchard's Leadership and the One-Minute Manager, and Billy B. Sharp with Claire Cox, Choose Success: How to Set and Achieve All Your Goals

CHAPTER 11 – CARE FOR SELF & OTHERS

[64]English Heritage (n.d.). History of Stonehenge. Retrieved from http://www.english-heritage.org.uk/visit/places/stonehenge/history/

[65]Banyal, I. (1995). Zoom. NY, New York: Viking Books for Young Readers; Library Binding edition.

Banyal, I. (1998). Re-Zoom. New York, NY: Puffin Books; Reprint edition.

[66]William Shakespeare, Hamlet Quotes. (n.d.). Quotes.net. Retrieved April 11, 2019, from https://www.quotes.net/quote/42920.

CHAPTER 12 – FULL VALUE & ACADEMIC CONTENT AREAS

[67]Egan, K. (n.d.). Lesson plan was used with permission and with gratitude.

[68]Lummer, T. (n.d.). Lesson plan used with permission and with gratitude.

[69]Kinnelon Borough Public Schools, Kinnelon, NJ. (n.d.). Used with permission and gratitude.

[70]Lowry, L. (1989). Number the stars. Boston: Houghton Mifflin.

[71]Lesson Planning Template for use in the school setting developed by Richard Maizell, Psy.D. & Jim Schoel.

[72]Schoel & Maizell, Op. Cit., pgs. 29-30

CHAPTER 13 - MINDFULNESS & FULL VALUE

[73]Luskin F. (2001). Forgive for Good: A Proven Prescription for Health and Happiness. San Francisco: HarperOne.

[74]Lozzio, J. (2015, September). An Introduction to the 4 Foundations of Mindfulness. Nalanda Institute's Contemplative Psychotherapy Training.

[75]Kabat-Zinn, K. (2012). Mindfulness for Beginners: Reclaiming the present moment and your life. Canada: Sounds True, Inc.

[76]Exploring the Problem Space. (2017, January). Counting Thoughts, Part 1. Retrieved from https://www.exploringtheproblemspace.com/new-blog/2017/1/1/counting-thoughts-part-i

[77]Greater Good Magazine (n.d.). Mindfulness Defined. Retrieved from https://greatergood.berkeley.edu/topic/mindfulness/definition#why-practice-mindfulness

[78]Ekman, P. (2009). Emotional Awareness: Overcoming the Obstacles to Psychological Balance and Compassion. New York: Holt.

[79]ibid

[80]Killingsworth, A., & Gilbert, D. T. A Wandering Mind is an Unhappy Mind. Science 12 Nov 2010: Vol. 330, Issue 6006, p. 932 DOI: 10.1126/science.1192439.

[81]McSpannen, K. (2015, May). You Now Have a Shorter Attention Span Than a Goldfish. Time Magazine.

[82]Luskin, Op. Cit., pgs. 47-49.

[83]Rechtschaffen, D. (2014). The Way of Mindful Education: Cultivating Well-Being in Teachers and Students. New York: W. W. Norton & Company.

[84]Duhigg, C. (2016, February). The Work Issue. What Google Learned from Its Quest to Build the Perfect Team. NY Times Magazine.

[85]Barron, B., & Darling-Hammond, L. (2008, October 8). Powerful Learning: Studies Show Deep Understanding Derives from Collaborative Methods. Retrieved from https://www.edutopia.org/inquiry-project-learning-research

[86]Rechtschaffen, Op. Cit., pg. 17.

[87]World Health Organization (2014, August). Mental Health: a state of well-being. Retrieved from https://www.who.int/features/factfiles/mental_health/en/

[88]MacLean, P. (1990). The Triune Brain in Evolution: Role in Paleocerebral Functions. New York: Springer.

[89]Siegel, D. (2007, August 9). Dr. Siegel's Hand Model of the Brain Retrieved from https://www.youtube.com/watch?v=f-m2YcdMdFw&feature=youtu.be

[90]Germer, C. (2016, February). Lecture on compassion at the Nalanda Institute, NYC program in Contemplative Psychotherapy.

[91]Neff, K. (2014, October). The three components of self-compassion. Retrieved from https://greatergood.berkeley.edu/video/item/the_three_components_of_self_compassion

[92]Empathy Defined (n.d.). Retrieved from https://greatergood.berkeley.edu/topic/empathy/definition

[93]Luskin, Op. Cit., pg. 119.

[94]Jellaludin, R. (1995). How is the Mind Field experience like the Guest House? The Essential Rumi. (C. Barks, Trans.). Pg. 109. New York: Harper Collins.

CHAPTER 14 – SUSTAINABILITY

[95]Responsive Classroom (n.d.). Retrieved from https://www.responsiveclassroom.org/about/principles-practices/

[96]Dreikurs, R., & Grey, L. (1970). A Parent's Guide to Child Discipline. New York: Dutton.

[97]Dejong, W. Building the Peace: The Resolving Conflict Creatively Program (RCCP). (1993). Department of Justice, Washington, D.C. National Institute of Justice. Report number NJC149549.

[98]Kiddie, J (2018, December 8). Whole-School Restorative Approach Resource Guide. Vermont Agency of Education.

[99]What is RTI? (n.d.). Retrieved from http://www.rtinetwork.org/learn/what/whatisrti

[100]Bernat, D. H., & Resnick, M. D. Healthy Youth Development: Science and Strategies, Journal of Public Health Management and Practice: November 2006 - Volume 12 - Issue - p S10–S16.

Griffin, K., & Botvin, G. (July 2010). Evidence-Based Interventions for Preventing Substance Use Disorders in Adolescents. Child and Adolescent Psychiatric Clinics of North America. 19:3, Pgs. 505-526.

Index

A

ABC Triangle, 21
Adventure Wave, 62, 66
Abstract Reasoning, 18
Acknowledgments, 297
Activity Difficulty Level & Materials, xviii
Activity Resources, 268
Assessment & Reflection Strategies, 47

B

Be Here, 4, 74; Activities, 74
    Blob or Add-on Tag, 74
    Chicken Tag, 76
    Claytionary, 76
    Coming and Going of the Rain, 77
    Everybody's It, 79
    Fire in the Hole, 80
    Flungee, 81
    Gotcha or Finger Tag, 82
    Help Me Tag, 83
    HI, YO, LO!, 83
    Hoop Relay, 85
    Hustle Handle, 86
    Impulse, 86
    Island of Healing Circle, 87
    Knee Tap, 89
    Look Up – Look Down!, 90
    Meteors, 91
    Near – Far, 92
    Pairs Tag, 93
    Peek A Who, 94
    People to People, 95
    Robot Tag, 96
    Speed Snap (or Whistle), 97
    Surf's Up, 97
    Toss a Name Game, 98
    Ultimate Zombie (12 years old and up), 99
    Zip Zap, 100
Be Honest, 6, 121; Activities, 122
    Back-Stabbers, 123
    Blindfold Square, 124
    Compass Walk, 125

　　　　Human Camera, 126
　　　　Have You Ever?, 128
　　　　Moving Without Touching, 130
　　　　Spin the Yarn, 130
　　　　Scavenger Hunt, 131
　　　　Sweet & Salty, 131
　　　　Truth Drawings, 132
Be Safe, 5, 102; Activities, 103
　　　　Air Traffic Controller, 103
　　　　Blindfold Walk (Sherpa Walk), 104
　　　　Cross the Mall, 105
　　　　Evolution, 107
　　　　The Gauntlet, 108
　　　　Hands Up!, 110
　　　　Mine Field, 111
　　　　Star Wars, 113
The Trust Sequence, 114
　　　　Two Person Trust Fall, 115
　　　　Three-Person Trust Fall, 117
　　　　Wind in the Willows, 118
　　　　Levitation, 119
Best Practices in the Schools, 255
Bloom's Revised Taxonomy, 63

C

Calling Group, 67
　　　　Rapid Groups, 73
Care for Self & Others, 11; Activities, 193
　　　　Accepting Yourself, 193
　　　　All Aboard, 195
　　　　Holy Alliance (Four Way Tug o' War), 196
　　　　Hospital Tag, 197
　　　　Human Ladder, 198
　　　　Letters of Appreciation, 200
　　　　Panic Evac, 201
　　　　Stonehenge, 204
　　　　The Balance of Full Value, 206
　　　　Trust Line, 207
　　　　Web Wave, 208
　　　　Yurt Circle, 209
　　　　Zen Count, 211
CASEL Core Competencies, xv
Challenge By & Of Choice, 44
Co-Creation, 28
Content Areas & Full Value Activity Connections, 222
Control to Empowerment, 14; in Calling Group, 69

Creating Small Groups Activities, 267
    Categories, 267
    Draw a Dog, 267
    Picture Puzzle, 267
    What's the Same, 268
Cross Categories, xviii

E

Elias, Maurice, xxi

F

Fear of Transformation, 10
Four (4) Square Goal Setting, 141
Full Value, 1; and CASEL Core Competencies, x; and Academic Content Areas, 213
Full Value Commitment, 36
    The Being, 36
    The Village, 37
    Full Value Boop, 29
    Full Value Speed Rabbit, 31
    Full Value Call, 33
    Full Value Human Sculpture, 33
    Mind Mapping, 33
    Toxic Waste, 34
Full Value Communities, LLC, 272
Full Value Communities Website, 297

G

GRABBSS, 47

H

Harassment, Intimidation, and Bullying (HIB) Data, 259
High School Programs, 57; and Middle and High School Goal Setting, 13
How and Why Do I Find Time for This?, xix

K

Kinnelon Borough Public Schools, xii

L

Let Go & Move On, 11, 168; Activities, 168
    Alligator River, 168
    Balance Broom, 170

  Bridge-It, 171
  Change Up, 175
  Cross the Line, 176
  Elbow Tag, 178
  Lost at Sea, 179
  The Luminaria Circle, 180
  Negotiations Square, 181
  Paradigm Shift, 183
  Personal Coat of Arms, 183
  Rearrange the Furniture, 185
  Red, Yellow, Green, 185
  Run, Shout, Knock Yourself Out, 187
  Stepping Stones, 187
  Turning Over a New Leaf, 189
  Zoom and Re-Zoom, 190
Life Cycle of Groups (Tuckman), 47

M

Mindfulness & Full Value, 226; In schools, 236; Activities, 239
  Evolution of the Triune Brain, 239
  Evolution of Compassion, 241
  The CASEL 5 Hoop, 243
  Neural Pathways – Neurons that fire together wire together, 244
  Mind Field: Partner Meditation, 246
Mindfulness Resources, 269

N

No Discount Contract, 1
Now What, 64

P

Peer Leadership, 260
Primary Prevention, 254
Printable Materials, 274
  Lesson Planning Template, 274
  Full Value Behavioral Norms & Desired Outcomes, 275
  SMART Goals Planner, 276
  Goal Planning Sheets, 277
  Four (4) Square Goal Setting Worksheet, 278
  Bridge-It Language, 279
  Bridge-It Timeframes, 280
  Alligator River Rankings, 281
  Accepting Yourself, 282
Project Adventure Physical Education Cycles & Full Value, 224

R

Reflection Practices, 60
Rogers, Fred, xi

S

SEL - A Different Way of Being Smart, xiii
Set Goals, 7, 134; and Activities, 142, and Asking for Help, 141; and Full Value Commitment, 135
    Helium Hoop, 135
    Balloon Trolley, 143
    Calculator of Keypunch, 144
    Duct Tape, 145
    Electric Fence, 147
    Goal Partners, 148
    Great Egg Drop, 148
    Group Juggling, 150
    Human Knot (Tangle), 151
    Leaning Tower of Feetza, 152
    Moonball, 154
    Phil Le Basquette (Fill the Basket), 156
    Pipeline, 158
    Star Gate, 160
    Team A Vs Team B, 162
    The Flying V, 163
    Traffic Jam, 164
    Warp Speed, 166
So What, 64
Sustainability, 265

T

To Go For The Perfect Try, 46
The What, 63
Training Wheels, 158, 269
Trauma, xviii; and Full Value, 15; and Challenge of Choice, 46; and Co-Creation, 28; and Calling Group, 73; and Goal Setting, 142
Triune Brain, 238

U

Under the Big Tent of Full Value, 248

ACKNOWLEDGEMENTS

Richard Maizell

My friends Jim Schoel and John Grund for their essential contributions to this book, for sharing my passion for service, and for their dedication to making the lives of children better. Iris Wechling, with her critical editor's eye and original contributions, makes the book accessible to educators. For her advocacy and support of experiential learning, and for all of the children whose lives have been changed through her efforts. Sonya Maizell for her encouragement and editing support. Ben Maizell for his professional video production and editing expertise of our Full Value interviews. Dr. Clarence Steinberg for his editing excellence. The Kinnelon Board of Education, Superintendent James Opiekun (retired), Superintendent Diane DiGiuseppe, Principals Jodi Mulholland, Pat Hart (retired), and Mark Mongon, who all vigorously supported Full Value in Kinnelon. I am in your debt. Assistant Superintendent Jack Hynes (retired), who has continued to champion Full Value and recommend our program to school districts. Your rigorous expectations and intellect give credibility to what we do. The teachers and paraprofessional educators of Kinnelon who embrace Full Value and understand the importance of social emotional learning. Sarah Tinney, for her promotion and sharing of our program with colleagues and students. Dr. Vincent D'Elia for his longstanding belief in the importance of social emotional learning. Paul Radcliffe, for his activity contributions, mentoring, friendship, humor, and selfless dedication to the mission of Project Adventure. Most importantly, my grandchildren; Arden, Rhys, Merjeme, Juniper, Everett, and Landon. It is my abiding hope that our Full Value work will make the world a kinder and safer place for them to live.

John Grund

A special thanks to all my colleagues in education who have cared for, valued, and taught our youth. I especially want to thank Bernards High School's retired Principals Lynn Caravello and the late Lewis Ludwig. I am grateful to the thousands of adolescent students that I have been connected with as a counselor, coach, peer leader advisor, and friend. Thanks to all at the Nalanda Institute in New York who continue to support my growth in the contemplative practices. I want to especially extend my gratitude to my friend Sundar Das Giron for his wisdom and feedback on the Mindfulness Chapter. I want to extend a deep appreciation to all the trainers and staff from Project Adventure who I've known since 1991. I am deeply grateful to Richard Maizell and Jim Schoel and honored that they included me in writing this book. I want to thank Jim for his unwavering belief in me and encouragement. I am most grateful to Richard Maizell for introducing me to Full Value and Project Adventure. Richard has been an inspiring mentor, patient collaborator, and esteemed friend. My thanks go to my friend Craig Meyer. He has been an inspiration in living a fully valued life and the creative power of a good walk and talk. Thanks to my son Sean for his feedback on my writing and for keeping me always on my toes. To my son Colin, for his feedback on activities and creativity. I admire their commitment to serve others and I am inspired by them every day. Lastly, I want to thank my loving wife Amy for her patience, support, and belief in me. She has been a model of compassion and the power of personal connection.

Jim Schoel

For my mentors and colleagues, who helped make Full Value Communities a reality: Herb Wostrel, former Superintendent of Gloucester Pubic Schools, and pioneer supporter of Adventure Learning. Barry Orms and Buddy Orange, creators of the Full Value Being, in Harlem, New York City. Cindy Simpson and Lisa Galm for their inventive and courageous work developing, teaching, and practicing the "Adventure Group Process" with Youth at Risk in Covington, Georgia. Robert Beau Bassett, Alaska Youth Leadership. Robert Natti and Bill Goodwin, former principals of Gloucester High School. Peter Natti, the first Gloucester student to participate in a month-long Outward Bound program. Dick Prouty, co-author of Islands of Healing and longtime director of Project Adventure. Nicole Richon Schoel, therapist, writer, editor, idea person, and advocate for victims of domestic violence. Yuki Abe and Toshio Hyashi, for advocacy, and adaptation and translation of Full Value practices in Japan. Tham Yew Cheong, Director of Adventure Learning in Asia. Carol James, Amy Kohut, Tom Knackstedt and Bob Fleming, for adaptation of Full Value learning in schools and universities. Tedd Benson, Mikio Takagi, and Lee Strauss for their support of the Full Value Tsunami mitigation Bamboo Resilience endeavor in the wake of the Fukushima and Minami San Riku disasters. Richard Maizell and John Grund, my co-authors and Adventure colleagues, for their wealth of expertise and for providing inspiration, guidance and support throughout this entire creative project.

Full Value Initiatives, Inc.

Doing Business As:

Full Value Communities

www.fullvaluecommunities.org